Clint Eastwood

About the author:

Minty Clinch, one of Britain's foremost experts on the
movies, is the author of highly-praised biographies of
James Cagney, Burt Lancaster, Harrison Ford and
Robert Redford. She writes regular articles on film for
several national newspapers and magazines including
The Sunday Times, the *Observer* and *She*.

Biographies by Minty Clinch

Cagney
Burt Lancaster
Harrison Ford
Robert Redford

Clint Eastwood

Minty Clinch

CORONET BOOKS
Hodder and Stoughton

First published in 1994 by Hodder and Stoughton,
A division of Hodder Headline plc
First published in paperback in 1995 by Hodder and
Stoughton
A Coronet Paperback

10 9 8 7 6 5 4 3 2 1

British Library Cataloguing in Publication Data
Clinch, Minty
Clint Eastwood
I. Title
791.43028092

ISBN: 0 340 63831 1

Typeset by Phoenix Typesetting, Ilkley, West Yorkshire

Printed and bound in Great Britain by
Cox & Wyman Ltd, Reading, Berkshire

Hodder and Stoughton
A division of Hodder Headline PLC
338 Euston Road
London NW1 3BH

Contents

List of Illustrations

With Sondra Locke, in *Bronco Billy* in 1980 (*Rex Features Ltd*)

Clint Eastwood as golfer (*Rex Features Ltd*), skier (*Rex Features Ltd*), racing car driver (*The Kobal Collection*)

With Frances Fisher in 1992 (*Rex Features Ltd*)

With Wolfgang Petersen on the set of *In the Line of Fire* in 1993 (*Rex Features Ltd*)

Meeting Prince Charles and Princess Di in London (*Rex Features Ltd*)

With son Kyle (*Rex Features Ltd*)

A mayor in the making during the run-up to the 1986 election (*Rex Features Ltd*)

Unforgiven takes top honours at the 1993 Oscar ceremony (*Rex Features Ltd*)

Clint Eastwood directs himself in *A Perfect World* (*Rex Features Ltd*)

I

The Price of Power

'I am a perfect Californian – modern, individualistic, liberal. I believe in citizens' rights.' Clint Eastwood provided this self-portrait in 1987 in the middle of his term as mayor of Carmel, his tiny adopted hometown on the coast of the state where he was born. He was then fifty-seven years old, one of the wealthiest men in the film industry, but held in only moderate esteem as an actor. He was a father of three, two in wedlock and one outside it, but living with Sondra Locke, the waif-like actress from Tennessee. And he was at a turning-point. He could go into national politics – George Bush, then Vice-President, wooed him for his running-mate for the 1988 presidential election. Or he could go on acting and directing in the hope of capitalising on a groundswell of opinion that he was rather better at both than anyone had previously imagined.

Evidence of this re-evaluation had started coming in a few years earlier when there had been retrospectives of his work at the Museum of Modern Art in New York and at equally prestigious venues in Paris, London and Munich. Since then, he'd put his film career on the back burner to stand as mayor, mostly because he'd been frustrated by his fellow Carmelites over planning permission for a prime piece of real estate he owned in the centre of town. Although the dispute had been settled out of court before he was elected in April 1986, Clint Eastwood was not amused. In his films, those who zapped his alter egos never went unpunished, and success as a director had made him seriously unaccustomed to people denying his slightest whim. Now a bunch of schoolteachers, many of them female, had dared to stand in the way of what he saw as progressive commercial practice, so he rode into town, metaphorical Magnums blazing, and got himself elected to show them that he had citizens' rights too.

Does fame mixed with fortune make Clint Eastwood a perfect Californian? Maybe, provided you define perfect as a charming, rugged, self-made billionaire and Californian as a White Anglo-Saxon Protestant male. And many do, despite its being the ultimate melting-pot state, developed as part of the Spanish Empire and with a huge Hispanic population and a substantial Sino-Japanese one, so Eastwood was in little danger of contradiction on that score. Nor would there be many quarrels with individualistic. He grew up as a loner and a drifter with a strong sense of independence which served him well once he'd established himself as an outsider in an insider's town. Modern is a relative term, though not one readily applied to a business creed based on old-fashioned appreciation of the Protestant work ethic and the notion that it's every man for himself. So Eastwood loves animals, and never squashes an insect in anger, but does that make him modern? Not really. As for liberal, the answer is no politically, for he is a lifelong Republican who switched allegiance to Ross Perot in the last election, but yes sexually, at least in the sense that he swaps partners in a thoroughly modern manner.

I remember the day on which I was first exposed to Eastwood's magnetic charm as if it were yesterday. It was a bright windy one in April 1969, and he was my first – and only – interview on my first visit to Hollywood and my first-ever contact with a film star of any description. At the time, he was known primarily as the Man With No Name in Sergio Leone's spaghetti western trilogy, *A Fistful of Dollars, For a Few Dollars More,* and *The Good, The Bad, and The Ugly,* so it was relatively easy for a rookie reporter to get an audience. But still terrifying, as I realised far too late as the barrier rose to admit me to Universal Studios. As the descendant of military folk, my upbringing had emphasised steadiness under fire as a supreme virtue; there could be no turning back now.

At the Eastwood bungalow, headquarters of his fledgling Malpaso production company, I was introduced to the actor and the late Jean Seberg, his co-star on his most recent film, *Paint Your Wagon.* She did not look pleased to see me, nor did she leave the room, deliberately adding to the awkwardness of the occasion as she was not to be included in the interview. In sharp contrast, Clint was graciousness itself. A quarter of a century ago and just short of his fortieth birthday, he was gorgeous, his greenish eyes and blondish hair set off by his perpetual tan, his lean frame relaxed in casual clothes. 'How about a brew?' he asked. I nodded dumbly, eagerly, and warmed to him for it was 4 p.m., an hour at which I expected tea rather than beer.

As I gulped the ice-cold Bud, he ran through his life to date, his tough Depression childhood, his roving adolescence, the lucky break in the corridors of Universal when he was spotted for Rowdy Yates in *Rawhide* after several years as an unemployed actor, the decision to go to Italy to work for Leone although they had no common language, the return to California, the films he was making there now. This was the age of violent student protest in Paris and Berkeley and Cornell, so we touched on politics – Republican on his part, Labour on mine – and did not agree. And we touched on marriage – sixteen years for him, none for me – and he told me how secure and happy he was with his wife, Maggie, and their year-old son, Kyle, while Seberg shifted in her chair and looked bored and doubtful in turn. Clearly my questions were

not original and he had no option but to answer them
as if he'd been this way many times before, but he smiled
and tried and I liked him a lot for that. My verdict? A
decent ordinary bloke, no great intellect, excellent manners, not much sense of humour.

Twenty-one years would pass before we met again at
the Edinburgh Film Festival in 1990. His publicists claim
that Eastwood never forgets a face, but he certainly forgot
mine, perhaps because, as a six-footer, I don't have so far to
look up to him as most women do. After years of research
in the field, students of his sexual history have credited
him with a preference for elfin blondes like Locke and
his current partner, Frances Fisher. Can it be that those
who don't conform don't get remembered? Maybe, maybe
not, but he was still charming and polite as he rose to his
feet and stretched out his hand in greeting. It closed on
mine like a trap, a bonecrusher that left me surreptitiously
shaking the blood back down my arm. He was no longer
quite so lean; age had given him a profile hacked out of
granite and the green eyes were much cooler and more
amused than those of yesteryear. On this occasion, they
were muddied by the tones of an American in Scotland
outfit – earth-coloured tweed jacket, a moss-coloured tie.
Fashion has never been an Eastwood priority.

The most striking thing about the sixty-year-old Clint
was how powerful he had become and how totally he was
in control. In large things, like amassing a fortune from
producing, directing and acting in his own films, he'd
moved from milestone to milestone, never deviating from
his chosen image as the contemporary face of traditional
American values. Sometimes it had been the fearsome
vengeful face of Dirty Harry, on the rampage against
universal evil; at others, it had been an expressionless
face like the Pale Rider, an anonymous hero fighting
the forces of oppression; occasionally, it had been a

despairing face like the Honky Tonk Man, at odds with himself and the world. As a director, Eastwood admired Ford and Hawks, Kurosawa and Hitchcock, though he was not often mentioned in the same breath as them. As an actor, he felt in tune with Bogart and Cagney, short wiry toughies with ready trigger fingers and a shared taste for wry humour, but was more often compared to John Wayne. His natural heir, the analysts claimed, but Eastwood has always denied it vehemently, even venomously at times.

On a personal level, he'd been divorced by Maggie in 1985, after a six-year separation, and sued for palimony by Sondra Locke in 1989, after bitter accusations that he'd forced her to have two abortions and a sterilisation operation. That same year the world had learned of the second family he had been hiding for twenty-five years. Kimber Tunis was born in 1964 to actress, Roxanne Tunis, a bit-part player in *Rawhide*, and, as her birth certificate had it, to Clinton Eastwood Junior. In 1983, she'd married a tree surgeon called Anthony Gaddie and given birth to an Eastwood grandchild called Clinton. By 1990, she'd divorced him and married Denver businessman Doug McCartney. Even after his legitimate children, Kyle and Alison, were born in 1968 and 1972, Eastwood stayed in touch with Roxanne and Kimber, keeping his promise of financial support in exchange for silence.

That silence was still in place in Edinburgh because he likes to be as in control of small things, like talking to me, as he is of big ones. There were questions he seemed not to hear – he said he was a little deaf – but when they were repeated, he paused for however long it took to think of the precise answer he required. The confidence that comes with success had brought humour into his repertoire, and he used it deftly, with a keen appreciation of the deflective power of wit. 'Sure, I play antiheroes. An element of failing is more fun when you're as unflawed as I am.'

When no wisecrack occurred to him, he slid off at a tangent and, as befits a big fish, he'd become very slippery indeed. I asked a simple question, 'Have you drastically cut down on alcohol?', and he replied, 'I like a glass of wine, a jar of beer. I don't drink hard liquor, just a shot of tequila now and then because I like the taste, but I can't knock it back like they did in those scenes that look so good in westerns.' Did this mean he drank less than he used to? 'Probably.' And did he feel better for it? 'Probably. Yes, I'd probably have to say I feel better because everyone has had a few moments in their life when they've had enough whisky to feel bad the next day and I don't like to feel bad the next day.' Did that mean more or less drink than formerly?

An informed guess would be less. Clint Eastwood does have an addictive side to his personality but it is focused primarily on work. By his own account, he has never taken drugs, never even tried cocaine in the days in the eighties when it was served along with the amuse-gueules at every Hollywood dinner party. He has never smoked except in movies, but he has always been an enthusiastic social drinker. It was an evening of beer-drinking that first brought him to Carmel as a young soldier, and many evenings of beer-drinking with his mates that kept him in town rather than back at one of several homes he has owned there. At play, he has always been a man's man, owing to inclination and a convenient supporting conviction that a woman's place is in the home while a man's is on a golf course.

Under pressure, he admitted he'd come straight to Edinburgh from a sybaritic holiday in the South of France. 'I keep myself in good shape and work out most of the time but the last two weeks it seems all we did was eat, then go on and eat some more. I fell in with a group of people who go from meal to meal.

It's quite awesome! I like being free of any ties and I do like to party once in a while, but not often. One of the problems about Hollywood is that you talk to the same people about the same things all the time. When I'm not working, I prefer to talk about . . .' He seeks inspiration in the Edinburgh skyline as seen through the windows of the Caledonian Hotel, and comes up with '. . . masonry, architecture, history.'

Not about Locke or Kimber or Roxanne? The big fish becomes a very committed human clam. How about Kyle, who is studying music, and Alison, who is working as a model and considering a career in the cinema? 'I'll encourage them, but whatever they decide to do, they'll have to put their best foot forward.' Paternal, certainly, but hardly original. Tears, then. What makes Clint Eastwood cry? Surprisingly, he is keen to elaborate on this. 'I'm emotional about many things, more than you would expect probably. It's weak men who are afraid to let their feelings show. I can be manipulated just like anyone else and I can be a slob in a sad movie.' What sad movie would that be? '*Pinocchio, E.T., Snow White*.' *Snow White*? 'Sure, I'd weep at the end of *Snow White*. When the Prince wakes her up at the end, you gotta weep.'

Or was he thinking of *Sleeping Beauty*? My knowledge of Disney movies was too scanty for me to be sure, but I scanned the lean cheeks and the crow's-feet round the eyes and tried to imagine the tears coursing down. Failed. Far easier to picture him skiing, which he does regularly in Sun Valley, Idaho, where he has a third or fourth home. Or powering his motorbike down the winding coast road from Carmel to Big Sur, a passion since his adolescence. Or flying his helicopter, the one he bought at the Paris Air Show after he got his licence in 1988. 'I love it up there,' he said, with the bogus wistfulness of the very famous. 'Up there, I'm just a number in the sky.' Or waiting for approaches from 'hip pocket rockets', as he allegedly calls the women who stake out the streets and bars of Carmel with intent to seduce him. If they can.

If they can't, it's not because he hasn't got the energy. 'I don't feel any different at sixty than I did at fifty-nine, nor at thirty come to that. You can feel good at thirty and miserable at thirty, and it's the same at sixty. I'm more even-tempered nowadays, more tolerant, and I realise that health is more important than making movies. Life gets better if you want it to get better.'

And, in the three years before our most recent meeting in October 1993, it did. The palimony case was settled in 1991, with Locke exchanging an undisclosed amount of money for a lifetime of silence. Her live-in replacement, Frances Fisher, had borne him a third daughter, Francesca Ruth Fisher Eastwood, on 7 August, but the couple had no plans to marry. 'I tried that once and it didn't work out,' Eastwood had quipped to a volunteer for his hand a few years earlier, and he has shown no signs of giving failure a chance to recur. However, it was work that brought him his greatest reward. Coming on top of a bunch of lesser prizes, the Academy Awards for Best Picture and Best Director for the western *Unforgiven* vindicated his long-held conviction that films didn't have to be arty to be good. As he held the statuettes aloft in the Dorothy Chandler Pavilion on 29 March 1993, the tears coursed freely down his cheeks, the tears of an emotional man who'd been a long time coming into his kingdom.

This last meeting with Clint Eastwood was in his offices at Malpaso, on the lot at Warner Brothers, and he still didn't recognise me, nor even my name, which few people forget. Every inch the perfect Californian in a plain white t-shirt, black pants held up with a narrow leather belt and black and red trainers, an outfit that must have cost all of $150, he looked more athletic than ever, with a spring in his step and a sparkle in his eye. I was there to talk to his executive producer, David Valdes, about Malpaso as part of an article about the Eastwood business empire for a prominent British newspaper. Comments from the man himself were a bonus and, as he gave them with his customary charm and politesse, I warmed to him once more.

It was only when I arrived in Carmel later in the week that I learned the true extent of his power and the lengths he will go to make sure no one flouts him, even in the most minor of ways. My first appointment was with representatives of the Carmel Business Association, an organisation that promotes the town as a tourist destination. Up to this point, they had been extremely welcoming, scheduling a series of meetings over the weekend with local people who had agreed to talk to me about Eastwood's tourist-oriented interests for the other part of my article. They included people who had worked with him when he was mayor and people connected with the Mission Ranch, a semi-derelict lodging-house when he saved it from developers in 1987 but now restored as a luxury hotel.

The offices of the Carmel Business Association are upstairs in the Eastwood Building, the same one that triggered his shot as mayor. Today it stands in wood-shingled splendour overlooking his bar-restaurant, The Hog's Breath. All very welcoming, but not for me because all my meetings had been cancelled. I asked why, was told that Malpaso had made enquiries with Mr Eastwood's office in London and instructed the Business Association to shut me out. Asked what office, I was told Warner Bros. Asked why, I was told that Warner Bros said that I hadn't been commissioned by the paper concerned. Untrue, as it happens, but difficult to prove as it was 10 p.m. on a Friday night in London. Further enquiries with Eastwood aides at Malpaso confirmed that the shutters had indeed come down. Mr Eastwood had already left his office, probably to fly himself up to Carmel for the Doris Day celebrity golf tournament in aid of her Pet Foundation in which he played the next day. However, he'd left words: 'not interested'.

Fair enough, but why was he zapping a mosquito with such force when his public image suggests that he wouldn't hurt a fly? As Malpaso's films contribute eighteen per cent of Warner's revenue, and as the Carmel Business Association exists in Eastwood's back pocket, it is hardly surprising that they dance so readily to his tune. But it is disappointing that a man of his stature should order them to do so, especially as those chosen for the interviews by the Business Association were by definition pro-Eastwood. And especially when he plays it so polite, so charming, so goddamn nice . . .

2

An Itinerant Youth

Clinton Eastwood Jr was born on 31 May 1930 in St Francis Hospital in the City and County of San Francisco to parents who were young, poor and struggling. His father, Clinton Sr, was a stocks and bonds salesman who had to take work as and where he found it. His mother, Ruth, was a housewife. They were twenty-three and twenty-one respectively when the first of their two children was born. His father's family was Scots English, his mother's Dutch Irish, a mongrel heritage from which Clint claims his innate sense of independence. His first complaint was being named after his father. 'I didn't even get my own name.'

Nor were he and his sister, Jean, ever going to get a stable childhood. In the aftermath of the Wall Street crash in 1929, selling stocks and bonds to its victims was the ultimate low-credibility occupation. The Eastwoods were middle-class – Clinton Sr had trained as a cost accountant – but, in the climate of bankruptcy and despair that followed the crash, jobs were at a premium and inexperience was not the best qualification for getting them. By 1930, California was no longer undeveloped desert, as it had been at the turn of the century, but it wouldn't reach its economic heyday until the defence industry moved in after World War II. In the early thirties, finding work required fast footwork and a flexible approach to location as the stranglehold of the Depression tightened.

Clint's earliest memories of life in Beacon Street, Oakland, just outside San Francisco, were soon replaced by images of other places, other towns, among them Spokane, Redding, Sacramento, Pacific Palisades and Seattle. 'It seems to me now', he said in 1969, 'that we didn't live much in houses at all: we lived in cars.' No doubt he exaggerated, because he also said that he has no memories of poverty or hardship. However, it is unlikely that his father would have uprooted his family from Sacramento, the Californian capital in the centre of the state, to Pacific Palisades, on the outskirts of Los Angeles, to take a job as a petrol pump attendant if there had been a viable alternative.

On the positive side, the Eastwoods were a close and happy family, drawn together by the isolation that comes with constantly moving on. Clinton Sr was a worker with the will to put groceries on the table, no matter how much it cost in blood, sweat and tears. 'Maybe my father did have his worries,' Clint comments, 'but neither Jean nor I ever knew about them. When I look back, I know he had to think pretty fast at times and he often moved from one company to another in order to better himself.' Clinton Sr was tall and athletic, with a good record on the football pitch and the track, and he took time out to teach his boy to shoot and fish and swim. Clint also found stability of a kind on his grandmother's chicken farm near Livermore. The family visited it regularly and there were times when Clint and Jean were billeted there for longer periods while their parents toured the Pacific states in search of work.

The property was set among lakes and hills, with opportunities for fishing and riding. With his long, slim build, Clint was a natural in the saddle and he developed a liking for going off by himself into the countryside, so establishing the persona of the lone cowboy that would serve him so well when he came to test for Rowdy Yates in *Rawhide*. Typically, he admired his grandmother for scratching a living out of rough country. 'She was quite a person, very self-sufficient, lived all alone on a mountain.'

The negative side of Clint's upbringing was that his education and his friendships were constantly interrupted. He grew tall and thin and gangly, reaching his adult height of six feet four inches by the time he was fifteen, and his dominant memory is of shuffling nervously into another classroom to meet new teachers and new peers. These meetings were rarely a success, either academically or socially. 'Somehow the standards were different or they were working on different phases of a subject. So although it wasn't that I wasn't bright, I was never out front. I always seemed to be behind and running to catch up. At school, I was never the one in my class to make things go. In the first place, I was about a foot taller than the rest of the kids. There were even occasions when I'd have lopped myself off at the knees if that had been possible.'

Clint's first opportunity to lead a normal life came when his father got a permanent job with the Container Corporation of America and the family returned to Oakland, across the bay from San Francisco. In the low ebb of adolescence, height combined with shyness can be intimidating, and it is easy to imagine the awkward youth striking fear into the hearts of the children he hoped would be his friends. Initially, the effect was to push him into greater solitude. When he was attacked by macho boys with points to prove, as large newcomers invariably are, he'd fight back and win. When he was left alone as a result, he'd take refuge in stories that gave him a hero's role. 'I dreamed of being a great air pilot. I rescued a lot of people from drowning. I was the world's greatest surfer. And I guess I saved more people on the operating table than any surgeon who's ever lived.'

Two things stand out in these daydreams: most of his heroes are outdoor types and his ambition is to be them, not to play them. At no stage did acting come into it. No doubt he is grateful to an English teacher called Miss Jones, who dared to insist he took the lead in a class play, but he wasn't at the time. Today he credits her with good casting instincts and good amateur psychology, but it can't have been too difficult for her to pick the introverted class loner to play 'a rebellious kid who didn't want to be involved; who felt a little bitter because he had this sense of rejection.'

Persuading Clint Eastwood to do it was another matter, as she soon discovered. 'The prospect terrified me. I didn't think it was possible to act – even in a school play – unless you were an extrovert. I asked to be let off. She tried to convince me I'd enjoy it. I enjoyed it so much through rehearsals that I almost ran away from school. My parents were pleased and anxious to see me perform; I suppose they knew I needed drawing out. Still, the closer it got to the actual performance, the more terrified I became.' He has vivid memories of going to the drugstore with his friend Harry Pendleton, who was to play his father, the evening before the show. The two boys talked through their dilemma and decided their classmates would laugh them off the stage. At the end of the discussion, Harry suggested they pull out rather than make fools of themselves and Clint agreed.

In the event, it was Clint who showed the less rebellious spirit by ringing Harry the next morning to renege on their deal. 'They'll murder us if we skip it,' he said, apparently with sufficient conviction to persuade his partner to join him on the stage. Nowadays he recognises that the play was the turning-point in his life. 'I remember drying up suddenly when the first laugh came. But then I realised it had come in the right place and that all the kids in the audience were laughing with me – not at me. I suppose it was the first time

I realised you could act extroverted without really being so, and also that being self-confident didn't mean people took an instant dislike to you or laughed at you. I was fifteen – but it was the day I grew up.'

The two other factors that brought him confidence in his teens were cars and success with girls. Cars came easiest but girls came first, if only because Californians started dating at a much earlier age than their European counterparts in the forties. Clint can barely remember a time when he didn't have his eye on a girl, starting in grammar school and working up through junior high and high school. His first crush was a red-headed teenybopper called Joan, the most popular girl in his class at Glenview Grammar School. He never dared ask her out, but for a time he abandoned his daydreams of derring-do to fantasise himself into the seat next to hers. For a man who has become one of the legendary womanisers of the late twentieth century, it was not a promising beginning. 'She never showed any signs of being intrigued with me and she never knew how I felt about her. In fact, so far as she was concerned, I was a big zero.'

The best way of attracting American girls in that era was to be a football or track star, but although Clint had an athlete's physique, he deliberately stood aside from any kind of group activity. In his own mind, he was an introvert out of necessity rather than choice. He'd watch enviously as all the girls hero-worshipped the champion of the moment and pray that he'd get to be an extrovert too, but the answering of his prayers was still some way off. 'I was the original hang-up man. I had a complex about jumping into anything with both feet. I stood back a bit too much, I guess; I just drew an invisible coat of armour round myself.'

When he did find the courage to invite girls on dates, he felt hopelessly inadequate as an entertainer. On one occasion, he talked incessantly about whatever came into his head, so much so that his partner never wanted to see him again. On the next date, he spent the evening in an amusement park in almost total silence. 'Somehow I could never get it right. I guess I was just too nervous around women at that time. I was pretty scared of making a fool of myself. It was just being afraid of women – which is the way a lot of kids are in adolescence.' His first breakthrough came when he was at Piedmont Junior High in Oakland. He recalls a stiff chaperoned birthday party and a stolen kiss with a girl called Marge. It was followed by dates at the drugstore and the swimming-pool, but the relationship ended abruptly when Marge's mother started talking about marriage. 'I just drew on my invisible armour and faded away.'

Much of his transitory sense of inadequacy was in the mind, according to the producer Fritz Manes, who remembers him as the cynosure of all eyes in junior high school. 'He had a kind of natural charisma that was really maddening. You could sit in class and do all the little tricks of flirtation, flex your muscles, shuffle your ten-dollar bill, and nothing would work if Clint was in the room. He'd be sitting there doing nothing, just looking at the floor, and all the girls would be looking at him as if they were in a trance, locked in on some secret magnetism he had. It was very demoralising for the rest of us.'

Not that he spent much time doing nothing because he always believed in his father's work ethic. As soon as he was in his teens, he financed his dates with newspaper and grocery rounds. His father bought him his first car when he was fourteen. It was a battered jalopy he picked up for twenty-five dollars but for Clint the freedom it represented was pure magic. For the next two years, girls came a poor second to cars as he drove around town illegally on a learner's permit. Thanks to his height, the cops never stopped him, not even when he took off for the summer to southern California. His game-plan for his first solo adventure was simple: take the first job that was offered. Employment came easily and he spent the summer baling hay on a large ranch, gruelling labour that left him barely fit to crawl into his bunk by nightfall. 'I'd be absolutely dead to the world but it sure toughened me up. That was about the happiest time of my life till then.'

With his confidence boosted by his success in going it alone, Clint returned to school and started making friends. His closest buddies, Bob Sturges and Jack McKnight, shared his passion for cars and soon they were deeply into drag racing, the current rage among teenagers with a liking for looking death in the face. The cars were assembled on a build-it-yourself basis, using whatever components could be picked up cheaply. The prime requirements were a powerful engine, a light frame, wide truck tyres on the back end and narrow motorbike tyres on the front. The aim was to produce a machine that would reach 110 m.p.h. in a few hundred yards and hold together until the race was over. Sometimes they burned out, sometimes the tyres blew out and the cars rolled off the track, sometimes they made it in one piece. Whatever the outcome, they made a hell of a racket, so meets were planned in secret to avoid interference from residents, farmers or the police. The favoured time was 5 a.m. on Saturdays and Sundays, but sometimes word leaked out and the contestants had to scatter across country on foot at short notice.

Clint had always been a speed freak so this kind of hell-raising came naturally, but he credits Bob and Jack with expanding his horizons in other directions. He likens them to the Three Musketeers in their 'one for all, all for one' approach to girls. Their main theatre of operations was the local swimming-pool and they trained hard so that they'd look impressive. At sixteen, Clint was filling out into a magnificent hunk, as even he had to

recognise. 'I knew I looked good on a diving-board and
I wasn't easy to beat in the water. I began scoring a few
successes.' Many of the girls had wealthy parents with
swimming-pools in their backyards where parties were
held at weekends. Recognising that any three men in
swimming-trunks look much like any other three men
in swimming-trunks, the Musketeers developed strategies
for gatecrashing the parties. 'The food was generally buffet-
style, so there was nobody to check on you there, either. But
it wasn't the food we were after – it was the girls.'

As soon as he was confident of his allure, male bonding
became as important as female bonding, and he felt able
to give up the fleshpots in favour of adventure in rugged
places. When Oakland Technical High School broke up
for the summer in June 1946, Clint headed north to the
Lassen Volcanic National Park with Bob and Jack. It was
an area he knew well from the time his father worked in
Redding, and he soon found jobs for the three of them with
the fire service. Their area of operations was the heavily
wooded slopes around the base of Mount Lassen, one of
the few active volcanoes on the American mainland. The
trio arrived too late to get spaces in the bunkhouse so
they unrolled their sleeping-bags in the garage among the
fire-fighting equipment.

Discomfort was the least of their problems during a
long dry summer in which a carelessly thrown cigarette
or an inadequately extinguished campfire could result in
raging conflagration. Clint and his gang were employed
to clear away stretches of undergrowth so that the flames
were halted in their tracks. Usually it worked, but on one
occasion the fire got out of control and it was all hands to
the hoses. For four long days, they tried to stop the inferno
by widening the breaks and cutting new ones, pausing only
for an occasional dried-up sandwich, but finally they had to
cut and run in the truck. As it accelerated down the slope, it

was pulled up short by a hose that had wound itself round a tree. In what could have been a pre-credit sequence for many a future action movie, Clint grabbed an axe, sprang to the ground and hacked through the hose, only to see the freed truck career off down the hill without him.

'There was no question of backing up. The truck had no more than thirty seconds to get clear itself. To the right of the trail, I noticed a big clearing – and a house in the middle of it. I went through a brush hedge like a tank and found myself running around in a field of pumpkins. All around me, the heat was intense, with smoke and sparks everywhere. I threw myself down on the grass and lay there, panting and scared, until I got my breath back. Then, sparks still falling around me, I staggered towards the house.' There he found succour in the form of coffee and pumpkin pie from a farmer's wife who took forest fires in her stride. Nor did his gang waste any time worrying about him, as he learned when he showed up later that night. 'They figured I'd fend for myself all right.'

Those first two summers in the great outdoors gave Eastwood a taste for living rough with his peers. On a dangerous job, he had to develop the team spirit that had been missing in his school athletic career. In the evenings, swapping tall stories with his friends as they sprawled around the bunkhouse stove, he began to communicate more freely, at least with men. He would never be one to talk off the top of his head, but he did learn to make conversation work at his pace. At weekends, the firefighters would hit Redding in search of relaxation in the form of a few beers, a few girls. To Clint, it seemed like an ideal life.

At times, the exhaustion that comes with hard labour during adolescence would put him out like a light so that he slept around the clock. At others, the adrenalin burn that comes with danger would keep him tense and twitching until dawn. In the dark watches of the night, he would

prevent himself re-running the firefights in his head by
pondering on an uncertain future. His school results were
adequate but not so brilliant as to cry out for a university
education, and his list of careers consisted only of those he
wouldn't consider at any price. No way was he going to be
a doctor, a dentist, a clerk, a lawyer or a businessman. He
liked taking girls to the cinema, and especially to westerns
or gangster films, but he had no thoughts of following up
on his one stage appearance with a career as an actor.

If he had gone for the entertainment business at this
stage, it would have been as a musician. His lifelong passion
for jazz began in 1945 when he heard the young alto sax
player, Charlie 'Bird' Parker, at a Jazz at the Philharmonic
concert. The experience would eventually inspire one of
Eastwood's most personal films, but in the meantime, he
decided to learn the trumpet and the piano. He made
sufficiently rapid progress to get a job playing the piano
at the Omar Club in Oakland in 1947, but there was
no cash return, just 'all the beer I could handle and all
my meals'. He had no difficulty deciding that it was not
enough. His parents were patient with his indecision and
with his wish to look around before committing himself.
'They were great parents and I was lucky to have them. I
never saw my father in a specific profession so I was never
really raised with the idea that you grow up thinking you
want to be a druggist or a physician or whatever.'

Ironically, it was in his son's late teens that Clinton
Sr, now aged forty, began the sales career that would
eventually make him a wealthy executive in the Georgia-
Pacific timber-shipping company. The family moved to
Seattle and Clint decided it was time he struck out on
his own. He heard that there were some good prospects
in lumbering in the Pacific North-West, and his father was
able to point him in the right direction, which turned out
to be the Willamette River in Oregon. 'My dad didn't object.

I guess he thought a little drifting around would be good for me.'

As far as lumberjacking is concerned, Oregon's wild unspoilt forests represent the top – and the most dangerous – end of the profession. The famous Douglas firs are six feet in diameter and they rise 250–300 feet above rough terrain. Lopping off the high branches requires more than a head for heights if the lumberjack is to survive. In those days, the forest giants were felled by the traditional method of cutting a big V in one side with an axe, then working a two-man saw through the trunk so that the tree fell in the required direction. The giant logs were then floated down to the sawmills for further treatment. Log-rolling, or riding them in midstream, was another procedure in which to fall could easily be to die.

Working the the sawmill was the best-paid part of the business, but Eastwood preferred to accept lower tree-felling rates in order to work outdoors. His most life-threatening moment came when he and his crane driver failed to secure the logs properly. Hearing a panicky yell of 'Timber!', he looked up to see a load of giant logs poised to fall on his head. 'I don't think I've ever reacted faster in my life. Yet even as I started to run, down came the logs. Any one of those great logs could have crushed the life out of me. I just barely jumped clear. As the logs hit the ground, they jammed against the crane.'

In essence, lumberjacking was not so different to firefighting. The days were long and tough, the accommodation basic and the food plentiful. The workers, as seen through the eyes of a conventional teenager from Oakland, were 'like wild characters out of a novel', but Eastwood soon adapted to their company. He particularly enjoyed Saturday nights in and around Eugene, a small place with a frontier-town mentality. The gang would drink a few beers and listen to live country and western music, badly but enthusiastically played. Eastwood recalls that they'd turn the place pretty much upside down before heading back to the hills, but that was what the citizens expected from the loggers. 'Maybe our manners were not quite the Ritz Hotel but they were usually glad to see us. We were a lively bunch, just out to whoop it up a bit.'

During this period, Eastwood was biding his time as far as girls were concerned. In the late forties, it was quite normal for school-leavers to settle on a career and get married before they reached their twentieth birthday, but Clint's itinerant childhood had made him aware of the dangers of taking on family responsibilities at too young an age. He was also smart enough to realise that a teenage crush might not be the perfect basis for a happy marriage. 'Occasionally I'd talk to a girl. I can't say there was anything serious, though. It was the wrong time for me. It wasn't that I was consciously steering clear of involvement but mentally I was still drifting. I'm glad I didn't rush into marriage like some of the other kids. They really didn't know what they were doing. Kids ought to give themselves time to look around a bit, to discover other standards. What looks good to you at fifteen or sixteen can look like crow-bait at twenty-one.'

As a Californian, Eastwood found the humidity of the temperate rain forest, where the sun could be hidden for six months on end, increasingly oppressive, so he moved back to Seattle before a second winter closed in. His worst job was filling out order forms for parts at the Boeing plant at Renton, but the night shift at the Bethlehem Steel furnaces ran it a close second. He was also employed as a truck driver, a swimming instructor and a lifeguard before he decided he would go to college after all and major in music.

The gods had other plans, as he realised as soon as the Korean War broke out. Knowing that nothing could stop him being called up, he headed south to San Francisco for a few last weeks of hell-raising before bowing to the inevitable. He partied so intensively that he arrived for his medical in a state of exhaustion but passed anyway and started his basic training at Fort Ord, on the Monterey peninsula. For a man accustomed to physical work, it was tough but bearable, much more so than the thought that he might soon die in a country he knew nothing about six thousand miles from home. 'I don't like the idea of getting killed, of anybody getting killed, but especially me. I'm against war, all war, and when I was in the Army, I was against the Korean War.'

No doubt his fellow recruits felt the same way, but while they found themselves on transports across the Pacific, Eastwood remained at Fort Ord. In an enterprising moment, he'd run through his varied work record with the captain in charge of the Division Faculty classes and asked if there was anything he could do. The captain asked him if he could swim. 'Sure,' said Eastwood confidently. As a result of this exchange, he was appointed swimming instructor in the Olympic-size pool. With typical bureaucratic overkill, it was already run by a lieutenant and four sergeants, but Eastwood organised classes and pulled out anyone who looked as if they were about to drown.

When their names came up, the lieutenant and the sergeants left for the theatre of war while Eastwood set about making himself comfortable for the duration. He moved out of the barracks into one of the pool huts and ran the place as efficiently as he could so as not to draw attention to himself. 'I was on my own, a private with a swimming-pool, wearing khakis and a sweatshirt, and a year and a half later, I was a corporal.' His basic pay was seventy-six dollars a month, inadequate to fund even low-key womanising, so he broke the rules by taking civilian jobs after he knocked off at 6 p.m. The first was loading sacks at the Spreckles Sugar Company, but after four months he was so exhausted that he fell asleep in the water. The second was as a bouncer at the junior non-commissioned officers' club, a rowdy place where a hundred or so men drank beer mixed with illicit liquor and fought over any girls foolish enough to go there.

His nearest dice with death during his army days came not as a result of action on a foreign field but of hitchhiking to Seattle. On a buddy's advice, he put on his uniform and went out to the naval air station near Monterey to see if there was a spare seat on a plane flying north. There was so he visited his parents and took a girl on a date before returning to the air base to look for a ride back to Monterey. With no planes available he was in a predicament, because he'd be declared AWOL if he didn't get back to camp in time and he had no money for the commercial fare. In desperation, he squeezed himself into the radar compartment of a naval torpedo bomber headed for San Francisco.

From his very cramped viewpoint, the flight seemed doomed from the start. First his door flew open and he had to secure it inadequately with a cable. Then his oxygen supply failed and he nearly blacked out as the plane rose above thickening cloud. Although he couldn't speak to the pilot, he overheard him telling his base that he had enough fuel for two and a half hours. That seemed okay at the time but not so great when the pilot dived towards the sea through a hole in the dense Californian fog; with the fuel gauge on red, he preferred to skim the waves rather than risk flying blind into a mountain or crashing over the city. When the engine finally cut, he had no option but to come down about a mile off the shore.

'I started wondering if the plane would float,' his passenger recalls, 'and began preparing for the moment we hit the water, wedging myself in so that I would ride the shock. I saw the water was rough. It was going to be

3

A Foot on the Bottom Rung

It is typical of Clint Eastwood that he should meet the woman who would become his only wife on a night when he had a choice of dates. He was in the shower when he received the telephone call from his friend Don Kincaid. Don had plans to go out with a girl from the University of California at Berkeley and she wanted to bring her friend along. Clint was easily persuaded to abandon his 'tentative' plans to see another girl and accompany him to the sorority house on a blind date. What he saw was a fairly tall athletic blonde with a model's body and lively humorous eyes. Her name was Maggie Johnson. Although Clint's first-ever crush was on a redhead, his subsequent track record shows that he is most attracted by slim blondes. Maggie was not the first and she would by no means be the last, but on that May evening in 1953, she suited him just fine.

'Maggie is the kind of girl I really like. There's nothing phoney about her. She has natural looks and, like me, she loves the outdoors. She and I hit it off at once but I can't say there was anything special about that night. At least I had no idea of marrying her.' When she graduated a month later, Maggie returned to her parents' home in Los Angeles. Eastwood had completed his two-year stint at Fort Ord so he was free and sufficiently intrigued to follow her south. He had $110 a month from the Army under the GI Bill, just enough to enrol in a business administration course at the Los Angeles City College. The course was for 'any student who hasn't the faintest idea what he wants to do when he graduates', but Eastwood showed some aptitude for it by doing a deal with the landlord of his apartment in Beverley Hills to halve the rent in return for managing the whole block. True to form, he took extra-curricular jobs in the afternoons, pumping gas at a Signal Oil station on Santa Monica Boulevard and delivering cars to General Service Studios.

He spent his earnings on exploring the city with Maggie at weekends. Their favourite relaxation was hanging out on Newport beach, part of an easy crowd of bronzed, cheerful young Californians kicking a ball around, preparing a barbecue and dancing on the sand to a radio, but they also liked films, theatre and jazz. In such a favourable climate, mutual liking led to a whirlwind courtship and marriage on 19 December 1953. They spent their honeymoon in Carmel, the time-warped resort near Monterey that Clint had fallen in love with at first sight in his early days at Fort Ord. 'Beautiful green mountains, well timbered, coming right down to the shoreline and some clean white beaches. I decided then and there that if I ever made a few bucks, I'd come back and settle there.' They were prophetic words, though not for some years yet.

In the meantime, the young couple had to come to terms with married life, which proved far more difficult than either of them could have imagined. Eastwood was as undomesticated as any other man of his generation, and then some. He had never had an enduring family home and, for the last six years, he'd either lived alone or dossed down with a gang of labourers. With male roommates, each staked out his territory and kept within it. With a wife, sharing was expected. Clint was not the sharing kind, not then, not now, not ever. He was and is private, egotistical and, above all, supremely old-fashioned in his attitudes to a woman's position, in general and in his life in particular.

'The first year of marriage was terrible,' he revealed to *Photoplay* in 1963. 'If I had to go through it again, I think I'd be a bachelor the rest of my life. I liked doing things when I wanted to do 'em. I didn't want any interference. I just didn't like to be pressed down, or having to go out of my way to cater to somebody, which I don't do. I'm not going to be that way. I never have been. You see, I'm a person who's never been gifted with a particularly easy-going temperament. I wasn't going to be submerged by the whole thing, so that being married was everything in the world because it isn't everything in the world. The whole marriage relationship consists of learning about one another. One thing Mag had to learn about me was that I was going to do as I pleased. She had to accept that because if she didn't, we wouldn't be married.'

She also had to accept that while she was to earn most of the money from her dull job at Industria Americana, a small firm supplying car parts, he was to lay down all of the rules. The one he enforced most strictly was the one about not opening his letters, whether they were personal or not. 'Mag did it twice, and then we put the roof back on the building,' he remarked laconically. 'I'm going to run the show. That's pretty well laid out. That's cut and dried. She's stuck with it. A man either runs the show or not. If I'm staying home and she's supporting me or something, then I shouldn't be running the show.'

Realising that these words invited charges of hypocrisy, Eastwood decided to give up easy come, easy go jobs and choose a real career. The foundations for his decision to become an actor had been laid when he'd chanced upon a film unit on location during his final days at Fort Ord. When he stopped to see what was going on, he attracted the attention of the assistant director, who hustled him in to meet the director, Arthur Lubin. He, in his turn, was impressed enough with the ruggedly handsome corporal to

ask him to contact him at Universal Studios. 'Did they ever
run a film test on you, Clint?' he asked when Eastwood
took him up on the invitation.

A date for the test was fixed for the following week and
Eastwood got his first real insight into the industry that
would take over his life. As he watched actors working
on the sound stage and talked to members of the crew,
he realised that he was watching a process that mixed
the familiar rigours of hard work over long hours with the
unfamiliar challenge of artistic achievement. Suddenly
he wanted to be an actor very much indeed. When the
test was done, he took Maggie out to a restaurant and
tried to heed her warnings. 'She was very sensible about
it,' he recalls. 'After all, thousands of people are tested and
only a handful ever turn out successful. Still, it could be the
break I was waiting for and neither of us felt like putting
a damper on the celebration.'

After two white-knuckle weeks and three unanswered
calls to Lubin, he was resigned to rejection, but three days
later the phone roused him from sleep in the early morning.
Universal Studios had a contract for him to sign: seventy-
five dollars a week for six months. Not bad, he thought, and
yet he hesitated. His business-studies course was unfinished
and he would have to give it up, along with his nice little
earners at the gas station and the apartment block. What's
more, he had a wife to support and she was against him
going into a profession with such a high divorce rate. In a
summit meeting with his father-in-law, he learned that the
Johnsons were definitely in favour of him getting steady
work of a decent professional kind, not tempting fate by
going into an industry none of them knew anything about.

In the end, it was sheer bloody-mindedness rather than
the strictures of his in-laws or his own impulse to take
risks that tipped the balance. By his account, the world
can thank an old woman in the apartment block for his

glittering career. Whenever he saw her, the nagging tenant would tell him to paint her walls and he'd explain that he was the manager, not the interior decorator. 'Every time I saw her, she'd bug me a little more,' he remembers. 'I think that settled it. "You're twenty-four," I told myself, "and you've been bumming around all your life, just drifting and sort of hoping something would turn up. So maybe it won't work out – but isn't it worth taking a chance?"'

Put that way, the answer could only be yes, and Clint Eastwood, actor, was finally on his way. Okay, so he was an untrained hunk who got photographed bare-chested on the beach with a starlet on each arm, but it was a start. While the contract was running, he went to Universal's workshop school and learned the rudiments of his new profession. When the contract was renewed for a second six-month period and then a third, he started taking outside drama classes at his own expense. He didn't think he had much aptitude for acting and he didn't join in much with the other contract players, but he watched and he listened and he learned.

He even got to play fourteen bit parts in what he has described as 'movies it would be kinder to forget'. The first was Jennings, a laboratory assistant in *The Revenge of the Creature*, a sequel to the low-budget horror classic *The Creature from the Black Lagoon*. Its star was John Agar, better known as Mr Shirley Temple, and its director was Jack Arnold, following up on his success with the earlier film. Once he'd been cast, Eastwood learned that Arnold had deep-rooted objections to Jennings's only scene whereas the producer, William Alland, insisted that it should be shot as written in the script. The two men fought the point fiercely for two days while Eastwood waited nervously for a decision.

As is customary, the producer won and Clint donned his white coat and walked into the lab to speak his only

line, 'I've lost my white mouse.' The head technician
replied, 'Look in your pocket.' Jennings looked and found
the missing mouse. 'It was terrible!' Clint remembers,
embarrassed years later by the idiocy of the exchange.
However, the film was something of a cult hit and Arnold
hired Eastwood for another tiny part in his next movie,
Tarantula. Again the budget was low, the star John Agar,
and the plot about man terrorised by beast predictable, but
Eastwood enjoyed taking over the controls of a jet plane to
bomb the malevolent spider in its hideout in Arizona. He
may be unrecognisable in helmet, mask and goggles as
he speaks his single line, but he's in there and he plays
his first hero's role by destroying the baddie.

He also worked for his original patron, Arthur Lubin, in
Lady Godiva as a drawling First Saxon, the last character
to appear on the credit list. The title role went to Maureen
O'Hara, but fifties prudery being what it was, she concealed
much more than she revealed in a thoroughly dull movie.
John Agar also headed up the cast in the first ever Eastwood
western, *Star in the Dust*, for which he received no screen
credit at all. However, he found that much less humiliating
than *Francis in the Navy*, the sixth in the *Francis the Talking
Mule* comedy series, with Donald O'Connor as the resident
lead. Again the director was Arthur Lubin and this time
he gave his protégé a part as a sailor with several lines
to say. 'If you remember it, you'll do me a favour by
forgetting as the whole thing looks pretty funny now,'
Clint comments wryly.

For Eastwood, the process was a valuable learning curve
and he made good use of it. When he wasn't at the daily
classes, he hung about on sets, chatting to the technicians
and casting a shrewd eye over what was going on. 'None
of the movies I was in were top rank but I learned a lot. I
think you learn from seeing a bad movie as much as you do
from seeing a good movie. It's just like acting in a picture

with a bad director. It gives you some point of reference, some comparison, so that when you meet someone who is halfway adequate, you see what makes the difference.'

And so it went on for eighteen months, with his salary rising by twenty-five dollars a week after the first six months. He notes ironically that when his early films are shown on television nowadays, they are billed as Clint Eastwood co-starrers, but at the time his one-to-four-line bit parts made zero impact at the box office or anywhere else. Eventually Universal concluded that his performances didn't merit even the modest increase they'd promised him after a year with the studio, so they called him in and told him either to quit or continue working at the current hundred dollars a week rate. After an initial outburst of rage – 'What the hell, if they can't give me a raise, I'll take a hike' – he swallowed his pride and continued with his game-plan for as long as he could.

In fact, his days at the studio were numbered by the climate of the times rather than any limitations of his own. After the golden years in the thirties, the cinema was in a worldwide decline, threatened on the one hand by the inexorable rise of television and on the other by its own refusal to face up to the need for change. When the industry's founding fathers, the great producers like Jack Warner and Sam Goldwyn, bowed out, they had not been replaced by men of similar vision but by accountants and chisellers. European cinema was feeding on a new bright vision in the aftermath of war. In America, where creative people were victimised by the McCarthy witchhunts and potential viewers were locked into the mindset of the Cold War, the industry was content to churn out lesser variants on jaded themes while television snapped at its heels.

In the immediate postwar years, cinemas were selling eighty-five to ninety million tickets a week, but by 1956 the figure had come down to thirty-five million. Stars like Humphrey Bogart and James Cagney, who had aged out of the glamour side of the business, were replaced by conventional hunks like Charlton Heston and Burt Lancaster. At Universal, the talent was headed by Rock Hudson and Tony Curtis, both groomed expensively for stardom in the late forties. By the time Eastwood became a contract player, the studio was cutting down on young male actors. He was one of only fifteen on their books, compared to forty women. All through his time at Universal, he was criticised for not being more like Hudson and Curtis. He was too tall but he didn't walk tall, he was too quiet and too still, he was not a new Cary Grant or a new Spencer Tracy.

As part of his acting workshop, he'd occasionally been sent out on a horse to make as if he was a cowboy and the secretaries at Universal always called him 'Coop' because he was slow-talking like Gary Cooper. The western was still a major force in Hollywood in the mid-fifties and yet the higher studio powers obstinately refused to see that the tall, slim wannabe with the faraway eyes was born to ride the range. 'That's the trouble with the movie industry sometimes,' Eastwood recalls wearily. 'When a trend starts, they want it to continue. So in their eyes, if you weren't a carbon copy of a popular star, you were a huge nothing. After a year and a half, they booted me out, along with a lot of other contract players who afterwards became big television stars.'

So it came about that Clint Eastwood went out where he came in: as a laboratory assistant. His second shot at the white coat was in *Never Say Goodbye*, a sugary tale of divorced parents who come back together for the sake of their child. The father was played by Rock Hudson in a pair of glasses hijacked from Eastwood. He'd been asked to select one pair out of ten in order to make him look older. When Hudson saw what was happening, he wanted a pair too. 'You're the leading man,' said director Jerry Hopper, 'you don't wear glasses.' But Hudson was not to be denied. Faced with the same selection, he picked the same ones as Clint, leaving the newcomer with no option but to hand them over and reflect on the power of privilege.

It was a lesson he would absorb over the next two gruelling years, because his early luck had run out. It didn't happen all at once. When he first left Universal, Arthur Lubin got him a contract with RKO Radio Pictures to play Carol Channing's beau in *The First Travelling Saleslady*. The comedy was a prime example of the kind of movie that was dragging the Hollywood studios down, and none more rapidly than RKO, already on its last legs in Howard Hughes's ownership. The script was written by Stephen Longstreet as a serious piece of Americana, triggered by an item he'd read about the fencing of the West in accordance with new laws in the early part of the century. Barbed-wire salesmen had died at the hands of enraged ranchers, so Longstreet invented barbed-wire saleswomen on the premise that the West would show them more respect. RKO thought that was just fine as long as there was a strong element of comedy, so they brought in a second writer to graft it on.

They then cast Ginger Rogers as a corset designer who reacts to the closure of a Broadway show featuring her wares by setting off for Texas with her secretary (Channing) to sell the barbed wire. By the time Eastwood read it, plausibility was not the lynchpin of the plot, but he accepted the part of a young officer much taken with Channing's charms. His height may have helped because she is a tall woman, but the role gave him 'introducing Clint Eastwood' billing, his first close-ups, and his first notice in the *Hollywood Reporter*. It read, 'Clint Eastwood is very attractive as Carol Channing's beau', but not enough of the right people saw it because the first phase of his movie career had just one picture to go.

Again it was an RKO/Lubin collaboration and it took him to Japan in August 1957 to play Pilot Dumbo at $175 a day. That aside, *Escapade in Japan* had few advantages, other than as an extended travelogue for its host country. Eastwood's unconventional pilot triggered the plot, such as it was, by inspiring two boys, one American, one Japanese, to go looking for the American's parents after they'd been lost in a plane crash. By the time the picture was released, Hughes had sold RKO to new owners who pulled out of film production altogether. With the B-movie on its way out and overall Hollywood production figures on a downward curve from four hundred pictures a year in 1951 to less than two hundred in 1959, Eastwood realised that a change of emphasis was overdue. 'TV was like a younger brother, or a second-class citizen, but to me it was a logical place to really learn the business. Most of the people in television were doing the newest things, and in TV you had to work twice as fast, twice as hard to get half the credits.'

At the outset, it took his best efforts to get any credits at all. For a while, he managed to scrape along with a line here, a line there, in single episodes of the series that churned relentlessly off the production line. The motorcycle cop he played in an episode of *Highway Patrol* was typical of the jobs he got, but then even they dried up. Increasingly the television producers were using young actors they'd groomed themselves or buying in surefire names from Hollywood to head up ever more expensive series. With hindsight, Eastwood can see a logic in this, but at the time it was a bitter pill to swallow, leaving him with no choice but to go back to labouring if he was to keep putting groceries on the table.

As Harrison Ford would do a decade later, he picked a new line that kept him in touch with the grass roots of his profession. 'I took a pick and shovel and worked for a swimming-pool company which was installing filter systems in the stars' homes in Beverley Hills. Quite a few of my friends now don't recognise the fellow who used to dig up their back lawns.' Unlike the Harrison Ford bookshelf, the Eastwood filter system has never become a collector's item, but he dug them with the same relentless drive he brought to his search for acting work. Recognising that agents 'don't give a damn about young unemployed actors', he had little faith in his, but he rang him every day, often from pay phones during breaks from work. Sometimes the responses were more positive than the results. Eastwood has grim memories of sitting in a producer's office all day and never getting the promised interview for the lead in an upcoming series. 'Sometimes I was out of work for six months at a time, and I got pretty depressed about it.'

When work came, it was brief and inconspicuous, far removed from the showcase he needed to reach the next step on the ladder. Even lower-echelon typecasting demanded that he should play more laboratory assistants, along with cops, ensigns and soldiers. In 1957 and 1958, his career developed a military bias, with roles in *Navy Log*, *Man of Annapolis* and, more regularly, in *West Point*, a series about cadets at the Military Academy. When it failed after a short while, it came as no surprise to Eastwood. 'Think what West Point cadets actually do. They march, go to classes, play football, study and go to bed.'

Such roles as he got were invariably action-oriented, so he tried to increase his appeal by volunteering to do the stunts himself, and eventually it paid off. He'd been overlooked for westerns for so long that *Ambush at Cimarron Pass* came out of the blind side. Although it was a Twentieth Century Fox production, it had a ten-day shooting schedule, an obscure director in Jodie Copeland, and a low-level cast headed by the routine cowboy actor Scott Brady, and an unknown starlet called Margia Dean. Eastwood's name came third in the list, which made it his most prestigious credit to

date. He played a Confederate soldier who teams up with
Brady's Yankee cavalry sergeant to fend off the Apaches,
then fights him for Ms Dean.

Ambush at Cimarron Pass was shot in a new process
called Regalscope, which earned the undying scorn of the
third actor in the line-up. When he and Maggie went to see
the movie at their local cinema, Eastwood described the
photography as 'the most uneven I have ever seen. One
minute, it was so bright you needed sunglasses to look at
the screen. The next second, the print was so dark you
couldn't make out anything. It was probably the worst
movie ever made.' Like his other dogs, it refused to die,
re-emerging in the sixties on the back of the 'Dollar' films,
with Clint Eastwood at the top of the cast list.

Lafayette Escadrille, directed by a Hollywood legend
William Wellman, promised much but delivered little.
Wellman had won the first-ever Academy Award for *Wings*
in 1927 and launched James Cagney on his glittering career
in *The Public Enemy* four years later. He was revered in
Hollywood for his roisterous personality and his exploits
as a Foreign Legion ambulance driver and an ace pilot
during World War I. *Lafayette Escadrille* was conceived
as a memorial to a close friend in the volunteer American
pilot unit of the French Air Corps. The story of his last
days was scripted as a tragedy and the sentimental ballad
singer Tab Hunter was cast in the lead, with Eastwood
and his old army pal David Janssen as fellow heroes
George Moseley and Duke Sinclair.

The film was shot and previewed as a tragedy, but
then Tab Hunter made a record that sold two million
copies and the studio decided that he couldn't die.
'That dirty rotten bastard Jack Warner decided that
killing Tab Hunter was impossible,' Wellman recalled
with his customary outspokenness. 'He raped my *Lafayette
Escadrille*, the story of a very dear friend. All the

guys who were still alive from Escadrille thought I was nuts. I shot the happy ending, came away and went home and said to my wife, "Dotty, I'm tired. I've worked too hard and I made a deal with a man I hate, knowing he's wrong. I'm never going to make another picture." ' And he didn't.

Nor, for the next five years, did Clint Eastwood. The reason for his change of status was Rowdy Yates of *Rawhide*, the series based on the great cattle drives from Texas to the railheads in the Mid West in the 1860s. The producer was Robert Sparks and the creator Charles Marquis Warren, renowned in the business as the man behind the best-selling thirty-minute series *Gunsmoke*. His current ambition was to match NBC's high-profile sixty-minute series, *Wagon Train*, with one of his own for CBS. The new series was to be solidly based in history, much of it culled from George C. Duffield's *Traildrover's Diary*, so as to present as accurate a picture as possible of the working life of the professional cowboy in the nineteenth century.

As luck would have it, Maggie Eastwood had a good friend, Sonia Chernus, who worked as a story consultant in the script department at CBS. Eastwood had pressed his agent to get him a test when he first heard rumours of *Rawhide* during the making of *Ambush at Cimarron Pass*, but the man had told him they were looking for someone aged thirty-five to forty to play trail boss, Gil Favour. Rowdy Yates, his twentysomething partner, didn't come into the equation. 'My agent wasn't bright enough to find that out,' Eastwood remarked later. This certainly suggests that he was either lazy or inept because the Hollywood model for *Rawhide* was the Howard Hawks cattle-drive classic *Red River*, which had two leads in John Wayne and his much younger antagonist, Montgomery Clift.

There are various versions of how Clint was finally transformed into Rowdy Yates, but all involve a chance visit to CBS to have coffee with Sonia Chernus, and an element of luck. By one account, Chernus tried to introduce Eastwood to Sparks, only to be told by his secretary that he was too busy. Deciding that it would do no harm for him to work his magic on the secretary, she took him up anyway, only to have Sparks come through the office and stop short in his tracks. 'How tall are you?' he is said to have asked Eastwood, before whisking him into an inner sanctum to meet Warren. By another account, Eastwood and Chernus were sitting by the coffee wagon when a man came up and asked, 'Are you an actor?', to which Eastwood replied with an economical 'Yeah.' More dialogue followed in which Eastwood tried to puff up his credits as much as possible, though without any element of desperation because he still believed there was no major role for him in *Rawhide*. Only when the man called him into his office and introduced him to another man who looked as if he might be a cleaner – none other than Charles Marquis Warren, as it transpired – did he learn of the existence of Rowdy Yates.

That same afternoon a phone call summoned him back to the studio for a screen test. Three other actors were already going through their paces as Eastwood was handed a dense page of dialogue. 'It was pretty complicated emotional stuff and I knew I'd never get it right. So I decided to memorise the key points and more or less improvise the rest.' As the afternoon passed and the director became increasingly hostile to his off-the-cuff interpretation, he realised that he could have made the wrong decision. Not only had the director written the script but one of Eastwood's rivals was ingratiating himself by reading the lines word for word. 'I've blown it,' he yelled at Maggie when he got home that evening. 'There's no one more right for that role in this town than me – and I've just blown the whole thing.'

For a week, it looked as if he was right, but then he received good news from the projectionist who'd run the test footage for the New York executives who had to make the final decision. By eavesdropping on their conversation, he'd learned that the director wanted the actor who'd shown a proper reverence for his writing, but the executives had insisted on Eastwood because he looked the part. 'I was in! I didn't believe it until the next day when the studios called to confirm that I'd gotten the role. That was a great day in my life. The money looked to me as if I'd be in a league with Howard Hughes.'

So far, so good, but many more months would pass before *Rawhide* would be seen on networked television. First CBS had to decide whether to try to sell the series on a single pilot programme or a thirteen-episode package. Eventually the word came through that the studio would go with the package and the cast and crew went on location. Real cowboys were hired to contribute authenticity. Eastwood studied and imitated them as they showed how to work huge herds of cattle over Arizona's arid open spaces. He remembers these as some of the most fulfilling days in his life, but then the axe fell again. With ten episodes in the can, CBS cancelled the show on grounds of cost and consigned the footage to the studio basement. Not only would it not be shown on television, it could not be shown at all, not even to a feature-film producer who wanted to see Clint's recent work. 'There I was again, without job or prospects except to go back to digging ditches. I knew that if producers could see my work – the first time I'd ever got a chance to show what I could really do – that I wouldn't be out of work for long. But there was no way round the impasse. I was the star nobody had ever seen. I wasn't even the actor on the cutting-room floor. I was the player who was locked up in a vault. It was impossible to believe.'

This was the one point at which Clint Eastwood considered quitting and returning to his studies in business administration. He'd been in films and television for five frustrating impoverished years, often collecting unemployment insurance of twenty dollars a week, and he'd been stabbed in the back on the whim that dictated that sixty-minute western series were no longer in fashion. While he was trying to come to a final decision, he decided to spend the Christmas of 1958 in San Francisco. He and Maggie travelled north by train, a journey he spent staring out of the window in black depression. When a porter handed him a telegram, his gloom was compounded by fears that something had happened to one of his parents. 'I expected the whole sky to cave in on me. Somehow I tore it open. It was from my agent. All it said was, "*Rawhide* going on as replacement series early New Year stop Congratulations and Happy Christmas". Happy Christmas was the understatement of the century, so far as I was concerned.'

He remembers sticking his head out of the window and yelling profanities, then ordering up champagne, as was right and proper, because this magic moment signalled the end of poverty for ever. *Rawhide* aired at 8 p.m. on Friday 9 January 1959 with 'Incident of the Tumbleweed Wagon.' For the first time, the singer Frankie Laine belted out the memorable theme tune, 'Rollin', rollin', rollin', keep them dogies rollin' . . . Rawhide'. Then Eric Fleming, another unknown who was to carve out a much lesser career as the taciturn Gil Favour, and Clint Eastwood appeared, although so inconspicuously that *Hollywood Reporter* reviewer Hank Grant asked, 'Who stars in this series?' He would soon learn, because *Rawhide* accumulated 217 episodes over seven years, fourth in the table of all-time western greats behind *Gunsmoke's* twenty years, *Bonanza's* fourteen and *The Virginian's* eight. By 1960, it was among the ten most popular shows in America and the Fleming-Eastwood version of the classic duo, the honourable authoritarian older man and the impulsive, antagonistic but ultimately loyal younger one, had found their niche in television history.

As far as Eastwood was concerned, the work was immediately rewarding as he rode the range in the ramrod pose that would become one of his trademarks. He has always been well suited to buddy-buddy action roles and the outdoor life. Where others might have moral reservations about peddling American colonial aspirations in the untamed West, Eastwood's deep-seated patriotism made him proud to be part of it. He also appreciated *Rawhide's* verisimilitude. 'Occasionally I guess we hoke up a story for dramatic purposes, but generally speaking we're doing the things that guys on the cattle drives really did.'

Once he was locked into the series, Eastwood used it as a highly paid training-ground. As an actor, he played the nice guy with reliability and professionalism. He enjoyed the luxury of experimenting that comes with regular work. If he failed one week, he could try again the next without fear of being fired. As variations on the role became harder to find, he tried to liven up his part by suggesting stunts that Rowdy Yates might perform, only to learn, to his surprise, that CBS now considered him too valuable to risk. When he noticed that a stampede was being shot from the side, he was quick to offer to mix it with the cattle. 'I'd like to take an Arriflex, run it on my horse and go right in the middle of this damn thing, even dismount or whatever. But let me get in there and really get some great shots because there are some beautiful shots we're missing.' He was told curtly and incorrectly that it was against union rules.

On the positive side, he developed a rewarding partnership with the late Eric Fleming, a man with whom he shared top billing without animosity. If Gil Favour had the major part of a story, Fleming headed the cast list; if it was Rowdy Yates's turn, then Eastwood came first. 'When I hear about rivalries and tensions that are standard on a good many of the production stages in Hollywood, I just draw a deep breath and say, "Thank God for Eric Fleming",' he commented at the time. In particular, he thanked God for Fleming's intervention in the hours war that resulted from studio greed. The original schedule stipulated six days' shooting, with Sundays off, with work starting at 5.30 a.m. and going on for as long as it took, often close to midnight.

After a few months of shooting that week's lines while learning next week's, Clint and Eric were exhausted. 'So were the steers!' Eastwood recalls. 'The horses would have been in the same shape but for the guardian presence of the SPCA. As I crawled to my car one night, I told Eric, "One of the things that gravels me is that there's no Society for the Prevention of Cruelty to Actors."' As a result of this conversation, Fleming went on set the next morning and announced that he would be knocking off at 6 p.m. that afternoon and every afternoon thereafter. CBS reacted with furious threats but Fleming stuck with his edict. 'That's about all that kept the actors alive,' said Clint with feeling.

When he wasn't in front of the cameras, Eastwood was invariably behind them, learning the basics of the directing career he was increasingly sure he wanted. *Rawhide* was heavily into guest celebrities to headline individual shows, so he was able to observe more experienced actors at work, among them John Cassavetes, Walter Pidgeon, Ralph Bellamy, Lon Chaney, Claude Raines and James Coburn. The nature of the show in which women rarely provided anything more than a romantic interest, and that a fleeting one as it had to end in failure by the end of the programme, meant that actresses were fewer and farther between. However, Eastwood singled out Geraldine Page and Julie Harris for special praise from a group that included Margaret O'Brien and Barbara Stanwyck.

On a lesser level, it also included Roxanne Tunis, a stuntwoman and actress who joined *Rawhide* in 1959 when she was twenty-eight. Contemporary accounts agree that she was a tall, stunning brunette and that she was totally bowled over by Clint Eastwood. For the next five years, they behaved as a couple on set, showing their mutual affection openly. Eastwood made it possible for her to stay by negotiating larger roles for her but he always made it clear that he had no plans to leave his wife. When Maggie Eastwood came to visit, she chatted to Roxanne but she has never admitted to knowing about the affair at the time.

In 1964, Roxanne bore Clint Eastwood his first child, a daughter called Kimber. Legend has it that she was too scared to tell her lover she was pregnant so Eastwood didn't know when he went off to Italy to make *A Fistful of Dollars*. Kimber was born at the Cedars of Lebanon Hospital on 17 June 1964. On the birth certificate, her surname was Tunis but her father was named as Clinton Eastwood Junior. When Clint heard a baby crying on his first visit to Roxanne after his return from Europe, he allegedly said, 'I see one of your sisters finally had a blonde baby', but then the truth began to dawn. In another five years, the climate of sexual liberation would have made public acknowledgment easy, but in 1964 marriage was still relatively sacrosanct, especially for those who would be Hollywood stars. Accordingly Clint and Roxanne did a deal by which she shut up and he paid, a bargain that held up for a quarter of a century.

From a professional point of view, Eastwood was more interested in *Rawhide's* directors than its guest actors. Some were familiar, among them Jack Arnold, who'd been behind the cameras on the first two Eastwood films, *Revenge of the*

Creature and *Tarantula*. Others were notably efficient and innovative, among them Ted Post, who was later chosen by Clint to direct him in *Hang 'Em High* and *Magnum Force*. Others muddled through as best they could, often with sound advice from the cast and crew who knew the way *Rawhide* worked much better than they did. When Eastwood was sure he could do a good job, he cleared his game-plan with Fleming, then asked the producer if he could direct an episode himself. The answer was yes, provided he cut his teeth on trailers for the next season. He worked hard and for nothing on them, only to have CBS ban him because they'd had difficulties when another series star had taken over an episode of the show.

Eastwood had lost his first big battle with CBS but he would yet win the war, albeit on a different front. His second major confrontation was over the question of whether he should be allowed to work on feature films during the summer break from *Rawhide*. James Garner from *Maverick* and Steve McQueen from *Wanted: Dead or Alive* already had plans for extra-curricular activities and Eastwood demanded no less for himself. When his requests were repeatedly turned down, he spelled out his grievances to Hank Grant in the *Hollywood Reporter* in 1961 in terms that he knew would make the television studio sit up and take notice. 'I haven't been allowed a single feature or TV guesting offer since I started the series. Maybe they figure me as the sheepish nice guy I portray in the series but even a worm has to turn sometime. Believe me, I'm not bluffing. I'm prepared to go on suspension if necessary, which means I can't work here, but I've offers to do features in London and Rome that will bring me more money in a year than the series has given me in three.'

Perhaps he was being economical with the truth over his intention of going on suspension, but he never had to stand up and be counted because CBS realised they had no choice but to let him use his own time as he wanted. It took two more years for bluff to become reality, but when the call came it was from Rome and it was for the film that would switch his career back from television to the cinema. This time, the switch would be for keeps.

4

The Magnificent Stranger

Clint Eastwood was not Sergio Leone's first or even his second choice for the leading role in the presciently titled *A Fistful of Dollars*, but then neither was Sergio Leone a name to be conjured with in 1964. As the son of a pioneer in the Italian film industry, he had excellent connections which he had used to work for leading directors, starting with a bit part in Vittorio De Sica's *The Bicycle Thief* in 1947. When Hollywood came to Rome in the fifties to benefit from cheap rates at the Cinecitta Studios and tax concessions back home, Leone was employed as assistant on wide-screen 'sword and sandal' spectaculars like *Quo Vadis* (1952) and *Ben Hur* (1959). As he worked he learned and so came to direct an epic of his own, *The Colossus of Rhodes*, in 1961.

Curiously for a man who had learned no English, Leone's real love affair was with the American West, to which end he acquired the rights to Akira Kurosawa's *Yojimbo* (1960). Preston Sturges had already been this route with *The Magnificent Seven*, the adaptation of the Japanese director's *The Seven Samurai* (1954) which established Steve McQueen as a major player when it came out in 1962. Encouraged by the film's success, Leone set about funding a remake of *Yojimbo*, retitled *The Magnificent Stranger*, in case any potential backer should fail to spot the connection. In 1963, Leone raised a modest $200,000 from Jolly Film in Rome, Constantin Film in Munich and Ocean Film in

Madrid. An English-language script had been prepared in three weeks by Leone and two collaborators, using dubbed television shows as the model for their dialogue. By the end of the year, the Italian-German-Spanish co-production was ready to trawl for its star and, on the grounds of verisimilitude and pulling power, he had to be American.

After toying with the high-priced Henry Fonda, Leone's first realistic approach was to Charles Bronson. Like McQueen, he had made his mark in *The Magnificent Seven*, but in a supporting role which meant that he might still be cheap enough for Leone's budget. Maybe he was, but he definitely wasn't smart enough to go for it, as he later admitted. 'The script was so bad that I turned it down. It was just about the worst script I'd ever seen. What I didn't understand was that the script didn't make any difference. It was the way Leone was going to direct it that would make the difference. So Clint Eastwood got the part.'

But not until it had been offered to another *Magnificent Seven* veteran, James Coburn. He didn't know Sergio Leone either, but everything he'd heard about Italian filmmakers had been negative and he too thought the script was pretty indifferent. Accordingly he set his asking price at $25,000, which was more than Leone was prepared to pay and, unlike Bronson, he never learned from his mistake. 'I didn't know who Sergio was until he came down to Almeria in Spain where I was making a film, and he wanted me to do a film with Charlie Bronson, *Once Upon a Time in the West*. I turned that down as well and it made a star of Charlie Bronson! And I'd turned down the first film, making Clint a millionaire – and he's never thanked me!'

Sergio Leone had never heard of Clint Eastwood until he was mentioned by an expatriate American, Richard Harrison, employed as a sub-Schwarzenegger-type muscleman in assorted Roman epics at the time. When Leone watched an episode of *Rawhide* entitled 'Incident of the Black Sheep', he noted that although Eastwood barely said a word, he was good at getting on and off a horse and he had a way of walking with 'a tired resigned air'. When the script reached Eastwood, he was reluctant even to read it on the understandable grounds that he'd been making a western a week for the past six years. When he did, he was surprised by the atrocious dialogue but struck by the concept of a man who couldn't even be identified as the hero until halfway through the movie, and then only by the implication that he was less evil than the other protagonists. After years with the virtuous Rowdy Yates, Leone's gun for hire seemed like a gift from the gods. 'I'd been typecast as a nice guy. "You're a nice guy," they'd tell me, "so we'll look around for nice-guy parts for you." A guy can go nuts, not to mention broke, listening to that sort of flattery. Yet you can't just grab any part. It has to feel right.'

The more he considered The Man with No Name, the more Eastwood came to believe that it did feel right. In his opinion, the western genre was moribund in America, mostly because if was too simplistic in its differentiation between good and evil and too predictable in its outcome. Some years later, he summed it up in the following caustic terms: 'Usually the hero rides into town, sees a horse getting beaten, sees the schoolmarm, rescues the horse and you know who he's gonna get hitched with at the end – and it isn't the horse!' When Eastwood had seen Kurosawa's original film, with Toshiro Mifune as the Samurai with No Name who arrives in a community torn between conflicting factions and sells himself as a yojimbo – a bodyguard – to each in turn, he'd enjoyed the conspicuous absence of virtue. When the Samurai sees a woman in distress, he rides on. When he gets bored with playing one side against the other, he turns his gun on both of them. When he's creamed off the cash, he rides out of town, leaving the survivors to work out their future as best they can.

Eastwood identified with the gunman's lone disposition and his ability to maintain his cool in any situation, things he prided himself on in his own life. He asked Maggie for a female reaction to the screenplay and hers was extremely positive. 'Clint says I'm good at spotting the woman's angle to a story and I liked this one of the loner. Women want to be looked after and protected and a man who can dominate the scene, handle himself against the odds, has instant appeal to a woman.' Their marriage was already under threat from Clint's male chauvinism and his womanising but, at this relatively early stage, Maggie was prepared to reinforce her husband's self-image, and Eastwood needed no further prompting. In any case, what did he have to lose? He'd never been to Europe, he'd be paid $15,000 for a summer's work, modest by *Rawhide* standards but enough by his, and if he failed, no one would ever know. 'If the picture turns out to be a bomb, it won't go anywhere,' as he told his agent reassuringly when he signed the contract.

So it came to pass that Eastwood arrived in Almeria in May 1964 at the outset of the blazing Spanish summer to take the lead in *The Magnificent Stranger*. He may have thought he was tough but nothing in a life spent almost entirely in California and the Pacific North-West had prepared him for the ordeals to come. He spoke no Spanish or Italian and no one else spoke anything more than rudimentary English. The other leading actors were the Italian Gian Maria Volonte, and the German Marianne Koch. Volonte played the Mexican bandit, Ramón Rojo, and Koch the kidnapped woman, Marisol, but each spoke their lines in their own language, with a view to dubbing at a later stage, as is the Italian custom. It didn't take Eastwood long to decide that it was in his own and his character's best interests that there should be as few lines as possible. To this end, he pared down his part, just as he had when he'd first read for the director of *Rawhide*, extracting the essence by eliminating anything he considered surplus to requirements.

'I had got to the point where I had enough nerve to do nothing. My first film with Leone had a script with tons of dialogue, tremendously expository, and I just cut it all down. Leone thought I was crazy. Italians are used to much more vocalising and I was playing this guy who didn't say much of anything. Leone didn't speak any English so he didn't know what the hell I was doing but he got so he liked it. When I had a problem, I used my street psychology. I'd say, "Well, Sergio, in a B-western, you'd have to explain, but in an A-western, you just let the audience fill in the holes." I wanted to play it with an economy of words and create this whole feeling through attitude and movement. I felt the less he said, the stronger he became and the more he grew in the imagination of the audience. You never knew who he was, where he came from and what he was going to do next.'

Both Eastwood and Leone have taken the lion's share of the credit for the elusive nature of The Man with No Name. Leone insists that his original concept was to emphasise the fundamental loneliness in the stranger by having him stride silently through a town full of noise. An essential element in his strategy was the music which he discussed interminably with his childhood friend, the composer Ennio Morricone. 'Calling Ennio before the filming was arranged, I told him the whole story. For three or four months we would row violently. But in the third or fourth month after listening for the three hundredth time to every small detail of my film, Ennio began to bring from the piano keys the first three or four bars of the film score. At last I had my drug. Now I could shut myself in a room knowing what Ennio, with sacred patience, had prepared for me. All the scenes and the photography now began to take shape. The characters were all moving with the correct style and I put in the finishing touches. A film was born.'

Their blueprint was as far removed as possible from the traditional western soundtrack, which used swelling chords to announce tension or trigger emotion in the customary Hollywood manner. Morricone's score was as integral to the film as the cinematography, a double assault on the senses that gives the story its momentum. The results were described by Staig and Williams in *Italian Western: The Opera of Violence* as 'a musically surrealistic panorama of strange cries, savage guitar chords, jangling bells and the cracking of whips. Grunts, groans and Indian-like shrieks adorn the panorama. The form is totally unlike anything American. The music is as hostile as the action, the close affiliation enters the realm of Opera.'

In a decade in which popular music took on an unprecedented role as a catalyst for social change, Morricone's jagged score underpinned the contemporary nature of the 'Dollar' trilogy. As the old barriers came tumbling down in the increasingly turbulent sixties, the strident chords enhanced Leone's potent mixture of brutality, realism and black humour. Eastwood's individual theme tune was a carefree whistle, a minimalist expression of his laconic screen persona. The actor saw the films as essentially satirical, with the comedy coming from the inter-reaction between the stranger and the hyperactive gun-toting classes he eliminated with such chilling despatch.

When the films came out, he was surprised at the hostile reactions to violence that he always perceived as an essential element in the comedy. The Man with No Name exults not in bloodshed but in professional expertise. There is no hand-to-hand combat, just the crack of a bullet, the crumpling of a victim onto the sun-soaked sand. The arid landscape is the perfect backdrop to the languid figure with the capacity to move at lightning speed when the occasion demands. 'I knew they were tough films,' Eastwood said when the trilogy was completed. 'I'm not a person who advocates violence in real life, and if I thought I'd made a film in which the violence inspired people to go out and commit more violence, I wouldn't make those films. But I don't believe they do. I believe they're a total escape type of entertainment.'

Eastwood has always claimed that he designed his wardrobe before he left Los Angeles, buying his black Levis from a western outfitters on Hollywood Boulevard and distressing them to the state of decay he required. His dark brown hat came from a shop in Santa Monica and he used a gun belt, boots and spurs 'borrowed' from *Rawhide*. Only the cheap trademark poncho came from Spain and it went through all three 'Dollar' films without a double or a replacement or a wash. Leone had originally perceived his central character as an older man so he disguised Eastwood's youth with a straggly beard and a permanent cigarillo stuck in the corner of his mouth. 'This posed problems for him, to have a cigar constantly in one's mouth when one does not know how to smoke,' he commented. However, Eastwood felt that the vileness of the thin black weeds put him in the right mood. 'If I had to be in an unpleasant frame of mind, I took a couple of draws and, boy, I was right there.'

The main set for *The Magnificent Stranger*, as assembled in Almeria by the cheap labour of Franco's Spain, consisted of a hybrid border town, part Mexican adobe, part American timber. Many of the buildings had interiors, an economy measure in that most of the footage could be shot in a single location. Beyond the town, spectacularly empty plains provided a dramatically minimalistic backdrop for The Man with No Name, or Joe as he is called in the original screenplay, as he rides his mule into San Miguel. He is greeted by a noose hanging from a dead tree and a dead man tied to a horse with an 'Adiós Amigo' message on a card pinned to his chest. When a woman is dragged back into her home and her small child is kicked, he rides straight past, only to find himself galvanised into undignified action when four gunmen – seemingly the town's only other living inhabitants – shoot up the ground under the mule's feet. After leaping for a beam outside the saloon to avoid being trampled in the dust, he saunters inside and discovers that San Miguel is in thrall to rival factions, the Rojos, a gang of ruthless Mexican bandits led by Ramón, and their adversaries, led by the corrupt Sheriff Baxter. Once he's staked out the territory, he moves smoothly into action, killing Baxter's gunmen and selling himself to the opposition on the strength of this display of expertise.

From this point, the plot twists and turns with more virtuosity than credibility. It contains many familiar western elements, among them gold stolen from the American Army and a distraught Mexican wife, Marisol, who must be freed from bandits. Its revolutionary nature lies not so much in the detail as in the motivation of The Man with No Name. Where traditional western heroes are proof against profiteering, honour-bound to eliminate corruption and faithful to the concept of romantic love, he straightens out San Miguel for personal gain. He is a mercenary whose values would attract a fatal bullet in the first reel if Gary Cooper or John Wayne were in the movie. As they aren't, he gets to call the shots himself. And very accurate they are too.

This straight-down-the-barrel approach is reflected in Leone's no-frills production. The director entered into the spirit of his movie on a daily basis by turning up for work wearing a ten-gallon hat, cowboy boots and sideburns, and his quest for realism didn't stop there. All the characters look as if they live hard and dangerously and none more so than the women, in startling contrast to Hollywood counterparts who are fussed over by hair and make-up people as they trip immaculately from their trailers to their marks.

While the sun blazed down over eleven exhausting weeks, the actors sweated under exterior arc lamps set up to intensify the already brilliant light. Their effect was to rack up the heat quotient still further, and it has been said that Eastwood acquired his trademark squint by looking painfully into the dual glare of natural and artificial sun. Although the production was chronically short of cash, Clint was usually grateful enough for his lead role not to protest too much. 'There were always arguments about paying the crew,' he commented pragmatically, 'but then I wouldn't have been in Spain if they'd had a lot of money. I'd still have been back in Hollywood with Maggie waiting for the breaks. They'd have gone for James Stewart or Bob Mitchum if they'd been loaded, so I figured I'd have to put up with the disorganisation.'

For the most part, he contrived to show as little emotion away from the cameras as The Man with No Name did in front of them, behaviour that was reinforced by the language barriers. He described his Italian colleagues as coming from the '*Hellzapoppin*' school of drama, in contrast to his own laid-back approach to his craft. 'In real life, Clint is slow, calm, rather like a cat,' Leone recalled. 'During shooting, he does what he has to do, then sits down in a corner and goes to sleep immediately, until he is needed again. It was seeing him behave like this on the first day that helped me to model the character.'

However, there was one occasion when Eastwood's fuse blew and he ran for home. At the outset, it had seemed a day like many another, with Leone and the crew arguing the hours away as if they had all the time and money in the world. 'The talk was all in Spanish and Italian. I didn't understand a word, but I could tell there was a violent discussion going on about something and I hoped they'd get it straightened out before we blew the whole morning without getting one shot. Finally Sergio called me over and said through his interpreter, "Okay, Clint, you can start making up."'

The make-up job in question simulated the results of a savage attack from the whole Rojos gang, an elaborate collection of swellings and bruises covering most of his face. As such, it would take a couple of trying hours in sticky fly-infested heat. When Eastwood walked grimly back onto the set, it was to find it totally deserted. 'I'd always been a loner but suddenly I was literally the most alone man in all Spain. No producer, no director and no crew. Only the big arc lamps standing there like Spanish vultures. It seems the crew hadn't been paid for two weeks, and they had left the set until someone came through with their money. This wasn't the first time this had happened. It was just one foul-up after another. But this time, with one eye sealed shut with make-up and all the other junk on my face, I'd had it.'

Even so, quitting went against the grain. 'I remembered that my father once said, "Nothing comes for nothing, son, and don't plan on anything because no one can give you anything in life. Of course, it you get lucky and something rolls your way . . ." On this occasion, paternal common sense was not enough to stop him leaving a message for Leone to say he was going to the airport. 'Maybe I hurt too easily inside, or react too quickly: I used to flare up at the drop of a hat until I learned better. Maybe I just don't shove around too easily. Anyway, I made a decision. Fortunately Sergio caught me before I left the hotel. He apologised for the ordeal I'd been put through and promised it wouldn't happen again.'

And it didn't, not to the same degree anyway. After the outstanding interiors were shot at Cinecitta and the dubbing completed in Rome, Eastwood made his way home for the seventh series of *Rawhide*, due to start shooting in the autumn. He had no great expectations of the film he still knew as *The Magnificent Stranger*, not even when he saw an item in *Variety* saying that Italian westerns were all the rage after the phenomenal success of *A Fistful of Dollars*. 'So what?' he thought as he returned to work on a series he now felt was overdue for retirement. Two days later, he learned the truth when he read a further dispatch from Rome: '*A Fistful of Dollars*, starring Clint Eastwood, is going through the roof here.'

What had actually happened was that the producers, Arrigo Colombo and Giorgio Papi, had decided that their film, with its taciturn hero, had more chance of success if it was billed as an American western rather than an Italian one. They changed the title to *Per un Pugno di Dollari* and Americanised the credits so that Sergio Leone became Bob Robertson, Ennio Morricone Dan Savio, and Gian Maria Volonte John Welles. Even with this bizarre window-dressing, they were far from optimistic, so they opened the English-language version with Italian subtitles as quietly as possible in a small cinema in Naples and waited for the worst. Instead they got the kind of word of mouth that producers dream of, and the film was still on its first run a year later.

'The producers hadn't bothered to write to me since I left, saying thank you or go screw yourself, or whatever,' Eastwood commented caustically when he learned of his change of status. In Italy, where he was now known as 'Il Cigarillo' because of the ubiquitous cigar, he was established as the ultimate symbol of machismo in a nation that couldn't get enough of it. As the months passed, *A Fistful of Dollars* became a hit throughout South America, another bastion of male pride where an anonymous self-confident hero who has no truck with women can never fail to become an icon.

According to the mythology, when Leone and Morricone saw their film for the second time, they agreed that it was good but not good enough, and so decided to make a second one. Fortunately Leone had already devised another story so he was ready to write the new screenplay – inevitably it was called *Two Magnificent Strangers* – with a collaborator, Luciano Vincenzoni. He had also found a new backer in Alberto Grimaldi, a lawyer who had established his own film company in 1962. Next on his checklist was Clint Eastwood, who had never expected to see him again. Luckily for Leone, the American release of *A Fistful of Dollars* was delayed until 1967 by copyright problems with Kurosawa over *Yojimbo* and a degree of scepticism among home-based distributors. As a result, Eastwood was a hero in Europe but a second lead in a stagnant television series in his native land.

Whether he would have returned to the chaos of working with Leone if he'd already become the toast of Hollywood is open to doubt, but in the circumstances he was happy to accept Leone's offer of a £50,000 fee, plus a percentage and a new Ferrari, to star in *For a Few Dollars More*. Leone offered the part of the second Magnificent Stranger to Charles Bronson, who still failed to understand what the Italian director was about. 'This time I turned it down because I said it was just like the first movie. It was, but what I didn't understand was that everybody wanted it to be just like the first movie.'

This opened the door for Lee Van Cleef, a familiar Hollywood baddie since he'd exuded silent menace as one of the gunmen in *High Noon* in 1952. His career had been subject to ups, like *The Man Who Shot Liberty Valance*, and downs, like being unemployed and broke when Leone approached him in 1965. Like Bronson, he wasn't overjoyed at the prospect of playing Colonel Douglas Mortimer in darkest Spain, but Leone's was an offer he couldn't refuse.

'I accepted because I had nothing more exciting to do,' he said after he signed on for his $17,000 fee, but, according to the biographer Michael Munn, the sum represented thirty per cent more than anything he'd ever earned before. When the production manager gave him his advance, he rushed home and threw the bundle of notes at his wife. 'The rubber band broke and there were greenbacks all over the room. It was two weeks' pay. She was crying and laughing and she counted it four times. The day before was our wedding anniversary and I couldn't give her anything. We were living on TV royalties and unemployment and what she made as a secretary. I didn't even have the money to pay the phone bill.'

He'd already met Eastwood briefly on *Rawhide* and reckoned that they'd be able to capture the somewhat ambivalent relationship between The Man with No Name and Colonel Mortimer. *For a Few Dollars More* was not so much a sequel as an opportunity for Leone to develop the themes and the style of *A Fistful of Dollars* with a lot more cash in the bank. The budget of $600,000 allowed for extensive sets in Almeria, including the frontier town, Tucumcari, the Mexican village, Agua Caliente, and a replica of the town of El Paso. In *A Fistful of Dollars*, San Miguel seems deserted even for a semi-ghost town locked into sudden-death conflict on a daily basis. In *For a Few Dollars More*, the easing of the economy permitted an appropriate number of extras and a range of period pieces, including a railway track with a steam train and a selection of stagecoaches and wagons.

The Stranger is still unnamed but he is now a bounty hunter, a freelance operator who collects posted rewards for bringing in criminals dead or alive. Self-evidently it is work he is well suited to and clearly he is good at it because the droopy mule from the first film has been replaced by a sleek high-stepping chestnut horse. In other respects, his appearance and his character are unchanged. Sergio Leone's storyline starts with a partnership between the stranger and Mortimer, two bounty hunters in pursuit of the same quarry, El Indio, a psychotic killer who has just escaped from jail.

The first twenty minutes of the film are spent establishing the three main characters in unrelated incidents before the strands twist together for the main story. As far as his two hunters are concerned, the only way El Indio can regain his status as the most ruthless operator of them all is to rob the bank in El Paso, the Texan equivalent of Fort Knox. All they have to do is ambush him during the hold-up and collect the rich bounty on offer for his corpse. The bank robbery is also a useful device in that it provides a safe full of cash on the loose to test the limits of the alliance between the Stranger and Mortimer. After assorted events that suggest there is little honour among any of these thieves, the three men and the money end up in Agua Caliente – hot water in Spanish – for the final showdown.

It is only when Mortimer has killed El Indio that his motive for hunting him down is revealed: revenge for the rape of his sister, the murder of her young husband and her subsequent suicide. Up to this point, Leone keeps us guessing as to whether Mortimer and The Man with No Name will fight for the booty. Their alliance is superficially friendly – they call each other 'old man' and 'boy' – but there is a hard edge to it that keeps the option of a duel to the death open until they finally go their separate ways. The plight of Mortimer's ageing gunman underlines the fact that The Man with No Name is a man with no future beyond his present, despite his stated ambition to invest the proceeds of his bounty-hunting in farmland.

Shooting on *For a Few Dollars More* began with interiors in Cinecitta, then moved back to Almeria for the bulk of the location work. This time, there were no strikes, no pay crises and fewer tantrums all round. Eastwood's dark golden looks made a fitting contrast with the slim, saturnine Van Cleef, a killer dressed all in black, as they competed to see who was fastest on the draw. Eastwood is credited with 0.45 seconds to draw, cock and fire, but Van Cleef claimed he was better still. 'Well, I believe that in actuality I'm faster than Clint,' he told Munn. 'They discovered it took three frames for me to draw, cock and fire. That's one-eighth of a second.'

Although Gian Maria Volonte had died as Ramón Rojo in *A Fistful of Dollars*, he was resurrected to play the archvillain El Indio, a drug-racked sadist who is first seen butchering his elderly cellmate as he is sprung from prison. Where the Colonel and the Stranger are career killers, he exults in death, pumping up his rage on an adrenalin high as bullets tear through flesh. His extremes of viciousness provide a kind of justification for his killers. In a Leone western, the presumed realities of mid-nineteenth-century America ensure that no one comes out squeaky clean, but there are grades of evil that clear the way for the survival of the antihero at the expense of the psychopath.

The increased budget for the second film allowed Leone to elaborate on a distinctive style that contrasted wide open spaces with extreme close-ups, not only of faces but of hands on guns and banknotes. The editing mixed languid long shots of insect-sized horsemen in arid country with staccato fights in which all is noise and bustle. Again there was the Morricone score, brilliant and intrusive as it reinforced, and at times even pre-empted, the visuals. *For a Few Dollars More* has been described as the ultimate horse opera, with its three separate establishing scenes as the arias and its three-way confrontation as the tragic climax. It is also the film in which Eastwood starts to emerge from his shell by giving the first hint of the narrow green-eyed smile that was to make him a superstar in years to come. As David Downing and Gary Herman wrote in *Clint Eastwood, All-American Anti-Hero*, 'It is the smile that makes you a hero because it sets you above both the common herd and the authorities, the physical morass of the one, the moral morass of the other.'

Back in Rome for dubbing at RCA Italiana studios, Eastwood was flattered to be asked by Vittorio De Sica to play a cameo role in *The Witches*, a compilation devised by the producer Dino De Laurentis as a showcase for his wife, Silvana Mangano. De Sica's segment, 'A Night Like Any Other', was the last of the five, a contemporary fantasy in which Eastwood plays Mangano's husband. Wearing modern clothes and glasses, he appeared in a short dream sequence showing the various stages in a marriage. 'I don't know what I've got going for me but Vittorio De Sica thought I appealed to foreign audiences because I depicted their idea of a rangy American, the same way I guess Gary Cooper might have done.' *Variety* was rather less enamoured, describing Eastwood's segment as 'the dismal, pointless De Sica bit at the end'. *The Witches* was never shown outside Europe, mostly because United Artists bought it in order to suppress it once they had Eastwood on their books.

Before Eastwood left for America for what had now become the annual *Rawhide* drudge, he struck a deal with Sergio Leone that would pay him $250,000 plus ten per cent of the net in the Western hemisphere to return in the spring of 1966 for a third spaghetti western. Back home, a quarter of a million dollars could make a man bullish, even boastful, as veteran Hollywood columnist Sheilah Graham learned when she spoke to Eastwood. 'I'm probably the highest-paid American actor who ever worked in Italian pictures. Only Mastroianni gets more in Italy. I don't want to make all my westerns in Italy and Spain, but in Europe I'm in a better position to get the films I want and to work with people like De Sica. For the first time in my life, I can pick the parts I want to play.'

When he learned that Eric Fleming had been fired from *Rawhide* by CBS for accepting a role opposite Doris Day in *The Glass Bottom Boat*, Eastwood sensed that the gods were finally getting in behind him on a permanent basis. Initially he allowed Rowdy Yates to be promoted to trail boss, a position he filled uneasily for a few more episodes until the inevitable falling ratings caused the show's cancellation in mid season. Not only was Eastwood relieved of the burden of carrying a moribund series on his own but, on a red-letter day, 8 February 1966, he received a pay-off cheque for $119,000 from CBS. As there was a feeling that 'an American actor making an Italian movie was sort of taking a step backward', he was not exactly in demand at home, but he was rich and he was free.

'*Rawhide* was great fun at first and it was certainly a great training-ground,' he told *American Premiere* by way of a wrap-up some years later. 'You shoot so much film in such a short period of time that you can really learn a lot if you want. But after seven years of playing the same character in the same wardrobe you get kind of edgy and the wardrobe begins to stand up all by itself. I mean, it's the same horse. After a while, you have to think of things to keep yourself amused. And when you find yourself putting lipgloss on your horse you know you're becoming ill. But there are so few acting jobs around that when you get one, you tend to want to hang on to it and ride it out. Fame is not that appealing, but keeping your job is.'

It comes as no surprise to learn that the third Leone western started life as *The Magnificent Rogues*. The first two films are set in the years of expansion after the Civil War, but the film that came to be known as *Il Buono, Il Brutto, Il Cattivo – The Good, The Bad and The Ugly* – takes place during the war itself. In this sense, it is a prequel, but once again, The Man with No Name is the only common factor in a story written by Leone and Vincenzoni. As the title suggests, Leone indulges his fascination with the threesome, but in a different psychological permutation. Whereas *For a Few Dollars More* matches cool with cool against psychotic, *The Good, The Bad and The Ugly* pairs cool with chatty against cool. Eastwood, as Il Buono, gets a new partner, Il Brutto (The Ugly), otherwise known as Tuco, while the clinical Il Cattivo (the Bad), also known as Angel Eyes, goes it alone.

Lee Van Cleef was glad to accept a second Leone assignment as Angel Eyes, a gun for hire who is happy to share a meal and learn a secret from a man he is contracted to kill. The persistent Leone hoped it would be third time lucky with Charles Bronson when he asked him to play Tuco, but the actor was already involved with *The Dirty Dozen* and regretfully turned the part down. The celebrated fifties Broadway 'Method' actor Eli Wallach agreed to do it instead, much to Leone's delight, because he had always dreamed of directing a major American star. As a result, he shifted the focus of attention towards Tuco at the expense of The Man with No Name, an adjustment that was not lost on Eastwood. 'In the beginning, I was just about alone. Then, there were two. And now there are three of us. I'm going to end up in a detachment of cavalry,' he commented drily.

The budget for *The Good*, *The Bad and The Ugly* was a handsome $1,200,000, which allowed for locations in parts of Spain Leone hadn't reached before. These included the environs of Burgos in the much greener north, but the hard core was still in the tiny patch of Almerian desert that he had made his own. Geographical variety was matched by a new style of clothing, with the long brown duster coat replacing the poncho. Near the end of the film, Eastwood covers a dying soldier with his cattleman's coat and puts on his poncho in exchange, a simple but effective way of establishing that The Good and The Man with No Name are one and the same man. As always, Eastwood took as active a part in the shooting as possible, especially when there were stunts to be done. When The Man with No Name was supposed to ride up behind Tuco and hoist him into the saddle, Wallach backed out fast on the grounds that Broadway actors aren't accustomed to such exertions. However, Eastwood had no hesitation in sweeping the stuntman, hands tied behind his back, on to his galloping horse.

Like *For a Few Dollars More*, *The Good, The Bad and The Ugly* starts with independent episodes designed to establish the three protagonists. Tuco, the Ugly, is the first to show, with Wallach leaping out of a window with a gun in one hand and a chicken leg in the other. He is a totally unreliable Mexican bandit, greedy and garrulous in equal proportions. Next into the limelight is Angel Eyes, The Bad, who establishes his *mala fides* by fulfilling his contract, then double-crossing the contractor. Last in line is The Man with No Name, saving Tuco as he stands on the scaffold by shooting the rope around his neck. Once again he is a bounty hunter, but this time he has a new game-plan: whenever the opportunity arises, he hands Tuco over to the authorities, collects the price on his head, and uses his gunmanship to save him on the gallows.

Based on deceit as it is, the alliance can only be a shaky one, with No Name abandoning Tuco in the desert and Tuco ready to repay him in kind until he realises that No Name knows the whereabouts of $200,000 of missing Confederate gold. The story contains familiar elements from the earlier films, with money in the melting-pot and three men due for the final carve-up, but it is placed much more precisely in American history. This is because Leone, who well remembered his adolescence during World War II, had points to make about the pointless suffering that comes with fighting other men's battles. In a European context, this is a particularly Italian perspective, but it translates effectively to the American Civil War, a no-win situation for the individual Yankee and Confederate soldiers involved. Even No Name, the totally efficient killing-machine, is moved to say, 'I've never seen so many men wasted so badly.'

This may be supposed to provide a rationale for a future as a gun for hire, but the point is not laboured in Leone's screenplay. Instead the alliance between No Name and Tuco is revived by the race for the gold they believe lies buried in Sad Hill Cemetery. This is a fitting arena for a brilliant final confrontation between three greedy men. Leone spins it out for five long speechless minutes as the camera plays over restless eyes and fidgety gun-hands and the Morricone score booms across the graves of war victims laid out in circles as far as the eye can see. In the cheating spirit of the contest, No Name has emptied Angel Eyes' gun, but neither he nor Tuco know this, which leaves the balance very much in No Name's favour. When the fingers finally hit the triggers, Il Cattivo dies and Il Brutto survives, but it is Il Buono who rides off into the sunset with his share of the money, abandoning his horseless ex-partner to find his way out as best he can.

While *The Good, The Bad and The Ugly* opened with the by now familiar razzamatazz and bumper bookings in Europe and Japan, Alberto Grimaldi was trying to sell the trilogy as a single package to United Artists for release in America and Britain. It was at this late point that The Man with No Name was born, a marketing device designed to provide continuity for a character who was fleetingly referred to as Joe in the first film and Blondie in the last. The name, like the character and indeed the films themselves, was very much in the spirit of the sixties, a period of restless rebellion in which people either opted out altogether or opted in with a view to destroying the social barriers that had sustained the status quo through the fifties.

As repressiveness was replaced by permissiveness, the western heroes of yesteryear were among the first to lose their credibility. The new generation of moviegoers had no sympathy with strangers who rode into town to destroy corrupt administrators, only to pin their marshals' stars to their own breasts at the end of the film. Nor did they have much time for honourable sheriffs who fought off bank robbers: in tune with the fashionable contempt for corporate greed, they were much more likely to wish the thieves godspeed. Least of all did they empathise with the hunky cowboy who hung up his gun to embrace homesteading, marriage and fatherhood. As the spread of the birth control pill paved the way for levels of sexual freedom that would have been unthinkable ten years earlier, family life was not what heroism was about.

In the Sergio Leone films, there was absolutely no danger of anything like that happening. As corruption is endemic in Italy, administrators are evil per se, so The Man with No Name can rip them off with impunity. If he enters into a deal with them, it is to use and betray them. If he doesn't he kills them, but not before showing them up as the scum they are. The towns he passes through are far removed from the tasteful quaintness of American western outposts, with their neat white churches, their decorative wooden buildings and their swing-door saloons. In the spaghetti westerns, the towns are desolate and dangerous. It is impossible to imagine anyone wanting to settle down and raise children in them.

When it comes to relationships, The Man with No Name is as isolated as his environment. He is the master of the clean kill but he never has fist fights, never touches an adversary and rarely makes any gesture of goodwill to anyone. In *The Good, The Bad and The Ugly*, he is

humanised to the point of offering a dying soldier a puff
on his cigar before taking his poncho and riding on. As the
film is the first in the chronological scheme of things, this
only suggests that he sheds any residual warmth towards
his fellow man as he gets older, possibly as a reaction to
the war. At no time does Leone provide him with any kind
of love interest, and his male companions are there out of
necessity rather than friendship. When women appear, they
are peasants oppressed by poverty, men and motherhood,
with no possible attraction for the passing stranger. At the
start and the finish of each of the films, he is always alone.

This too was in tune with an era in which revolutionaries
like Fidel Castro and Che Guevara became international
icons for resisting the yoke of American imperialism. In
photos, they appear grim and committed, but the popular
perception was that they were cool and self-sufficient, the
qualities that underpin The Man with No Name. Eastwood
does smile in the 'Dollar' trilogy, but it is a detached,
sardonic smile, with no warmth in it, at best an expression
of amused contempt, at worst a prelude to further rapid
despatch.

When Grimaldi finally had his deal in place, United
Artists opened *A Fistful of Dollars* in eighty cinemas in
New York on 2 February 1967. The night was locked in
a blizzard and the reception from the critics was at least
as chilly. It was too imitative, too cheaply made, above all
too violent. 'An ersatz Western dedicated to proving that
men and women can be gouged, burned, beaten, stamped
and shredded to death,' wrote Judith Crist, adding, 'Mr
Eastwood shows a talent for squinting and mouthing a
cigarillo.' Other critics were outraged by Leone's attempt
to outscore Hollywood in its own backyard. Where *Yojimbo*
had been accepted as art, *A Fistful of Dollars* was dubbed a
'pop western' and slated for it. Not that the public cared:
as in Italy, word of mouth spread and United Artists were

able to announce that they had a hit on their hands. In
May 1967, they trumpeted the return of The Man with No
Name in *For a Few Dollars More*. *The Good, The Bad and
The Ugly* came out the next year.

As the films gathered momentum, the critics became
increasingly confused as to how they should react to a
phenomenon that refused to go away. Should the trilogy be
condemned as amoral or applauded as satirical? Certainly
the second two were considered long, though they were
not as long as they should have been owing to censorship
cuts that curbed the violence at the expense of the plot,
especially in Britain. Andrew Sarris, of *Village Voice*, an
initial doubter who crucified *A Fistful of Dollars* for its crude
dubbing and monotonous settings, had a change of heart
when he saw a way of using the trilogy's on-going religious
imagery as an intellectual peg. 'The sheer duration of the
suffering makes Eastwood a plausible lower-class hero
whose physical redemption is the contemporary correlative
of Christ's spiritual redemption,' he wrote of the scene in
The Good, The Bad and The Ugly in which Tuco takes his
revenge on The Man with No Name.

America's most celebrated film critic, Pauline Kael, went
the other way, starting out with positive remarks about the
larger-than-life quality of the films, then changing her mind
at a later date after she spotted the embryo of Dirty Harry in
Leone's Stranger. 'Apart from their aesthetic qualities, and
they did have some,' she wrote in the *New Yorker*, 'what
made these Italian-produced Westerns popular was that
they stripped the Western form of its cultural burden of
morality. They discarded its civility along with its hypocrisy.
In a sense, they liberated the form: what the Western hero
stood for was left out and what he embodied (strength and
gun power) was retained. This is no longer the romantic
world in which the hero is, fortunately, the best shot;
instead, the best shot is the hero. And that could be what

American audiences, grown derisive of the triumph of the good, were waiting for. Eastwood's gun power makes him the hero of a totally nihilistic dream world.'

And what did Eastwood himself think? '*Fistful* established the pattern. It was the first film in which the protagonist initiated the action. He shot first. Everybody knows that nobody ever stood in the street and let the heavy draw first. It's me or him. To me that's practical and that's why I disagree with the [John] Wayne concept. I do all the stuff Wayne would never do. I play bigger than life characters but I'd shoot the guy in the back.' No kidding. He's been doing it ever since.

5

A Profitable Learning Curve

'A lot of people thought I was a bit crazy to go off to Europe to make a western – and for an Italian company! But I've learned to back my own judgment and my hunches now.' As these words suggest, Eastwood returned from Italy flushed with the confidence that comes with success. In a daring coup, he'd broken the mould. Now he would re-write the ground rules. Essentially that meant he would take control of his career with a view to profiting from the studio system while keeping it at arm's length. To this end, he set up his own production company, Malpaso, initially in a bungalow at Universal Studios. It was named for a creek he owned in the Monterey Peninsula, but the irony in a name that means 'bad step' in Spanish appeals to Eastwood, especially as it has been one of the best steps he has ever taken.

In line with the principles of good housekeeping that have always underlined his career as a director, he kept his over-heads to a minimum, employing just four people and buying as little office equipment as possible. It was from this base that his trusty lieutenant, Irving Leonard, was charged with launching Clint Eastwood into the Hollywood mainstream without selling his soul to the devil. The first Malpaso production was *Hang 'em High* for United Artists, naturally keen to follow up on their profits from the 'Dollar' trilogy with further Eastwood appearances. Accordingly they agreed to the kind of deal that no major studio would have touched at the time, though such complex co-productions have since become commonplace. In essence, *Hang 'em High* was a collaboration between Malpaso and Leonard Freeman Productions for United Artists. Leonard Freeman, an old friend from Eastwood's Universal days, came up with the story and got sole credit as producer, although he shared the production work with Eastwood and Irving Leonard, who was billed as associate producer.

Hang 'em High is an overt attempt to cash in on the Leone films, an American spaghetti western with a theme of vengeance supported by up-front violence and obsessive historical detail. Its $1.6 million budget included a $400,000 fee for its star, plus twenty-five per cent of the gross. Eastwood chose Ted Post, who'd worked with him on episodes of *Rawhide*, to direct, although he'd not done a feature for ten years. The qualities he admired in Post, efficiency and technical expertise, come through in the finished film, but the American veteran was never able to match Leone's flair and off-the-wall humour.

The film opens with a near-lynching as Eastwood, playing stone-faced ex-St Louis lawman Jedediah Cooper, herds his newly purchased cattle across the Rio Grande. Enter nine hostile horsemen led by Ed Begley's Captain Wilson. After accusing Cooper of stealing the cattle and ignoring his proffered bill of sale, they drag him by lariat across the river, a painful stunt that Eastwood made all the more effective by doing it himself. After that, they hang him and leave him for dead. It is his good fortune that a roving US Marshal, played by Ben Johnson, passes by and cuts him down, then swears him in as a deputy marshal so that he can legally pursue his attackers.

Much of the action takes place in Fort Grant, standing in for Fort Smith, Arkansas, known historically as the arena for a notorious hanging judge called Parker. In the film, he becomes Judge Fenton, similarly enthusiastic about capital punishment and therefore ready and willing to provide the film with its most dramatic set-piece, the public hanging of six men. Fort Grant was built with dedicated accuracy on an old western set at the MGM studios, and many of the scenes were shot there. Its centrepiece was the huge gallows, a working replica of the ones at Fort Smith. The location work was done out of Las Cruces, New Mexico, much of it in considerable discomfort among shifting dunes in the White Sands National Park. The young Bruce Dern, cast as one of Cooper's many opponents, vividly remembers crushing Eastwood's face into the fine powdery sand, then getting his own crushed as the star got the upper hand. 'I pushed his face in that sand and he came up spluttering and trying to blow sand out of his mouth, and he just got on with the scene,' Dern recalls admiringly.

It is easy to see the heavy hand of Hollywood in a scenario which has Cooper pursuing his aggressors through a maze of confused plotting. Unlike The Man with No Name, Cooper is never fully in control, either of himself or his destiny, so he has to muddle through as best he can. He channels his revenge through a legal system whose most powerful representative, Judge Fenton, is in favour of carnival-style public executions. Along the way, he falls in with a woman seeking vengeance on the man who killed her husband, a contrived love interest of the kind Tinsel Town can never resist. 'I think, on the screen, men like it better without a female; and sometimes, women do too,' Eastwood commented but, after three years of non-involvement on the wide screen, he agreed to love scenes in *Hang 'em High*.

Cooper and Rachel get to know one another when she nurses him back to health after he is ambushed by Wilson during the executions. She is effectively played by the tragic Swedish actress Inger Stevens, an Eastwood favourite until she killed herself in 1970. 'She was a doll, a real good woman to work with,' he said in final tribute, and her quiet, strong performance as Rachel confirms this obituary. Unfortunately neither their relationship nor the film comes to any particular conclusion, as it ends abruptly with Cooper riding off into yet another sunset in pursuit of yet another of his aggressors. Presumably this was to avoid the cliché of him settling down with his cattle and his bride, but the lasting impression is that the filmmakers had run out of ideas. 'It was a western in the old tradition, only tougher,' was Eastwood's verdict. 'It was not a Dollars picture. It wasn't satiric. It had a comment on law and justice and capital punishment. Not a pro or con statement, but it analysed these things and let the audience draw its own conclusions.'

Whatever these conclusions were, the public had no hesitation in coming to make them when *Hang 'Em High* opened early in 1968. Despite indifferent reviews which included the cruelly accurate 'Mr Eastwood, with his glum sincerity, isn't much of an actor' from Howard Thompson in the *New York Times*, the film made United Artists their fastest-ever profits. As it also served its purpose by proving that Clint Eastwood was a star in America as well as Europe, he had no difficulty in shrugging off the insults. 'I'm not overly affected by the critics. I figure everybody's entitled to his opinion, and reviewers are employed by publications to express these opinions. I've even seen unfavourable reviews of my pictures that I agreed with. I've always felt, though, that it's easier to write an unfavourable review than a favourable one, because it takes more knowledge to write a good review. Anyone can do a pan, but to say what really works – that's tough.'

It may be that *Hang 'Em High* was one of the films in which some of the criticism struck home. When he fulfilled his ambition of becoming a successful director, Eastwood cited three main influences on his career. From Sergio Leone, he acquired his insights into the nature of violence, and especially the motivations and imperatives that make it so compelling. Leone also developed the laconic, succinct screen humour that has become a trademark in such widely differing films as *Dirty Harry* and *In the Line of Fire*. From Post, he learned about technical precision and the need to work within the budget by shooting efficiently. It was a valuable lesson and he absorbed it well, but *Hang 'Em High* proved that, on its own, it was not enough. It is to Eastwood's credit that he drew the correct conclusions from his first four features and identified the American who would complete his learning curve. His name was Don Siegel.

Although Siegel was born in Chicago in 1913, a wandering youth had made him cosmopolitan in a way that appealed to his future collaborator. The son of a mandolin player, he was educated at public schools in New York, then at Cambridge University in Britain and the Beaux Arts in Paris. The money to pay for this kind of privilege ran out when Siegel was twenty, at which point he tried to work his way around the world as a merchant seaman. When he ended up broke in Los Angeles in 1934, he found a toehold in the film industry, thanks to producer Hal Wallis, who gave him a job as a film librarian at Warner Bros at the request of his uncle.

His progress up the ladder was limited not so much by his talent as by his dislike of studio domination, a viewpoint he shared with Eastwood. Although he was directing features by the time World War II came to an end, they were always B-movies with budgets small enough to be left alone. *Riot in Cell Block 11*, which he made for Warner Bros in 1954, became a blueprint for the future in that it established him as a minimalist director with the ability to touch chords of social realism. The film's liberal perspective came not from Siegel but from its producer, Walter Wanger, in search of a righteous crusade against the prison system after a recent spell in jail. Siegel's own preference was for macho antiheroes who took justice into their own hands. Whether they did this inside or outside the law was a matter of indifference to him but, genre being genre, they were more likely to be outside it.

Although *Riot in Cell Block 11* was little more than audience fodder in America, it attracted acclaim in France from Eric Rohmer, Jean-Luc Godard and François Truffaut, the New Wave directors of the future who were cutting their critical teeth at the influential *Cahiers du Cinéma* at the time. Siegel's career progressed along these understated lines through most of the sixties, its landmarks being *The Killers* in 1964 and *Madigan*, his first film with a commercial star (Richard Widmark), in 1967. By this time, the inspiration of studio tyrants like Sam Goldwyn and Jack Warner had long since given way to the pusillanimous concerns of the accountants and lawyers who took over Hollywood in the fifties, leaving Siegel as a self-styled 'prophet without honour' in his native land.

It was at this point that he met Clint Eastwood, who had contracted to make *Coogan's Bluff* for his old studio, Universal, partly because he owed them a picture and partly because it would launch him into the present. Eastwood had the good sense to realise that his first contemporary role shouldn't take him too far away from the cowboys of yesteryear. He might wear modern dress, but it should be western dress. He might act in a modern theatre of war, but it should be one in which he was a stranger and one from which he felt alienated. All these factors were present in *Coogan's Bluff*, a script about an Arizona sheriff who is punished for cruelty to an Indian prisoner by being sent on a routine mission to New York City to bring in another prisoner.

The only problem was that by its eighth draft, Eastwood and the slated director, Alex Segal, couldn't agree on the final form. When Mark Rydell turned down an offer to take over, he suggested Siegel in his place. Jennings Lang, the executive from Universal in charge of the project, liked the idea on the somewhat tenuous grounds that Eastwood had clout in Italy and Siegel in France. A first meeting well lubricated by beer led to a level of relaxation that resulted in Siegel agreeing to direct the film if he could produce as well. 'Why not?' said Clint with typical economy, but the easy accord dissolved into anger when the ninth draft, as commissioned and endorsed by Siegel, was rejected abruptly by Eastwood. Only Jennings's intervention and the hiring of a regular *Rawhide* writer Dean Riesner resulted in a rapprochement and eventually in a tenth draft that was acceptable to all parties.

In the interests of running a tight ship, *Coogan's Bluff* was made almost entirely on location, initially in the Arizona desert and then in New York City. The opening scene is a classic, a direct lift from the 'Dollar' films which is overtly designed to transform Eastwood from ancient to modern with maximum impact. The panoramic shot of a featureless desert surrounded by mountains is a fitting stadium for The Man with No Name, but it is an Indian in a loincloth who is first seen climbing over the rocks, rifle with telescopic sight in hand. As he halts and turns it on his pursuer, the camera closes in through the cloud of dust to reveal the contemporary crusader hidden behind dark glasses at the wheel of a powerful jeep. Only when he has his own gun trained on his quarry, after tricking him into wasting his bullets on empty air, does Walt Coogan allow himself the luxury of speech.

'Put your pants on, Chief,' he says laconically before handcuffing his prisoner to a hitching-rail while he takes his own pants down for the benefit of a married woman whose husband is out of town. This action is both arrogant and racist and it earns an early reprimand from his superior when he catches Coogan preparing for sex by soaking in the bath tub. For the first time, audiences

see the prototype of an Eastwood character they will come
to know and love, the maverick cop whose independence
earns the censure of his superiors. Although he officially
operates within the law, many superiors will suspend him
for insubordinate behaviour. However, this one leaves him
with his badge when he sends him to New York to reel in
James Ringerman (Don Stroud).

This is a scenario that invites a dramatic visual clash
between the old and the new, the wide-open Indian terri-
tories that have been systematically raped by the ranching
brotherhood and the cramped urban landscape that has
risen out of the greed of property developers. Again, Siegel
proves more than worthy of his hire as a helicopter touches
down on the Pan Am pad in the heart of Manhattan and
Walt Coogan, in cowboy boots and stetson, emerges to
survey a world in which he is as alien as a visitor from
Mars. It is the confrontation between the country boy and
the urban jungle that gives *Coogan's Bluff* its power in
that the sheriff, who should be disadvantaged by being
out of his element, is able to fight more effectively for what
he believes in than those who are on their own terrain.
If his methods make him an antihero, his achievements
make him a hero, in his own eyes and the eyes of all those
who approve of clean-ups that ignore the body count.

These certainly include Don Siegel and Clint Eastwood
who condone Coogan's actions in a whole series of adventures in which he combats red tape, represented by
Lieutenant McElroy (Lee J. Cobb) of the New York Police
Department, and the Social Services, represented by social
worker Julie Roth (Susan Clark). People may call him 'Tex',
and taxi drivers may cheat him, but he's never shown as a
hick when it comes to the sharp end of the manhunting
business. That's not to say that he doesn't meet with re-
versals as he bluffs Ringerman out of the security of his
hospital bed and into the mean streets where he can catch

him, only that there is never any doubt as to who will win in the end.

'I like those characters myself,' Eastwood explains. 'That's why, maybe, I carry them to other extremes than my predecessors. In other words, in the complications of society as we know it today, sometimes a person who can cut through the bureaucracy and red tape – even if I'm playing in a modern film – a person who thinks on that level is a hero. A person who can do that, a man who thinks on a very simple level and has very simple moral values, appeals to a great many people.'

Like Jed Cooper from *Hang 'Em High*, Coogan has a strong libido, but he has less luck when it comes to sleeping with the women he encounters. His liaison with Julie starts badly when he outrages her by seeing off one of her pestering clients with extreme prejudice. For Coogan, a man who insults a lady is simply a punk who deserves punishment. For a late sixties social worker like Julie, he is a focus for her compassion and understanding. Yet however much her mind warns her against him, her body responds to Coogan's redneck charm and only an intrusive phone call prevents them having sex. Their relationship reinforces Coogan's simplistic approach and it points the way to a series of Eastwood affairs that often promise more than they deliver. Coogan's relationship with McElroy is also written to underline gulfs that can never be crossed, with the Lieutenant as the weary operator who knows his limitations within the law and Coogan as the loose cannon who doesn't play by the rules.

Once the cameras were rolling, Eastwood and Siegel put their script differences behind them and enjoyed the give and take of a collaboration based on mutual respect. Eastwood liked Siegel's economy, his ability to get what he wanted on the first take and then dispense with the insurance policy of unnecessary repetition. 'He's willing to take a lot of chances that way,' he said later. 'I think it's true that there is a group of directors who do always want to "cover" themselves. The really great directors of the old days, like John Ford, Howard Hawks or Hitchcock, however, didn't do that. They knew in advance exactly what they wanted. Some, like Wyler and Stevens, did cover themselves, but those must have been boring films to work on.'

Boredom was certainly not a factor for Siegel and Eastwood as they developed their own shorthand and their own style. Recognising that Clint's pared-to-the-bone screen persona evolved directly out of his own personality, Siegel didn't try to give him much direction and Eastwood reciprocated by not treating him as either director or producer. Instead he offered technical advice culled from Leone and others and Siegel was smart enough to see that he knew what he was talking about. 'He has very good ideas about set-ups and things, and I call them Clintus shots. Now I'll try to figure out a shot to top it and if I do, it's called a Siegelini shot. Many times his ideas will lead me into another channel of thought, and I'll come up with another approach. It's a peculiar relationship but what we're trying to do is tell a story as well as we can.'

Eastwood agreed with this description of their modus operandi, although he put it slightly differently. 'He liked my ideas and had a running joke that he was happy to steal from anybody and put his name on it. He was always straightforward and knew what he wanted. He never got bogged down, even in a disaster. Sure he has an ego like everyone else, but if a janitor came up with something, Don wouldn't turn it down. He bred an atmosphere of participation.'

As an example of Siegel's tolerance, Eastwood cites a scene in which he was perched on the ledge of a building. Siegel said the studio had forbidden it because it would take four days to shoot, so Eastwood asked if he could have a go at directing it himself. The studio agreed, providing it took no more than two days. In the event, Eastwood did it in an evening. 'I just put a searchlight up there and ran everybody through the light, just as I had seen it happen on the TV news. I thought, "They've got the same camera and the same scene – why can't I just shoot it like I saw it happen?" except in our case, of course, we faked the guy falling.'

There is a certain irony in the fact that the one area of disagreement between the two men was not over how much Eastwood should usurp Siegel's role, but how much he should allow his own to be usurped by stuntmen. Clint was up for all the action sequences and especially for the motor-bike chase in which Coogan finally captures Ringerman. However, Siegel was too familiar with studio policy to buy that one and most of the bike work, including the rugby-style tackle that put Ringerman in Coogan's power, was done by stuntmen. When Siegel grounded Eastwood, the star was so incensed that he uncharacteristically stormed off the set in a rage. 'He's insane and childish about doing his own stunt work,' Siegel commented. 'I think he's actually very lucky never to have been hurt. Maybe he thinks he needs to prove to himself he's not frightened. Well, I can tell you he's not. He doesn't need to prove it.'

The stunt question arose again on Eastwood's next picture, *Where Eagles Dare*, which he scornfully re-titled *Where Doubles Dare* after being denied the opportunity to hang in space off a cable car in Austria. Again the project was in tune with his current game-plan of expanding his horizons in profitable ways. This time, the new ground was in England, the new period World War II, the new challenge working with Richard Burton and an all-star international cast. Eastwood's first brush with the Burtons came even before he was officially scheduled to meet them when his way through customs at Heathrow was inexplicably blocked. Enquiries as to why this should be revealed that Richard and Liz had just flown in from Geneva in their private jet, with all the official fawning and media attention that entailed. Nonplussed, Eastwood collected his bags from the carousel and headed for his connecting flight.

This incident indicates diametrically opposing attitudes to stardom, but neither the Burtons nor Eastwood allowed any little differences in approach to mar their pleasure in working together when they met in Austria at the start of 1968. Why should they when Richard was being paid $1,200,000 and Clint $800,000 for a film that required little more than being there. 'I'd never done a film with a major star and my agency thought it was time. They gave me this script. Terrible. Alistair MacLean. All exposition and complications. Brian Hutton [the director] told me not to worry. Though I'd never worked with him before, I'd seen *The Pad* and *Wild Seed* and figured he was talented enough to be trusted. So we sat down one day over in Austria and the subject of why we were doing the film came up. Brian pointed to Richard Burton – "Because he's doing it." I pointed to Burton – "Because he's doing it." It went round the room – "Because he's doing it." The thing was, we all knew Richard was doing it for the loot.'

The man they should have asked was the London-based agent turned producer Elliott Kastner. The story goes that he knew Burton wanted to make a film in the style of *The Guns of Navarone*, an action adventure based on Alistair MacLean's novel that became the highest earner for 1961. When Kastner noticed that MacLean was the best-selling paperback writer on a British Rail bookstall, he immediately asked him to prepare a script with a leading role for Burton. He got the actor to agree by telling him that MacLean was keen to write an original screenplay for him. Then he sold the package to MGM, who were as keen as Burton to cash in on the spin-off from *The Guns of Navarone* and *The Great Escape*. However, they were not as convinced as Kastner that Burton, then reeling after several major cinema flops, would pull in the crowds, so they made Clint Eastwood an offer he didn't refuse while he was working on *Coogan's Bluff*.

Where Eagles Dare was a typical product of its times, a mega-budget romp in colourfully dangerous surroundings which emphasises the decency of the special friendship between Britain and America in the face of dastardly Nazi chicanery. Alistair MacLean belongs to what has now become the Robert Ludlum school of thriller writing, in that his body count mounts alarmingly whenever the action threatens to flag. In *Where Eagles Dare*, this 'when in doubt, kill 'em' philosophy is applied to espionage during World War II. MacLean kicks off with the familiar premise that the British Secret Service has been infiltrated by Nazi agents. Burton, as Commando unit leader Major John Smith, is dispatched to discover the extent of the damage, although his true mission is initially masked by a daring assignment to rescue an American general carrying essential secret papers from a clifftop fortress in the Bavarian Alps. This provides an excuse for the arrival of Lieutenant Schaffer, the American Ranger who is drafted into the unit as Burton's second-in-command to help expedite this mission almost impossible.

In an attempt to explain his delphic storyline, MacLean interspersed his killing sequences with long speeches in which the principals discussed the balance of improbabilities for the enlightenment of the audience. At least that was the idea until Lieutenant Schaffer, a.k.a. Clint Eastwood, arrived in Austria to carve up the duties with his co-star. 'The character I played had tremendous amounts of exposition,' he explained. 'We'd stop and we'd talk for hours about what's going to happen and the director and I felt that this was very impractical. Talk about blue-pencil. I started scratching out my dialogue. Pretty soon I realised that I had no dialogue left. Brian got this strange idea. "Yeah, we'll make you this mysterious guy who doesn't say very much." Meanwhile Richard was complaining, "Do I have to talk so much? Everybody talks so much." Still, we decided to let Richard's character handle the exposition – he has a beautiful speaking voice and he's very good at that sort of thing – and I would handle the shooting, which they felt I was very good at.'

Burton readily concurred and added some kind thoughts of his own. 'It was instructive to watch Clint move around because he reduced everything to an absolute minimum. If he had a four-line speech, he would reduce it to four words and it was enormously effective. I'm afraid he used me a bit in those days; he allowed me to do most of the talking.'

These comments illustrate Eastwood's instinctive understanding of the ground-rules of his trade. He'd never played opposite a major star before and he rarely would again. What's more, he, a relatively untrained screen actor, was faced not only with Burton's Welsh magic but with the solid theatrical skills of a supporting cast that included Michael Hordern, Peter Barkworth and Patrick Wymark. How better to emphasise his cultural isolation than by making Schaffer as like The Man with No Name as possible? As for Burton, whose film career can at best be described as chequered, he was astute enough to recognise the real thing. 'Within three minutes of shooting time, we all realised we were in the presence of a very remarkable man. We made a great pair, he with his lanky frame and me with my stocky Welsh body. He's a fine actor and will become one of the big stars of the future.'

The Burton–Eastwood accord survived weeks of the brutal conditions that characterise a high Alpine winter. 'I finished *Coogan's Bluff* on 31 December,' Clint said at the time. 'I saw the New Year in on a plane to Austria and was acting with Richard in a raging storm on a mountainside for *Where Eagles Dare* on 2 January. Burton's great to work with, full of stories. And Elizabeth is fantastic. Nothing hurts her. She laughs at bad reviews, even points out which critics will give you bad notices!' In the interests of such good company, Eastwood was even prepared to put up with hold-ups as a result of Burton's drinking and conspicuous expenditure on a scale that conflicted with his frugal principles.

During location filming, the unit was based in the village of Ebensee, with access by cable car to Schloss Hohenwerfen. The leading actors stayed in a gasthaus where Clint was at pains to initiate time-passing conversations about home and family with colleagues and crew. As a result, he was extremely popular, especially with Peter Barkworth, who described him as 'immensely liked and respected.'

Back in England for the studio work, Clint was able to run on a longer leash when he surreptitiously bought himself a 750cc B11 Norton motorbike. On his first visit to Britain to do publicity work for the 'Dollar' films, he'd staked out a few pubs, among them Jack Straw's Castle in Hampstead, and he now extended his range considerably with a lot of enthusiastic help from Burton and one of the leading actresses, the Polish-born stuntwoman Ingrid Pitt. It didn't escape Clint that she was blonde and beautiful and flirtatious as well as daring, so he was happy to take her joyriding round Brands Hatch on the back of his bike. With the responsibility for a multi-million-dollar picture and the certainty that the insurance company wouldn't pay the price for such capers, Elliott Kastner was less amused when he angrily waved the errant couple to a halt on the side of the track.

As he travelled around, Eastwood realised that the junketing for the Leone films had worked so well that he was star-spotted wherever he went. 'Being human, one likes to be recognised,' he told Mike Hughes of UPI. 'At first, it was great but now I get embarrassed. I just wave and hope that will suffice. I like to travel and explore but in most places, that's not possible now, although I've had peace in London. The English respect one's private life and this has enabled me to see a lot of this famous old city.'

Four days before *Where Eagles Dare* wrapped in May 1968, Maggie Eastwood gave birth to her first child and Clint's only son, Kyle Clinton. Clint celebrated with the Burtons, then flew home as soon as he could, but not before he delivered a final accolade on the film. 'It became a wild, preposterous action picture that we didn't take too seriously but it turned out better than the script, much to my surprise.' As Elizabeth Taylor had probably foreseen, the critics were remorseless, but the public flocked to see it, reviving Burton's flagging career and setting the seal on Eastwood's international one.

No doubt Clint was pleased with his son but he certainly didn't allow his new responsibility to stand in the way of his old ones in that he almost immediately left his wife's bedside for another long location shoot, this time in Baker, Oregon. The film was perhaps the most unlikely one he has ever made, a musical called *Paint Your Wagon*, in which he starred with Lee Marvin and Jean Seberg. With the advantage of hindsight, it is hard to imagine how the canny Eastwood was lured into what appears to be an inevitable fiasco, but in the years after *My Fair Lady* had carried all before it there was a certain cachet in an Alan Jay Lerner and Frederick Loewe musical. Written for the stage in the fifties, *Paint Your Wagon* had been adapted for the screen by Paddy Chayevsky and Joshua Logan, who'd made the successful screen musicals *South Pacific* and *Camelot*, was slated to direct.

With these credentials, Eastwood was prepared to be impressed when Alan Jay Lerner showed him the script in London during *Where Eagles Dare*. 'It was really good but later they had it re-written and I didn't care much for that. I had been signed subject to material. So they changed it a bit and came back with a final script that was all right. It was very long, very elaborate. When they got down to shooting the film, a lot had to be condensed so they excised huge sections which made it a bit choppy.'

In an era of high-profile high-cost musicals, *Paint Your Wagon*'s budget of eight to ten million dollars must have seemed like something of a snip for Paramount, but their confidence proved fragile, perhaps because they failed to do their sums at the outset. Their initial agreement with Lee Marvin gave him a reported $1,000,000 plus a percentage, plus $20,000 a day or $100,000 a week overtime, to play Ben Rumson, the rollicking drifter who was to sing the slowest classic ever, 'I Was Born under a Wanderin' Star'. Eastwood, whose only singing credential was a ballad 'Unknown Girl', which sank without trace during his *Rawhide* days, was paid $750,000, plus a percentage, for his portrayal of the overgrown Midwestern farm boy, Pardner. The first choice for the Mormon maid they both marry was Julie Andrews, then the world's top warbler, but she preferred to take the title role in *Darling Lili*, another Paramount musical extravaganza that was to be directed by her husband, Blake Edwards. Logan's second best was the flaky blonde, Jean Seberg, whose lack of popularity in the United States at least had the advantage of keeping her salary low.

Even so, there was never going to be enough money in the original budget to fulfil Alan Jay Lerner's dreams of filming *Paint Your Wagon* over five months on location in the back of beyond. Logan's personal preference was for a more modest production on the back lot at Paramount, where he would retain the kind of control he'd become accustomed to during his distinguished stage career, but Lerner insisted on building sets from scratch in the Wallowa-Whitman

National Forest. The gold-rush town, No Name City, rose up slowly in East Eagle Creek on the slopes of Boulder Peak. The maze of rivers under the site had to be filled in by Forestry Service workers before construction could begin, and the city had to be collapsible so that it would fall apart at the climax of the film. The no-expense-spared approach extended to bringing in trees from Hollywood, horses from Nevada and oxen from New England, plus eight vanloads of props per week from Los Angeles.

Small wonder that the cast believed they were on a gravy train that would run and run, none more so than Lee Marvin, who rented a house for himself and his wife and staffed it with his own servants. Reasonable enough maybe, but his drinking habits weren't, and nor was his mounting paranoia over the way he was being directed. Marvin had won a Best Actor's Oscar for *Cat Ballou* in 1963 and enough praise for his role in *The Dirty Dozen* for its producer, Ken Hyman, to say to Logan, 'The fact that Lee gets drunk and stops the picture for a day or two is not important because he'll make it up to you in so many other ways.' For Logan, the words seemed progressively less prophetic as Marvin's distrust and, with it, his drunkenness increased.

When Don Siegel, who'd been Marvin's first choice as director after their collaboration on *The Killers* in 1964, came to visit, he found the film ground to a halt while the star fumed. Siegel tried to calm him down, then lost his temper, ground an avocado into his head, and left. Richard Brooks was then called, first by associate producer Tom Shaw, and then by Marvin himself, with a view to his replacing Logan as soon as possible. When Eastwood heard about this scheme, he told his agent to tell Paramount that he'd give them even more trouble if they changed director in midshoot. 'Clint Eastwood stood by me,' said Logan. 'It was a strong thing to do and I admired it.'

Acting on Brooks's advice, Marvin sorted out his problems with Logan and filming continued, but at an ever more profligate rate as Eastwood, who'd arrived on his motorbike with his golf clubs slung on the back, noted with horror. 'It was a disaster,' he told Rex Reed, 'but it didn't have to be such an expensive disaster. We had Learjets flying everyone in and out of Oregon, helicopters to take the wives to location for lunch, crews of seven trucks, thousands of extras getting paid for doing nothing, everyone living in ranch houses – twenty million dollars down the drain and most of it doesn't even show on the screen.'

He also noted that *Paint Your Wagon* was doubly doomed, in the editing room as well as on location. 'I saw it in four versions: the director's version, the producer's version, and then the coalition of all the studio executives and their versions. The director's version, the first one, was actually the best one. But that wasn't the one that was released.' The one that was released earned lukewarm reviews, especially for Seberg, who was considered lightweight. In Britain, its most successful aspect was Marvin's recording of 'I Was Born under a Wanderin' Star', which reached number one in the charts in an era dominated by The Beatles and The Rolling Stones, but the flip side, Clint Eastwood murmuring his way through 'I Talk to the Trees', never became a collector's item.

Paint Your Wagon notched up a couple of unsatisfactory firsts for Eastwood which he repeated in his next film, *Two Mules for Sister Sara*. One was that he played the fall-guy to dominant partners, Marvin's lovable rogue and Shirley MacLaine's revolutionary nun. The other was that the animosity he felt for both Marvin and MacLaine showed up as a lack of chemistry in the finished product. The original game-plan for *Two Mules for Sister Sara* had been hatched in Austria when Liz Taylor told Eastwood about the project and invited him to play opposite her. When Don Siegel was

added to the credits, Clint had no hesitation in signing on.
By the time he discovered that bankrolling the Burtons for
a four-month shoot in Mexico was beyond even Universal's
means, it was too late to withdraw.

MacLaine, whose track record underlined her skills as
a comedienne, seemed to be a reasonable last-minute replacement, though not to Eastwood, who thought that her
casting 'stretched the imagination a bit'. She re-wrote her
part to suit her style, but as Eastwood had already cut most
of his lines he had no problems with that. Nor, in the first
instance, did he mind that he was going to be bushwhacked
by a woman. 'It's the only western I know that has a great
part for a woman – not a dance-hall, ballsy broad, but a
woman. The average western isn't written for the female.
The cliché broad says, "Don't do it, Charley!", and Charley
answers "I've got to do what I've got to do!" Besides,
it's an outdoors show; it's hard to work with women –
make-up, wardrobe, all of it – while the guy, well, you just
stick him in some smelly outfit.'

Despite this positive approach, things went badly from
the moment the egocentric MacLaine and the sardonic
Eastwood met on location in Cocoyoc outside Mexico City.
It didn't help that they were both intensely interested in
politics, yet their views were polls apart. Their mutual hos-
tility resulted in them eating their meals in separate trailers,
the norm for MacLaine but a departure for Eastwood, who
was accustomed to eating with the crew.

On screen, the competition was no contest from the word
go. Eastwood's finest moments come in a brilliant opening
sequence in which his progress on horseback through the
desert is registered by the nocturnal creatures that live off
it – a snake, a mountain lion, a rabbit and an owl – as
they prepare to take cover at dawn. After a tarantula is
crushed beneath his horse's hoof, the camera pans up to
reveal another reincarnation of The Man with No Name,

a Civil War veteran called Hogan who is running arms to Juarez's Mexican rebels for use in their independence struggle against the occupying French forces. As his unkempt appearance suggests, he is a man without illusions who is ready to sell his soul to the highest bidder. Like No Name, he shoots to kill, in the back if necessary, as he proves when he saves a half-naked MacLaine from three drunken rapists. When she puts her clothes back on and mounts her mule, she is revealed as a nun and therefore as worthy of his protection.

Their partnership progresses through various romantic phases, with Hogan pulling back on sexual involvement out of respect for her habit and Sara saving his life by removing an Indian arrow from his chest, before a denouement that reveals that she is both a dedicated supporter of Juarez and the madame of a brothel. After a battle-scene that has little bearing on their relationship or on any other aspect of the story, Sara abandons both callings to lead Hogan, his packhorse laden with her hat-boxes instead of weapons, back to America. From her arrogant expression, it is clear that he is her trophy, a strong man brought to heel by a woman's wiles, which is not how Eastwood's growing army of fans were accustomed to seeing him. From the loner without sexual needs of the Leone westerns, he had progressed to the 'love 'em and leave 'em' conqueror of *Hang'Em High* and *Coogan's Bluff*, but now he was a sexual victim, outwitted on all fronts by a calculating woman.

With the help of the favourable Mexican exchange rate, Siegel bought *Two Mules for Sister Sara* in at four million dollars but the sixty-four day shoot was marred by sickness. At one stage MacLaine, who fought openly with Siegel throughout the production, had to stop work for a week, then returned rather sulkily, 'to finish the picture and get the hell back to humanity and civilisation'. Meanwhile Eastwood saved himself from the general malaise by eating fruit and sunflower seeds, a diet pretty much guaranteed to result in weight loss. 'It came off while I was waiting for my meals to arrive,' he joked, then added more seriously, 'I always get thinner and thinner when I'm filming, even it it's a fairly light schedule.'

In the cutting room, the lack of chemistry between the stars became clear. 'The film is really a two-character story, and the woman has the best part, something I'm sure Shirley noticed. It's a kind of *African Queen* gone West,' said Eastwood with some irony. MacLaine got her own back at a press conference in New York when she mocked Eastwood for his gun lust. 'You should have been there for the garrison scene. He gets those guns in his hands and really gets going. He's in there banging away after the camera stops! Really, the rest of us in the scene are doing all the work, and we're satisfied with the take. But he wants to do another. You should have seen the look in his eyes.' A judiciously balanced opinion or an actress jealous of a colleague's moment in the limelight? The jury may be forever out on that one, but it is easy to imagine that the episode Eastwood most enjoyed was handing a dead rattler to MacLaine. He'd killed it reluctantly for the cameras, at the insistence of the Mexican authorities who didn't want it left on the loose, but handing its headless corpse to his co-star must have carried a symbolism that appealed to his sense of irony.

The finished film was cheap enough to hold its own at the box office but it did little for Eastwood or Siegel, other than bring them together in adversity. Siegel was happy with the opening and closing scenes, but little else. 'The opening took two weeks to get but it was worth it because it established a feeling for the kind of animalistic man who was our hero,' he explained. 'I shot the battle as a montage, right out of my Warner Bros days. I had every shot tilted in the opposite direction from the one before. I worked very hard on making that battle sequence work because there was really nothing in the story that justified it. My goal was to make it justify itself by being very exciting.'

For Eastwood, the last stop in the learning curve that would definitively put him in control of his own destiny was Yugoslavia, where he joined *Where Eagles Dare* director Brian G. Hutton for *Kelly's Heroes*. 'It had the best script, a good cast, a subtle anti-war message,' he said of the picture he believed would be a mould-breaker in its genre. With the Vietnam War raging almost as fiercely as the American sentiment building against it, the time was certainly right. Eastwood's view of the war was tempered by the loss of contemporaries in Korea, the conflict he narrowly escaped during his military service, and his growing antipathy to killing living creatures of any kind, but his right-wing political stance prevented him joining the Vietnam antis who wanted to get out at any price. 'When I was in the Army, I was against the Korean War and I'm against the war in Vietnam. But I'm not among the people who say. "Let's stop Vietnam, zap!" If you're going to stop it, I'd like to say, "Here's a constructive way."'

One not entirely serious constructive way that he suggested was to send all the hunters to fight in South East Asia, leaving all the soldiers who wanted out free to come home. Another was to turn *Kelly's Heroes*, a story about four American soldiers who put personal gain above patriotism in the chaotic aftermath of World War II, into a parable about the futility of conflict. The screenplay, written by Troy Kennedy Martin, best known for his scripts for the BBC's *Z Cars*, depicted Private Kelly and his three associates as mercenaries who corrupt superiors and peers in the American Army with promises of a share in the Nazi gold they plan to liberate from a French-Italian bank. In a world in which everyone has his price, and a pretty low price at that, they have devoted their war years to survival, looting and maintaining their creature comforts, priorities as cynical as any Sergio Leone could come up with.

As Kelly, Eastwood was teamed with Donald Sutherland as Big Joe, Telly Savalas as Oddball, and Don Rickles as Crapgame in a five-month shoot that was as anarchic off screen as it should have been on it. 'How can Telly and I go to the producer and demand better treatment when Clint's happy with a room in one building, a toilet in another, and an ocean to shower in?' asked comic character actor Rickles, after being mocked by Eastwood for making an excessive fuss about a minor cut on his leg. He also described his fellow actor as 'the only man who can talk with flies on his lips', to which Savalas added, 'Clint belongs to the great tradition of American stars, Gary Cooper, John Wayne, Gregory Peck, Henry Fonda, James Stewart, who project one thing beautifully – pure Americanism.'

Predictably, Hutton had a rather kinder take on his star. 'On the screen, Clint Eastwood is a man who knows where he's going. He knows what he's after, and he knows how to get it. In an age of uncertainty in the arts, politics and everything else, people enjoy watching a man like this in action. They don't want to see the anguish of a Brando or a James Dean any more. They want to escape into something more positive. I think we went twenty years of film from 1947, when Brando hit, until 1967, when Clint hit, with actors who for the most part played characters who were confused. Now Clint is a throwback to the strong, silent men of the 1930s. Clint's character has always been a guy who knows where he is, knows what he wants and goes out and does it. Regardless if he's good or bad, at least he's certain.'

In *Kelly's Heroes*, Eastwood's initial certainty turned to doubt as what should have been a warts-and-all illustration of a corrupt and cowardly army engaged in a no-win war became a routine romp. While Mike Nichols's black comedy *Catch 22* was putting over the message of the moment, and winning audiences with it, Clint Eastwood was begging Jim Aubrey, the head of MGM, to hold off release of *Kelly's Heroes* until Brian Hutton could work on it some more. 'Somehow everything got lost. The picture got bogged down in Yugoslavia and it just ended up as the story of a bunch of American screw-offs in World War II. I told Aubrey "You're going to cut off maybe millions of dollars in box-office receipts." He said he'd think it over, but I'm sure when he hung up the phone, he said to himself, "What does this frigging actor know about millions of dollars? Forget it."'

If he did, he paid for his poor judgment in bad reviews and indifferent though not disastrous box office. As for Eastwood, he now had the cash and the clout to put the lessons he'd learned over the past ten years into practice. In 1968, he was number five on the list of top box-office attractions. By 1970, he was number two, a position of strength from which to prove that life really does begin at forty.

6

A Not So Simple Man

As is the way with late developers, the best part of Clint Eastwood's future was all before him when he reached his fortieth birthday in May 1970. This was because he had laid the right foundations with some care over the previous six years. In 1964, when he first went to Italy, he was a moderately prosperous television actor whose reputation was based on a single show. By 1970, he was an international star, with a solid commercial following at home and a reverential one in Europe, especially in France, where he was appreciated as an artist, and in Italy, where he was treated as an icon.

As the money that seeped in while he was making the 'Dollar' films turned to a flood with their success and then to a torrent as he converted his Man with No Name persona into cash in his native land, he found that he was rich. There was nothing accidental about this. Like many Depression children, he grew up with a nagging level of deprivation, though more of inessentials than essentials. There is no evidence that the Eastwoods went hungry and a man who can buy his son a car when he is fourteen, even a twenty-five-dollar car and even in California, is certainly not on the breadline. Deprivation may not be poverty but it is a sharp spur to developing an accumulator's instincts towards money. It also ensured that whatever Eastwood acquired, he increased and multiplied.

Like any sensible man who is newly rich, he put his

money initially into the things that don't go away – land, bricks and mortar. Clint and Maggie invested the proceeds of *Rawhide* in their first house in the northern Los Angelean suburb of Sherman Oaks, a ranch-style place overlooking the San Fernando Valley. At the end of the decade, Maggie described it as 'modest' but, as it had four bedrooms and four bathrooms, her opinion merely underlines the change in her expectations since they'd moved into it in the early sixties. As their fortunes improved, they added a swimming-pool, a gym over the garage, and a games room for pool and table tennis. 'Clint's pretty good at pool and even better at table tennis,' Maggie revealed when she visited London in May 1970. 'He doesn't like parties and enjoys himself most with small groups of people whom he knows well and likes to be with. He's something of a loner who prefers the rustic scene to city life and doesn't care too much about clothes. Ninety per cent of them are casual.'

In the *Rawhide* days, Eastwood liked to hang out with friends from the series, even when it wasn't shooting. Jill Banner, a young actress who used to meet him at the home of Kitty Jones, an established actor's agent with an ability to gather a cheerful, youthful crowd around her, recalls that 'he and his buddies were like a pack of wild college comedians, cracking jokes, telling risqué jokes, rough-housing and teasing the girls. I've read articles calling Clint a taciturn, close-mouthed, tight-lipped silent type. Bull!' she added. 'Clint didn't give a — about the la-de-da Hollywood crowd, or traditional status symbols. He drove an old pick-up truck and I never saw him wear anything but Levis, t-shirt, windbreaker jacket and tennies. Kitty's girlfriends were crazy about him, not because he was so young and good-looking or a television star, but because he was kind, intelligent and such a fun guy.'

Cash in the bank from the Leone films allowed Eastwood to fulfil his long-term goal of buying into Carmel. His initial purchase was a small vacation house. The five-acre site, a rocky spur sticking out into the Pacific with its own beach, was everything he'd ever dreamed of. Better still, it was 'about a driver and a five iron south from the eighteenth hole at Cypress', as Eastwood the golfer put it. By 1969, he had accumulated sufficient wealth to replace the original simple structure with what he may have hoped would be a home for life. The new house was made from redwood timber, rock and glass, and sheltered from prying eyes by established stands of cypress and pine trees. The master suite jutted out over the water, giving it spectacular ocean views and complete privacy. It also had an extra-long king-size bed and, as Clint has always preferred soaking to showering, a full-size Japanese bath. 'The Americans are the biggest people in the world with the smallest baths and the Japanese are the smallest with the biggest baths,' he rationalised.

With escalating prosperity, Maggie Eastwood found it easy to give up her career as an office worker and occasional swimsuit model. For much of the time she was apart from her husband, but she slipped easily into the kind of routine socialising and homemaking that befitted her new status. She was always elegant, an appropriate adornment to a rising actor, and she recognised and accepted her role in her husband's 'married bachelor' programme from the outset. The Carmel house had an art gallery which she filled with pictures and sculpture bought on her travels, and she also took up painting on her own account. 'I like paintings that create moods, feelings, rather than landscapes or profiles. I don't do it for a living, although people have offered to buy some of the things I've done.' She used the state-of-the-art Japanese camera her husband bought her to photograph objects for the new home, then sent him the pictures so that he would know what to expect. Their joint taste ran to English artefacts of the copper warming-pan variety.

Over fifteen years of marriage, the Eastwoods had learned what it took to live with each other on a part-time basis, and the turbulence of the early years had given way to a resigned tranquillity. 'Maggie and I no longer have to work at making our marriage a success; we just accept it and it works itself,' said Clint in 1969. 'I still get bugged once in a while and sometimes she does. But she knows exactly when to ignore my moods. We've never been a big togetherness couple in the sense that we've had to cling tight to each other all the time. She's quite an independent person and used to living or travelling on her own quite a bit. I'd certainly call it a successful marriage by any standard; and almost fifteen years together proves that we're right for each other.'

Clint had carte blanche to go on location wherever he wanted for as long as he needed, and he liked having his wife and later his son along, 'but only for part of the time'. If Maggie suspected that he had affairs with co-workers, she kept quiet about it. In return, Eastwood made sure they weren't in evidence when she came to visit. By mutual agreement, she spent a few weeks, usually between three and six, on her husband's films, always when he was well settled in and preferably when he had a bit of time to spend travelling with her. 'Maggie understands the strain of location work and knows there are times when I don't want anyone around. There are some days when I get mentally and physically exhausted and all I want to do is flake out. She is intelligent enough to understand what a difficult profession I'm in and make the allowances that are necessary.'

In some ways, Maggie's first big trip to Spain for *A Fistful of Dollars* set standards that could never be repeated. The Eastwoods drove north to Castile where they visited the Escorial and the medieval castles in Toledo, Segovia and Avila, towering memorials to repressive regimes of yesteryear that appealed to the primitive in Clint. 'Spain is for a man what Paris is for a woman,' he commented. He even suppressed his dislike of killing to watch the legendary El Cordobes, the matador of the moment, in action at the Plaza de Toros in Madrid. Maggie spent many hours in the Prado Museum, and they ate in a wide range of local restaurants, an adventurous programme considering that the food Maggie served at home was always very plain. 'Clint looks forward to coming back to healthy foods like fish, beef and poultry, with baked potatoes and salads,' she said, with wifely zeal. 'They're his favourites.'

As Eastwood's fame grew, such freedom became progressively less possible, especially in Italy, where Maggie joined him the next year while he was working in the studio on *For a Few Dollars More*. By this time, small children dressed in No Name ponchos were following him through the streets shouting 'Il Cigaro', and the paparazzi, with a cunning line in manufactured scandal which involved Eastwood posing with a beautiful oriental model, weren't far behind. 'Could this love affair end in marriage?' the headlines screamed, to which Maggie, wrapped in her false security, serenely replied, 'Never mind, this is all part of what is called fame.'

On the plus side of their relationship, Maggie helped Clint with his career, recommending scripts but always allowing him to take the credit, liaising with his agent in his absence, even forging his signature on photos for his fans. The Eastwoods also shared a passion for sports and an interest in preserving the body beautiful through healthy living. For Eastwood, the number-one sport has always been golf, which he played to a handicap of fourteen in the late sixties. His clubs went everywhere with him in case there should be delays during filming. On *Paint Your Wagon*, for example, he calmed his nerves during Marvin's drinking bouts by hitting his way round the local nine-hole course. Maggie's first choice was tennis, and her husband took it up so that they could play together. They also went skiing, a sport Eastwood and his sister, Jean, taught themselves in their teens, and took shooting lessons.

As the years passed, the Eastwoods eliminated red meat and cut down on fish and poultry to the point at which Clint could say in 1974, 'I'm a kind of vegetarian, you might say, but I'm not as avid about it as some people are. I do eat eggs occasionally and believe that milk is a good food, especially for kids. I never eat nutritionless junk food. Maggie and I don't care for the typical Hollywood parties, and so I'm infrequently exposed to that kind of stuff and, of course, we never have any of it around our own home. I like to eat fresh fruit and vegetables and avoid the canned or frozen varieties. Instead of candy or other sweets for dessert, I'd much rather grab an apple or an orange to munch on.'

The Eastwoods never smoked, although Clint gallantly carried matches to light ladies' cigarettes during the sixties, and they always drank herbal tea. 'I don't drink coffee or tea usually. Value my nerves too much. People who drink coffee, smoke, they shake, not with their hands or face; they shake with their eyes. Peppermint tea, no tannic acid, that's one of my wife's hang-ups.' After standing in line during his days in the Army, Eastwood hated to shop and he wasn't handy around the house, but he was an excellent cook, his speciality being a bone-marrow soup that took three days to prepare. When he could, he slept late and surfaced slowly, but he could get by on four or five hours when necessity or filming required.

He never drove when he could walk and he always followed a rigid plan for what he called 'sensible body maintenance' which included swimming, jogging and working out in the gym long before it became an essential part of southern Californian life. The plan also included special vitamins, another of his wife's hang-ups. His one cautious nod to vice was beer, which he called 'brew' and drank steadily and sometimes to excess. 'I've never left half a beer on the table in my life,' he once said in macho jest.

Although he insists that he escaped to Carmel as often as possible to 'get out of the smog and noise pollution', his one area of conspicuous consumption has always been high-decibel, high-emission machines. His first status acquisition was the gunmetal-grey Ferrari which he shipped home to Los Angeles at the end of the 'Dollar' trilogy in 1966. In 1968, he added the Norton motorbike he'd bought in England while making *Where Eagles Dare* to a collection that already included a Triumph and a Honda. After *The Great Escape* in 1963, Steve McQueen became Hollywood's Mr Motorbike, so Eastwood underplayed his fascination with what he has called his 'big hang-up'. 'On a bike, you control everything. You're out there in the wind. The speed is nothing. It's that you're by yourself on a vehicle in the free air and you manoeuvre it, lean with it. With a car, or a horse, you are always separate. With a cycle sometimes you feel you're part of it.'

Maggie confirmed that motorcycles were his favoured means of escape, of being entirely alone, yet within rapid reach of civilisation. 'I wouldn't like anyone to think that because Clint has made his name playing cowboys that he acts like a cowboy at home. He's an outdoors person, but he's not at all that wild about horses. He loves tracking down on Big Sur on his bike and rides one into San Francisco if the mood takes him. I ride pillion with him because he's a careful rider who loves the power of the bike and sometimes we ride off into the sunset on one of them, just like a fade-out scene in an old movie.'

Eastwood's sense of what was right was at its most unyielding when it came to a conscious decision to have children. 'I never really felt I had the right to bring a child into the world until I could be completely responsible for it,' he said in 1969. 'A friend of mine used to argue that whatever the circumstances, he and his wife would never

have a child of their own. He would adopt one. Why?
Because there were so many parentless children now who'd
been brought into the world and it was our duty to care for
them, rather than just add to the population by selfishly
reproducing ourselves. I figured he was probably right –
but I just didn't feel big enough to take that attitude. My
sister Jean, however, was able to do it. Anyway, one way
and another, we kept postponing that family.'

Once the embargo was lifted along with the financial
constraints, Maggie Eastwood did become pregnant, but
lost the baby in a miscarriage, so the couple had been
married for nearly fifteen years by the time Kyle Clinton
was born in 1968. 'We promised each other that we would
never pull baby pictures out of our wallets because of all
those years we saw other people's pictures of kids and
we didn't have any of our own to show,' Clint said, but
admitted that resolutions about besotted behaviour melted
away once he got to know his son. 'My wife is very beautiful
and our son Kyle is, in my opinion, and I am prejudiced,
absolutely handsome. He has given us a great deal of
extra happiness. He's a likeable little guy. They say he
has my eyes and eyelashes and Maggie's nose. With his
arrival, I'm no longer the loner I used to be. Even a
loner like me gets used to having company around, after
a while. If it's the right company.'

On the tricky question of upbringing when he was away
so much, he admitted to a degree of anxiety, but always
within a characteristically pragmatic framework. 'My kid
could be a teenager and screwing up before I get home,
and I'll have missed all the good times. I guess I'll play it
by instinct. You hope to inspire a certain set of values, but
it doesn't always work out. In some ways, I know I didn't
live up to my parents' hopes. I was a bit of a screw-up,
a loner, and it was a long time before I wanted to go to
college but, in some ways, I surpassed them.'

To what degree this public candidate for canonization is a private Lothario is well-worked, but not well-documented, territory. However, there is little doubt that his attitude to women verged on the Neanderthal, at least at this stage in his life. 'The worst thing is owning people,' he revealed to the *Daily Telegraph*'s Deedee Moore. 'It brings you down. I don't want to be owned by anybody – maybe share, but not owned lock, stock and barrel. To me, love for a person is respect for individual feelings. The beginning is infatuation. After that, it becomes other things. Love isn't across a room; it's a long time. Respecting privacy, accepting faults. But I don't believe it's a one-way street. I don't expect her to stand there and hold my coat.

'Sex is a small part of life,' he continued. 'It's a good thing, great, but 99.9 per cent of your life is spent doing other things. And if you accept a guy, you have to make that guy important so he gets satisfaction. It's selfish – you give love to get love. Women are always saying, "Why isn't this working for me?" A question of want, want, want. Men too. Women've got the toughest role. It's easier to be on the offensive than the defensive!'

In Eastwood's case, taking the dominant role was easy, if only because most women were all too ready to fall in with any plans he might have for them. One Hollywood dissenter dared to say that going to bed with Eastwood would be like computer sex on the grounds that he is more a personality than an actor, and too narcissistic to think of his partner, but it's not an opinion his wife would agree with. 'He isn't the type who has to keep proving himself. He is a man and he knows it.'

Speculation over his extra-marital relationships ranges from certainties like Roxanne Tunis and Sondra Locke to blatant falsehoods. In between, there are unconfirmed probabilities like Susan St James, a frequent visitor during *Two Mules for Sister Sara* after meeting Eastwood in Acapulco, and Jean Seberg, who was moving back to America at the time of *Paint Your Wagon* after ten tumultuous years in Europe.

She took the part in the belief that it would set her American career alight. 'It's a wonderful script, quite different from the play,' she told Rex Reed in the *New York Times*. 'I play a woman, a sort of nineteenth century flower child in the middle of the Gold Rush, who is deeply in love with two different men. I really dig that idea and believe it to be quite possible. Especially with Lee Marvin and Clint Eastwood, who are totally opposite. Lee is full of chatter and great tales he tells with his whole body – when I first met him, I thought I was talking to a Watusi. And Clint is the original quiet man. He stands back and says nothing, but then he comes out with a statement so intelligent you know he is aware of everything that is going on.'

During shooting in Baker, Oregon, Seberg became close friends with both her co-stars. 'Sure, we all sit around and have fun, and Jean gets a little juiced like everyone else,' Marvin confirmed. When they went out to dinner together, she'd pre-arrange for him to be served three gin and tonics 'to give him a buzz' and plain mixers thereafter. Apparently he never rumbled this strategy and even said, 'I love Baker. No matter how much I drink, I never get hangovers.' Or so the story goes, though reports of lengthy hold-ups suggest differently.

Of Eastwood, Seberg had this to say. 'He's guarded. People can't get close to Clint. He's not a buddy-buddy. Every moment he had out in Oregon, he was off alone . . . jogging in the woods, or in his trailer, or on a motorcycle. I think he genuinely likes solitude. He rented a farm outside Baker and he really lived like a farmer, got up in the morning to feed the animals, the hamsters, the ducks, the hens. People in this industry lose touch with nature. It's just something we use in our work. But Clint will get up at four-thirty

or five in the morning to watch the sunrise. He really is
somebody who has his knapsack at the foot of the bed. You
always have the feeling Clint is ready to hit the road.'

Did she share that isolated farm with him on occasion,
as on-set reports suggested? According to an item by Joyce
Haber in the *Los Angeles Times* in late August 1968, she told
the veteran film writer Roderick Mann that she broke up
her second marriage to the French writer-director Romain
Gary because she got a crush on someone else. 'I'm a bad
liar so I had to tell Romain about it. I said, "Divorce me."
There was no sneakiness about it and that's one of the
reasons we've managed to remain friends. The sad thing
is this other person was misplaced. It didn't work out. He
was the absolute opposite of Romain, an outdoor type, a
kickback to my days in Iowa perhaps. It was marvellous
while it lasted.' 'Who's the other man?' Haber enquired
by way of wrapping up. 'I'll give you a clue. It isn't Lee
Marvin.' Of course this is no more than a broad, and
possibly deliberately false, hint that the other man was
Eastwood, but the description certainly fits.

If they talked about politics, there must have been
considerable scope for disagreement, because the fragile,
sensitive Seberg was a civil rights activist from the age of
fourteen. When she had a baby more than a year after *Paint
Your Wagon*, the *Los Angeles Times* claimed that the father
was a member of the Black Panther Party. When the baby
died at birth, Seberg had it displayed in an open coffin
in her hometown, Marshalltown, Iowa, to prove it wasn't
black. A year later, she made her first attempt at suicide,
according to Romain Gary. In 1979, after her then lover
Hakim Jamal was murdered, she made a second successful
attempt, an early death made all the more tragic because
her body wasn't discovered for a week. Gary made a claim,
which was never refuted, that the Black Panther item had
been planted by the FBI, as part of a scheme to ruin her

reputation because of her connection with the Party.

Eastwood as always was economical with his verdict. 'She was fine to work with, a very sweet girl.' No doubt these ambivalent words could have been said of many of his fellow workers, but who was counting? Not him and not Maggie, not in those days anyway. 'Maybe married bachelorhood is one answer to many marriage and divorce hang-ups and heartbreaks. Though I haven't asked her, I think Maggie would agree.' On this point, time would prove him wrong.

7

The Female of the Species is Deadlier than the Male

'Hollywood is strange. Everyone is looking for a formula. One year, it's two guys on a motorcycle, the next year it's a girl dying of cancer and they flood the market with imitations. For years, I bummed around trying to get a job and it was the same old story – my voice was too soft, my teeth needed capping, I squinted too much, I was too tall – all that constant tearing down of my ego was bound to turn me into either a better person or a complete jerk. And I know that if I walked into a casting office right now and nobody knew I was Clint Eastwood, I'd get the same old thing. My voice is still too soft, my teeth still need capping, I still squint and I've been compared to a small redwood tree. But after the westerns I did in Spain, I was suddenly Clint Eastwood and now the other guys who are too tall and squint too much are the ones cursing me! You go figure it out!'

Although Eastwood never finished his studies in business administration, he certainly learned enough to figure out the best way of marketing himself from the moment his career went into overdrive. In what was described as a 'unique formula' at the time, he set up Malpaso in 1966 as a company in which he owned the controlling stock but took no official position. Its function was to hire him out to film productions in deals set up by its first president, Irving Leonard. In the late sixties, Eastwood's

fee per film was in the $750,000 – $800,000 bracket, but
percentage points upped each deal to at least $1 million. In
addition, deferred payment clauses spread the tax burden
to the further enrichment of the actor.

As Eastwood's fame grew, so did Malpaso's control over
the productions he appeared in. By the time he made *Paint
Your Wagon*, the company had enough clout to contract
all the featured actors, with the exception of Lee Marvin,
to MGM for the duration of the production. Although
Eastwood footed none of the bill himself, it was the blatant
overspending and the indifferent editing of that film which
made it imperative for him to expand Malpaso. 'As an
actor, you're very, very vulnerable,' he later told *Sunday
Times* film critic Iain Johnstone. 'They can make you look
like an idiot if they want to . . . *Paint Your Wagon* wasn't
the smoothest-running picture I've ever been in and, for
that reason, I started my own company and figured I'd try
some other approaches to production.'

When Irving Leonard retired in January 1970, he was
replaced by Robert Daley, whom Eastwood had met back
in 1954 when they lived in the same apartment block.
Daley, an accountant by profession, recalls sitting around
the pool discussing the economics of moviemaking with the
struggling young actor. Fifteen years later, he'd risen up
the corporate ladder at Universal but left willingly to join
Malpaso. 'Clint's extremely knowledgeable about the business,' he explained. 'One of the things I noticed when
he and I formed this company together, in the business
aspects, he would ask me a question and he'd never ask
that question again because once he'd heard the answer,
he'd never forget it.'

Something else he never forgot was a favour from a
friend, which meant that Sonia Chernus, the story editor at
CBS who had been instrumental in getting him the Rowdy
Yates role in *Rawhide*, was also offered a job in the fledgling

company. In the early months, the priority was to find screenplays that would expand and enhance Eastwood's screen image and allow him to start a parallel career as a director. At first, Eastwood even found it impossible to delegate the sifting of unsolicited scripts to his employees, but gradually a bond of trust developed. 'I'd read scripts from beginning to end, even if the first fifty pages were just awful. It takes an awful lot of reading to find the right material. You have to wade through miles to get one inch. I've been easing up, though. Sonia and Bob are doing some of the reading and I'm taking their word on more things.'

Another recruit to Malpaso was Fritz Manes, an old friend he'd kept in touch with since their days at Oakland Technical High. 'Clint hasn't really changed that much,' he commented, when he took his position as unit publicist on Malpaso productions. 'He was always a tall lanky kid and didn't necessarily dress the way the rest of the kids did. It was our first day in grammar school and it was just one of those things, we instantly identified with each other. We weren't that excited about going to school, both being sort of non-joiners, non-members of the pack.'

After the completion of *Kelly's Heroes*, the last opulent long-running shoot that Eastwood would undertake for many years, the era of belt-tightening began with *The Beguiled*, a small labour of love about a wounded Yankee soldier who finds a precarious refuge in a girls' seminary deep in Confederate territory. The money was raised through Jennings Lang at Universal, the producer-director was Don Siegel, and the soldier, Corporal John McBurney, was Clint Eastwood. The story deals with the cataclysmic effects of a lone male on an all-female community, with the emphasis on the fact that the female can be much deadlier than the male.

After a credit sequence of sepia photographs of the American Civil War, some of them genuine, some of them extracted from an earlier Universal film with Eastwood's head superimposed at relevant moments, the footage turns to full colour as the camera homes in on McBurney's blood-soaked foot. Next on the scene is ten-year-old Amy, a pupil who reports her discovery to the headmistress, Martha Farnsworth, and her second-in-command, Edwina Dabney. Refusing to do their duty by turning the enemy soldier in, they nurse him back to health, a kindness he repays by treating them as the women they would like to be rather than the frustrated schoolmistresses they have become. In this, he is the beguiler, they the beguiled, but unwisely he extends his patronage to the pupils as well. 'You lying son of a bitch, you bastard, you filthy lecher. I hope you're dead,' screams Edwina when she catches him *in flagrante* with nubile seventeen-year-old Carol.

Calling on the power of lust denied, she chases after him and hurls him down the stairs, breaking his leg so badly that Martha later declares it gangrenous and summarily amputates it with a hacksaw on the dining-room table. When McBurney wakes up from the wine and laudanum anaesthetic, he makes the literally fatal mistake of killing Randolph, a name he associates with a sexual rival until he discovers that it belongs to Amy's pet tortoise. In a world in which sexual peccadillos are punished by the symbolic castration of amputation, there can only by one response to the murder of a cherished pet. With the full agreement of her teachers, Amy gathers a plateful of poisonous mushrooms and McBurney eats and dies under the cold gaze of the sisterhood. The beguiler has finally become the beguiled.

In Siegel's hands, this moody scenario became a mine-field of sexual undercurrents. It is suggested that Martha's only previous experience is incest with her brother and that Edwina is indeed the 'virgin bitch' McBurney describes her as. McBurney is a liar as well as a cheat. He presents himself as a peaceful Quaker who deserves to be saved rather than the career soldier who delights in death that the flashbacks reveal. When he manages to lay his hand on a gun, the beast within is fully exposed, making the death sentence inevitable.

Although Eastwood thought of withdrawing from the project at one stage on the grounds that he wasn't the right man to play McBurney, the role stretched him in ways that would prove useful when he came to direct himself in his next film. The setting for *The Beguiled* is claustrophobic, with little scope for staring mesmerically into wide open spaces. Although McBurney is capable of violent action, his main theatre of operations in this context is seduction and his principle weapon is conversation. If Eastwood had pared his lines to the minimum on this occasion, he would have had no chance of sweet-talking the women into bed. It followed that he had to say them more or less as written, and a very effective seducer he proved to be. 'My role in *The Beguiled* was easier to play than the lone Westerner was. In those Leone films, I had to establish an image for the audience while saying very little, showing very little. In *Beguiled*, I was dealing with straight, normal emotions from my own standpoint, which were simply those of survival.'

As *The Beguiled* was a relatively low-budget film, shot in Louisiana over ten weeks, and as Eastwood's fee was slimmed down to $600,000, he was able to choose 'real' actresses rather than Hollywood beauties. Geraldine Page and Elizabeth Hartman played Martha and Edwina, with drab all-embracing costumes and seething Southern sensuality, and there was a full supporting complement of pubescent maids on which McBurney could work his evil ways. Although the film was succinctly condemned by Judith Crist as 'a must for sadists and woman-haters', the men were not significantly better, merely fewer and less prominent. As well as being incestuous, Martha's brother is a probable deserter while Edwina's father is a philanderer and the only other male on show, a visiting Confederate officer, is more seductive than protective.

'One reason I wanted to make *The Beguiled* is that it is a woman's picture,' Siegel explained, 'not a picture for women, but about them. Women are capable of deceit, larceny, murder, anything. Behind that mask of innocence lurks just as much evil as you'll find in members of the Mafia. Any young girl, who looks perfectly harmless, is capable of murder. There is a careful unity about the film, starting with the first frame. We begin with black and white and end with black and white; we start with Clint and the mushrooms, and end with them; we start with Clint practically dead, and end up with him dead. The film is rounded, intentionally turned in on itself.'

The Beguiled marked the consolidation of the core of what would be the Malpaso team for years to come. Bruce Surtees, the son of the celebrated cinematographer Robert Surtees, had worked as an assistant on earlier Eastwood–Siegel collaborations. Now he came of age with photography that made a forceful correlation between the damp Louisiana treescapes and the walls of the seminary and the hidden desire of the women who have no alternative but to live and work in this festering environment. There are moments when McBurney seems to be the liberator who will set the prisoners free, but ultimately the liberator becomes the captive, a victim of emasculation and death by a thousand cuts. Surtees brought out the underlying pessimism in this scenario with a sombre expertise that put him at the top of Eastwood's list of cameramen for the future.

Despite its display of talent, *The Beguiled* became Eastwood's least profitable film, partly because the public didn't want to see him crippled and dead and partly because the studio realised this too late and tried to recoup their losses with a hopelessly inept marketing campaign. 'It probably would have been a more successful film if I hadn't been in it,' the actor commented. 'I was terribly disappointed by the way *The Beguiled* was sold. I told the studio before I made it that it was a completely different kind of story, a psychological gothic horror film. Then they sold it as just another Clint Eastwood picture, me with a cheroot cigar and stubble beard, which was awfully unfair both to my regular audience and those who wanted something different.'

At least he was able to take some comfort from the 'positive criticism' he received, but Don Siegel was totally disgusted by the way in which the film he considered his and Eastwood's best work was treated. He perceived *The Beguiled* as arts film, a potential winner of the Palme d'Or at the Cannes Film Festival. His point of view was endorsed when it opened in Paris to ecstatic reviews and high box-office returns, but by then it was too little, too late for the home market. 'It's unfortunate that in this country, although we got some wonderful reviews on it, it was very badly handled from the publicity and distribution side. People were misled into believing that Clint Eastwood with a gun in his hand was going to win the Civil War singlehandedly. If that meant that it was the only way you could sell the picture, then you shouldn't make the picture. If we'd opened in a tiny little theater, winner of various festivals, Clint Eastwood co-starring with Geraldine Page, great reviews, we would have created a great deal of curiosity about the picture. As it was, it was opened up greedy. They wanted to make immediate money.'

As it happened, they made very little, but Eastwood was so busy setting up *Play Misty for Me*, the film that would fulfil his long-term ambition to direct, that he had no time for regrets over milk already spilt. According to the Director's Guild, the sole qualification for directing a picture is having a job, so Malpaso duly told Eastwood, 'Kid, you got the job', and Siegel co-signed his application. Raising the money was trickier because studios were traditionally reluctant to stake even a modest budget on a star's ability to take control of his own destiny. The basic sixty-page outline for *Play Misty for Me* had been written some years earlier by another old friend, Jo Heims. Eastwood remembered her from the lean years when she was trying to sell her scripts while working as a secretary. He'd initially optioned her treatment about a small-town disc jockey who finds himself victimised by an obsessive fan but later released her from their agreement when she received a much bigger offer from Universal.

'A few years later, when they'd abandoned the idea of making it, I went to Lou Wasserman, the head of the studio, and said I'd like to do it and I'd like to direct it,' Eastwood told me. 'I told him I'd make it with a budget of less than one million dollars in natural locations and he started to warm to the idea. "Take it and run with it," he said, then started voicing objections. "Why do you want to do a film where a woman has the best part? Why do you want to play a disc jockey?" Nonsensical things like that. When I talked to my agent, I discovered he wanted me to waive my fee and accept a percentage. That was okay, I'd have paid to do it, but eventually the percentage turned out okay.'

Setting up the production in six weeks was made easier by appointing Robert Daley as producer and by making the film in and around Carmel on the Monterey peninsula. Eastwood's familiarity with the area reduced the need for location scouting and he rapidly assembled a twenty-five man crew, headed by Bruce Surtees, from the ranks of those he'd worked with before. Dean Riesner, the *Rawhide* veteran who had beefed up *Coogan's Bluff* until it met Siegel and Eastwood's expectations, turned Jo Heims' treatment into a shooting script. 'Jo's story appealed to me for several reasons,' Eastwood explained. 'It was a small story that lent itself perfectly to being shot on natural sets. Working in realistic, authentic backgrounds in Europe during my years there as an actor had taught me the value of utilising such locations. The story had great entertainment value. In addition to the psychotic horror element, it made a nice comment on the relationships of the individuals to each other and the misinterpretation of commitment. I felt that all types of audiences could identify with the characters. When I added all these factors together, it seemed ideal for a first project.'

The budget didn't allow for fancy casting but even so, Eastwood went out on a limb by choosing Jessica Walter to play the dangerously amorous Evelyn Draper. The studio had little confidence in Walter after her previous films, *The Group* and *Pro*, but Eastwood was adamant. He then picked Donna Mills to play the pretty but vapid blonde who is DJ Dave Garland's true love. Last but not least he hired Don Siegel to play a barman so that he would have expert advice ready to hand. 'A lot of people thought I was using him in the picture as a buffer and subconsciously maybe that was the idea. I knew I'd have a really good director on the set if anything went wrong.'

The night before shooting started, he went to bed well satisfied with his preparations, only to wake with a start in the middle of the night. 'All of a sudden, I went, "Jesus! I got to be in this thing!" I turned on the light and started learning my lines, approaching the scenes all over again from the actor's point of view. Needless to say, I didn't get much sleep.' The next morning the camera rolled on an apprehensive Siegel making his debut in front of the cameras on a set in a derelict sardine factory in Monterey. 'I couldn't turn Clint down,' he said. 'First of all, we're close friends. Even more important, I had to give him my support in his first directorial effort. I had always encouraged him in his desire to direct, and if he insisted on turning me into an actor, I simply had to roll with it.'

But he didn't have to like it and, although he came to believe that his cameo was creditable, it was achieved with difficulty because he kept forgetting his lines. 'I had nothing to do with the direction,' he confirmed when the film was completed. 'Clint didn't need any help with the direction other than the certain idiocy of putting me in that part because it was the very first sequence he shot and the very first sequence I ever acted in. I was nervous that I might let him down. He's very knowledgeable cinematically speaking. He's very good with the camera and undoubtedly will have a successful career as a director. I think the big problem he faces is if he's in the picture himself. It's very difficult for a director to act in his own film. He's not fair to himself if he does.'

As Siegel had already warned Eastwood on this score, the experienced actor was ready to bow to the tyro director's will. His agent in this was the Video West TV Replay System, a high-tech means of checking out his performance as objectively as possible. 'The Malpaso company feel it is indispensable for a director who is directing himself because it is the only way to obtain an impartial view of his portrayal. The routine goes something like this: you line up the shot with the camera; you rehearse with the other actors; then you shoot the scene; and finally you run down the back to the sound truck and look at the scene on the Replay System.'

After a week in which he neglected his own reaction shots and close-ups, Eastwood realised that while generosity to other actors is admirable in theory, it is out of place if it hampers the proper telling of the story. Another vital early lesson was the need to keep the crew involved as much as possible at all times. Eastwood achieved this by explaining exactly where each scene fitted into the overall game-plan rather than issuing curt instructions. 'I had the distinct impression at first that they were all waiting for me to prove myself as a director, but that lasted exactly one day. By the second morning, we were all working together as a totally involved compatible unit.'

Once the ground-rules were established, things went pretty smoothly and very swiftly, with the film coming in four days under its five-week schedule and $50,000 under its $950,000 budget. 'My biggest surprise during the filming of *Misty* was when I discovered that Universal was giving me complete freedom on the production of the film, a situation which I deeply appreciated. I think our success reflected the fact that we were taking the new approach to moviemaking. It is no longer a ride that everyone goes along for. It is a serious job, one that can be fun, but nonetheless a job dedicated to making a profit. That means bringing the film in for a reasonable price and the only reasonable price is the lowest possible cost consistent with telling your story well. The twenty-week schedule seems to me to be an anomaly today. It is saddling a dinosaur. I think people in the industry are aware of this. Hollywood is in no present danger of becoming the LaBrea Tar Pits.'

Back in the editing room, Eastwood assembled a taut, compelling film that has become an enduring late-night classic. Dave Garland, a schmaltzy disc jockey who introduces five hours of 'music to be happy to' on a nightly basis, may not be a typical Eastwood character, but he has a contemporary quality that appealed to the youth-oriented culture of the early seventies. He'd originally been based on a local DJ whom Clint knew, and playing him came even more easily because he'd endured a similar case of infatuation in his own adolescence. 'I was nineteen, the gal maybe twenty-three,' he recalled, 'and there was maybe just a little misinterpretation about how serious the whole thing was. It didn't get into being homicidal or anything like that.'

Audiences who were not prepared to see their action-man hero killed by womankind during the Civil War were happy enough to see him persecuted by a woman governed by uncontrollable lust, a form of behaviour that had become publicly admissible in the permissive sixties. Better still from their point of view, Garland survives his difficulties and settles down with the anodyne girlfriend who has failed to get over him during an extended trip to Europe. In other words, *Play Misty for Me* is sugar-coated in a way *The Beguiled* never could be. Fifteen years later, it would prove to be an inspiration for an even more successful obsessive lust triangle in *Fatal Attraction*. 'They admit to stealing,' says Eastwood with a smile. 'I told Sherry Lansing [the producer of Fatal Attraction], "You owe me a beer" and she said, "Yes, I always liked that movie."'

When it was finished, Eastwood found he liked it too. 'After seventeen years of bouncing my head against the wall, hanging around sets, maybe influencing certain camera set-ups with my own opinions, watching actors go through all kinds of hell without any help and working with both good directors and bad ones, I'm at the point where I'm ready to make my own pictures,' he told Rex Reed in the *Los Angeles Times*. 'I stored away all the mistakes I made and saved up all the good things I learned and now I know enough to control my own projects and get what I want out of actors. So I directed this picture and I'm editing it myself and I think it's damned good.'

Many of the critics agreed and there was an encouraging level of support for Eastwood the director. 'There are a couple of hackneyed moments, notably a nude love scene, but Eastwood displays a vigorous talent for sequences of violence and tension,' wrote Jay Cocks in *Time* magazine. 'He has obviously seen *Psycho* and *Repulsion* more than once, but these are excellent texts and he has learned his lessons passing well.' Tom Milne, writing in the *Financial Times*, admired Eastwood's 'brilliant handling of his cast [memorably including Don Siegel as a barman], his easy way with the thriller medium and his cleverly underplayed use of music throughout.' John Russell Taylor concluded his review in *The Times* with 'altogether a very promising debut for Eastwood as a director.'

The luckiest beneficiary of the film's success was Roberta Flack, whose song 'The First Time Ever I Saw Your Face' rocketed from obscurity to number one in the charts when Eastwood used it to plug a nagging gap in his narrative. When his story editor told him that he needed a love scene between himself and Donna Mills, he characteristically refused to consider anything that involved a lot of talk. The solution occurred to him one morning when he heard Roberta's song on a jazz station as he drove to the Malpaso offices at Universal. Realising that the lyrics would tell the love story for him, he searched all over town for the album, *First Take*, which the singer had recorded four years earlier. When he eventually found it marked down from $4.95 to $1.35 in a supermarket, he bought it and approached Atlantic Records for the rights to use it in his movie – with dramatically happy results all round.

8

The Ultimate Shoot-'Em-Up

After playing second fiddle to various manifestations of the sisterhood twice in succession, Clint Eastwood took stock of a career that wasn't going exactly where he wanted and came up with the perfect answer: Harry Callahan. His choice may have been prompted by the visit to Italy he made when the cameras stopped rolling on *Play Misty for Me*. Its purpose was twofold: to attend the Italian premiere of *The Beguiled* in the Cinema Misure in Milan and to receive a bronze medallion for his artistic contribution to the Italian film industry at a gala held in his honour by Milan University. Before the presentation ceremony, he chatted easily with the students, then gave a simple speech of thanks in which he credited Sergio Leone and his compatriots with being the inspiration for his career. These dignified proceedings were in sharp contrast to the rapturous and at times hysterical welcome he received whenever his car appeared on the city streets. Although Eastwood has never sought or enjoyed overt emotion on this scale, he could hardly fail to notice how much more warmly he was received in Italy than in the United States.

No doubt the impression was reinforced when he found himself on the cover of *Life* magazine in July 1971 under the less than flattering catchline 'The world's favourite movie star is – no kidding – Clint Eastwood'. Significantly, this assessment came not from his fellow Americans but from The Hollywood Foreign Press Association and they confirmed it by presenting him with a Golden Globe award. Meanwhile, *Life* tried to come to terms with his popularity by asking, 'Who can stand 32,580 seconds of Clint Eastwood?' a sardonic question that elicited the response, 'Just about everyone.'

By this time, however, Eastwood was well into his shooting schedule for *Dirty Harry*, the film that would make him into the kind of brutish vigilante hero who most appealed to his target audience of eighteen to twenty-five-year-old American males. When he was asked to define a Clint Eastwood film, the actor once said 'any film with Clint Eastwood in it', but, after his first nine major American films had failed to make the spectacular box-office returns he wanted, he was forced to realise that he needed a more American version of The Man with No Name. At this point in his career, the 'Dollar' trilogy regularly played as a night-long triple bill to packed houses and his next most successful films were *Hang 'Em High* and *Coogan's Bluff*, the ones he'd made when he first returned to his homeland. Subsequent experiments with action adventures in which he shared the limelight with high-profile co-stars like Richard Burton and Lee Marvin, and pictures that explored the woman's angle as well as the man's, had proved relatively disappointing.

In 1971, Eastwood came second in the American box-office charts to John Wayne, a mythic figure who fully understood how to manipulate the deep-seated desires of his fellow Americans by playing heroes who believed that might is right. He'd taken control of his career in the forties and fifties by producing his own films and he'd been making sure they were created in his own image ever since. His attitude didn't always make him popular, certainly not with Don Siegel, who said, after directing him in *The Shootist*, 'I found him impossible. Don't let anyone tell you he's mellowed. I wanted to quit almost every day. But I think it turned out to be a good picture, and I think he gave the best performance of his life in it, but I wouldn't want to be in the same room with him ever again.'

However, Wayne's way did pull in the crowds and Clint Eastwood understood why. 'A guy sits in the audience. He's twenty-five years old and he's scared stiff about what he's going to do with his life. He wants to have the self-sufficient thing he sees up there on the screen. But it will never happen that way. Man is always dreaming of being an individual but he is really a flock animal.' In Harry Callahan, a rogue cop who took as much pleasure from his Magnum .44 as he did from the cold-hearted contempt with which he addressed his victims, Eastwood had found his means of tapping into the trigger-happy, violence-loving section of the American dream. By locating him in San Francisco, the most westerly city on the United States mainland, he hoped to add a frontier component to a modern cosmopolitan man.

The story that was originally known as *Dead Right* had been bought from its authors, Harry Julian and Rita M. Fink, by Warner Bros for Frank Sinatra, then approaching the end of his acting career. He saw Inspector Harry Callahan as a suitable swansong until a hand injury put him out of the picture during pre-production. The role was then offered to Paul Newman, the number-one box-office attraction in 1970, who said that the character was too scruffy but probably meant that he was too right-wing. He suggested Eastwood who agreed, subject to Warner Bros accepting a clean-up for Harry, a Dean Riesner re-write for the script, and a Malpaso package that included Don Siegel as director. A key piece of casting was Andy Robinson as Scorpio, the psychotic killer based on a serial killer called Zodiac who had terrorised San Francisco.

As *Dirty Harry* is essentially a duel between the cop and the killer, a strong presence was needed to balance Eastwood, and Robinson, an off-Broadway actor with no film experience, certainly provided it. After the re-write, Scorpio came out of the blind side, a madman with no specific motivation for horrific crimes that include the random shooting of a beautiful young woman in a swimming-pool and burying a schoolgirl alive. Siegel eliminated all reference to Scorpio's background so that he became an everyman assassin, the murderous impulse that is within us all.

'I have a theory that anyone can be a killer, is a potential killer,' said Siegel, returning to the argument he'd used to justify female murderers in *The Beguiled*. 'I took the situation as it existed, without going into the *raison d'être* for the killer's action. I tried to play the killer as normal-looking as possible, not with a wild face or appearance. He is on the loose and the police go after him. However, they have a great deal of trouble with him because I always like my villains to be brighter than my heroes. He's all by himself, and he's quite brilliant, mysteriously so. You never quite see how he gets into or out of a place. I hold that knowledge back, so that he's almost a cunning Superman, although not a physical one.'

The implication from Siegel's characterisation is that Harry has to make up for anything he lacks in brains with a conspicuous display of brawn, and that is exactly what happens. Scorpio is the first to show in a classic opening sequence involving panoramic shots of San Francisco's high-rise skyline. As Bruce Surtees turns his camera upwards from the top of an apartment building, he picks out Robinson with his telescopic sight centred on the woman in the turquoise blue water of the rooftop swimming-pool far below. The rifle cracks and she dies. Next in the firing position is Inspector Callahan, steely in his resolve to nail his man. As he reads a note demanding $100,000 or 'it will be my next pleasure to kill a Catholic priest or a nigger', his eyes narrow and we know the battle is joined.

As is the way in rogue cop movies, Harry Callahan has at least as much trouble with his superiors, represented by John Vernon as the Mayor and Harry Guardino as Lieutenant Bressler, as he does with his adversary. He is also burdened with a partner, the youthful Chico Gonzales (Reni Santoni), whose naive eagerness is in marked contrast to his own surly demeanour. By Harry's book, the liberal mayor is a mealy-mouth appeaser destined to fail in the great crusade for justice because he isn't prepared to bend the law in order to achieve the desired results.

'When an adult male is chasing an adult female with intent to rape, I shoot the bastard,' Harry tells him in their first encounter. 'That's my policy.' 'Intent? How did you establish that?' the Mayor enquires, and Harry has a brisk reply. 'When a naked man is chasing a woman through an alley with a butcher's knife and a hard-on, I figure he isn't out collecting for the Red Cross.'

This exchange establishes Harry Callahan both as the kind of cop who would rather shoot the wrong man than ask the right questions and as a master of the laconic riposte that would become his trademark. Many years and many sequels would pass before he would speak his most famous phrase of all, 'Go ahead, make my day', but *Dirty Harry* sets the tone for the future as he levels his gun at a lone surviving bank robber considering a last-ditch stand. 'I know what you're thinking, punk,' he says with controlled menace. 'Did he fire six shots or only five? To tell you the truth, in all the excitement, I kinda lost track myself. But being that this is a .44 Magnum, the most powerful handgun in the world and would blow your head clean off, you got to ask yourself one question, "Do I feel lucky?" Well, do you, punk?' Although the bank robber ducks the challenge, the words are repeated

to Scorpio in the climactic finale, with predictably different
results.

By this time, actor and director worked together so easily
that Eastwood was able to stand in for Siegel when he
fell ill with flu. The scene slated for the night of his absence involved Callahan rescuing a would-be suicide from
a sixth-floor window. The schedule allowed six nights for
this sequence, but Eastwood had other ideas as he climbed
on to the crane that would raise him to the shooting position
high above a downtown intersection. He'd worked out the
logistics of the rescue with stuntman and occasional actor
Buddy Van Horn, who'd masterminded the rather limited
stunts on *The Beguiled*. Now Van Horn would play the
would-be suicide who grabs at Callahan from his precarious
rooftop position and is then hauled to safety on the crane.
Both men played it cool and safe through the dark hours
before dawn and, sure enough, as the sun lightened the
summer sky at 5.30 a.m., the footage was in the can and
Eastwood was snapping the tab on a can of beer.

Under Siegel's command, he later completed an even
more dangerous stunt when he jumped from a bridge on
to the roof of a moving bus hijacked by Scorpio as the
action approaches its climax. Like *Play Misty for Me*, all the
filming took place in natural locations in a city he knew well
from his schooldays across the Bay. Some, like the Mayor's
office and the casualty department of the General Hospital,
were the real thing. Others were adapted as required, with
the seventh floor of the Pacific Gas & Electric Building
standing in for a working police department. Key confrontations were shot in Mount Davidson Park, where Scorpio
ambushes Harry, and the Kezar Stadium, where Harry
tortures the killer, an abuse of human rights that means
he is freed at the subsequent hearing. The grand finale took
place in a gravel works, a watery venue that provides a final
resting-place for Scorpio and Harry's rejected police star.

The manner in which the disgruntled inspector throws away this badge of office reflects the key differences in attitude between Siegel and Eastwood. Siegel always intended the contemptuous gesture to signify a parting of the ways for the San Francisco Police Department and its turbulent inspector but, for three antagonistic days, Eastwood refused to shoot it. Cynics would suggest that this was because he already had four sequels in mind, but it is generally agreed that the argument went deeper than that. Throughout the film, Harry Callahan abused his police star just as his adversary, Scorpio, abused the peace symbol he wore as a belt buckle. In Siegel's eyes, this made them two of a kind. As the war raged on in Vietnam against a groundswell of unpopularity at home, the use of a peace symbol by a man engaged in unlicensed killing not only for personal gain but for his own amusement was aberrant behaviour, but it found a mirror image in Callahan's illegal police work. By torturing Scorpio, Harry takes a parallel pleasure in causing pain. It follows that throwing away the badge is a symbolic act, a recognition by the director that Harry is a vigilante rather than a legitimate law enforcer.

Eastwood, on the other hand, always saw Harry Callahan as a force for good opposed by a force for evil. In his eyes, the means, however brutal and however illegal, justified the end, which was the elimination of criminals. Scorpio's callousness gives his adversary the right to match or even exceed it. The police star is the badge that confirms that right, the seal of his legitimacy, and Eastwood had no wish to see him lose it by throwing it away. Where Siegel wanted to comment on social evils of the era which included a significant breakdown of proper police procedure – there are references in *Dirty Harry* to the Escobedo and Miranda cases in which real-life policemen were censured for abusing citizens' rights – Eastwood was aiming for heroic status, not only for himself, but for Inspector Harry Callahan. He wanted him to be seen as an individual standing up for his values in a society that had gone soft on criminals.

As David Downing and Gary Herman point out in *All-American Anti-Hero*, Siegel's portrayal of abuses in police procedure was exactly in tune with the times. Using examples taken from an academic study of trends in American television, they noted an increase from 18.8 to 55.4 per cent in illegal seizures and searches and from 20.6 to 50.8 per cent in failures to advise suspects of their rights between 1969 and 1971. Dramatically speaking, showing the police smashing down a door has a lot more impact than showing them knocking on it politely, search-warrant in hand, but even so, the rise is startlingly large. In the sense that he is a loner who shoots to kill, Callahan is a direct descendant of The Man with No Name, but where the Leone character operated outside the law, the Siegel one is its official representative.

In the final analysis, Eastwood saw little fundamental difference between the two and the public voted for him with their money when the film opened in December 1971. However, the serious critics picked up on the issue of vigilante justice, as Siegel must have feared they might. As was usual in those days, the protest was led by the *New Yorker*'s Pauline Kael, who wrote, '*Dirty Harry* is obviously just a genre movie but this particular genre has always had a fascist potential and it has finally surfaced. If crime were caused by super-evil dragons, there would be no Miranda, no Escobedo; we could all be licensed to kill like Dirty Harry. But since crime is caused by deprivation, misery, psychopathology and social injustice, *Dirty Harry* is a deeply immoral movie.' The film was also condemned on the grounds that the criminals were predominantly black, proof not so much of a new trend as of a growing awareness of issues like racism and sexism in the early seventies.

Eastwood's defence of the emotive fascist charge was abrupt and dismissive. Critics, he said, were aged forty to fifty, audiences under twenty-five. If they liked it, as early box-office returns of sixteen million dollars insisted they did, that was fine by him. 'Jesus, some people are so politically oriented that when they see cornflakes in a bowl, they get some complex interpretation out of it. We made an action adventure film. If it commented on the fact that courts set guilty people free on occasion, well, that sometimes happens. It was a dramatic device, not a political one. We weren't doing a big thing about police being hamstrung. People on either side of the political spectrum tend to go overboard. One critic in L.A. actually wrote that because our killer hijacked a school bus in the movie, we were making an anti-bussing statement. Incredible. Who has time to think of all that crap? We're busy making a movie.'

Siegel justified the film on the grounds of realism, citing the fact that the Los Angeles Police Department expressed approval after a private screening the night before the San Francisco premiere. Again, cynics might say, 'Well, they would, wouldn't they?', since a proportion of them would agree wholeheartedly with Callahan's *modus operandi*, if only out of frustration at their own lack of results in the face of over-oppressive bureaucracy. The one thing they didn't approve was the ending, which they said could never happen because anyone who'd served in the police force for as long as Harry Callahan would balk at throwing away substantial pension rights along with his badge.

Siegel told Andy Warhol in an interview in 1972 that he modelled Dirty Harry on a friend of his called George Dyer, the head of a burglary unit who showed a much more human face when he brought his children over to the director's house at Easter. 'He's not a monster but his work is so tough that he becomes inured to brutality. They [the police] don't even realise when they're talking about the dreadful things they have to go through that it's shocking to someone like myself who hasn't been exposed to blood and physical violence. The difficulties a policeman has, not only in apprehending a criminal, but in how he apprehends him – by the time you follow all the rules and regulations, the criminal could have escaped long ago. You have also in *Dirty Harry* a time factor, which seems to be ignored by my left-wing critics; he had to find this girl or she was going to be dead. He didn't have time to go through all the petty nonsense of getting a warrant or worrying about breaking in or how he was going to get the information.'

If that sounds more like Eastwood that Siegel talking, it may be because the director lost control of his actor on this occasion. There is evidence that Eastwood became much more serious at this point in his career, partly because Malpaso's expansion gave him new powers and partly because he'd earned his own spurs as a director with *Play Misty for Me*. Where he and Siegel once had an equal partnership, he was now in the ascendant, as the director acknowledged when he said, 'My close associate and star of the picture and in a sense my boss is Clint Eastwood who is a registered Republican and I am a registered Democrat. Notwithstanding what Pauline Kael says when she refers to me as a former liberal, I would say that I certainly am liberal. I'm not saying that Clint is a reactionary but the interesting thing is that he leans to the right where I certainly lean to the left. Now we're making a picture where this never comes up. There's never been a discussion between us whether we're telling a rightist picture, a leftist picture, a racist picture, all we're interested in is telling a story as entertainingly as possible. We have no political discussion about the picture.'

Does Siegel protest too much? Probably he does, and although there were lengthy disclaimers of rifts at the time,

Dirty Harry was the only Callahan film he would direct. Although he worked with the actor once more, on *Escape from Alcatraz*, the most fruitful period of their collaboration, four films in four years, was over. For Eastwood, the time had come to look at the balance sheet for *Dirty Harry* and decide what to do next. On the plus side, he had found the home-based popularity he wanted along with considerable financial gain. The minus side of the equation was that he had still failed to establish a contemporary version of The Man with No Name. American audiences approved of Harry's obsession with getting the killer off the streets, they even accepted that the ends justified the means, but this tough, cynical cop who used his gun as an extension of his penis was not a person that many could easily warm to. Eastwood might have no doubt that Harry Callahan held the moral high ground, but his opinion didn't find universal favour. Amusing though they were, his efforts to sugar the pill with one-liners that smacked of sadism merely emphasised Callahan's essential callousness.

The core of the dilemma was that lawless actions that seemed appropriate for a western hero throwing back the frontiers of civilisation, and thereby extending the benefits of American culture into places previously deprived of it, were less acceptable on the streets of San Francisco in supposedly democratic times. Eastwood's solution was obvious: he dived back into the Old West where a man could do what a man had to do without interference from critics and other liberal wimps. His vehicle was *Joe Kidd*, originally titled *Sinola*. It was a re-make of Sergio Corbucci's *The Big Silence*, a spaghetti western that was never released in the United States, allegedly because Eastwood bought up the rights in order to prevent it.

The storyline is familiar, as is the setting, the small town of Sinola in New Mexico near the border where

Mexican and WASP cultures habitually clash. The bone of contention is the right to own land, something the American faction, led by Frank Harlan (Robert Duvall), takes for granted. The Mexicans, led by Luis Chama (John Saxon), dispute this by rioting at the courthouse, threatening the judge who refuses to listen to their case and burning the land records. Joe Kidd, who is already in jail overnight on a drunk and disorderly charge, rescues the judge and receives an offer of five hundred dollars from Harlan to track down Chama. He refuses, then accepts at double the fee when he discovers that the Mexican has stolen some of his horses. As the plot unfolds, Harlan and Chama are revealed as equally evil, which means that Kidd has to switch sides so as to support he who behaved least badly in the previous encounter. This makes for a hard road for a hero to hoe, as the critic Arthur Knight noted in the *Saturday Review*. 'Joe Kidd, in his single-minded purpose of turning the corrupt Mexican over to a corrupt justice, is demonstrably mad.'

Intriguingly, it has been pointed out that Joe Kidd, as fashioned in the image of Clint Eastwood by the novelist Elmore Leonard, has a background that ties in to some degree with the 'Dollar' trilogy. In *A Fistful of Dollars*, The Man with No Name is referred to as Joe, and Kidd admits to a long history of bounty-hunting, slender facts that have prompted the theory that Joe Kidd is a direct evolution of the Leone hero. If so, he is not a very good one because he lacks mystery, inspiration and focus. Like No Name, he changes sides, but not so much out of self-interest as out of a righteousness that seems progressively more misplaced. Nor does he use subtlety in pursuit of whatever goals happen to suit him at the moment. Like most Eastwood heroes, he is chronically trigger-happy, but his ultimate weapon is a train which he drives through several buildings to bring the final battle

A muscular display as cowboy Rowdy Yates in *Rawhide*, the long running television series that paved the way for the big time.

Nice work if you can get it, especially if your ideal woman is tiny, blonde and perfectly formed.

Maggie Eastwood - seen strolling with Clint through the streets of San Francisco in 1962 and with son Kyle at their home in Carmel some ten years later - may not have been quite tiny enough but she is the only woman he has ever married.

A gun for hire: the Man With No Name in Sergio Leone's spaghetti western trilogy (1964-67) set the laconic tone that persists today.

Play Misty For Me (1971) is a new ball game for a first time actor-director: as deejay Dave Garland, Eastwood steams it up with Jessica Walter's psychopathic admirer and plays it cool with Don Siegel's barman.

Getting used to a champagne lifestyle with Elizabeth Taylor and Richard Burton, his co-star on *Where Eagles Dare*.

A tough pool school for Jean Seberg during one of many shooting breaks on the megabuck musical, *Paint Your Wagon* (1969).

The sweet smell of success: 1973 brought a second outing for Dirty Harry - aka Inspector Harry Callahan of the San Francisco Police Department - in *Magnum Force* and a second shot behind the cameras on *Breezy*.

The rise and rise of Sondra Locke began when Eastwood chose her as the female lead in *The Outlaw Josey Wales* (1976) but that was just the start of the agony and the ecstasy.

between the Americans and the Mexicans to a bloody conclusion.

Malpaso's choice of director was John Sturges, a star in the western firmament after successes with *Gunfight at the OK Corral* and *The Magnificent Seven*. His work was in the liberal western tradition. In other words, his potential saviours wanted to collaborate with, rather than dominate, the victims of oppression. By displaying compassion rather than patronage, as reactionary western heroes like John Wayne invariably did, Sturges's saviours could be seen as equals rather than superior beings assisting a disadvantaged underclass. As this was never Eastwood's personal perspective, and even less so in the immediate aftermath of *Dirty Harry*, it must be presumed that he hired Sturges in the belief that he would make Joe Kidd into a classic and that he would learn something about directing westerns while he did it.

As things turned out, he was disappointed on both fronts. Sturges was past his prime and on a losing streak, yet Eastwood discovered that he could neither dominate nor collaborate with him to any useful degree. Shooting took place in dramatic country in the high sierra in California and the desert hills around Tucson in Arizona, scenery that was faithfully and magnificently captured by cameraman Bruce Surtees, but *Joe Kidd* remained obstinately pedestrian. This was because the hero lacked heroism, no matter which direction you came at him from. Even those who believed implicitly in the American dream balked at seeing it peddled by a righteous mercenary, however charismatic. Despite a faithful spaghetti-western score from another Malpaso regular, Lalo Schifrin, who'd worked on *The Beguiled* and *Dirty Harry*, *Joe Kidd* made a little money but few real friends.

For Clint Eastwood, the writing was on the wall: if he wanted to make a decent western, he'd have to renege on

his promise when shooting stopped on *Play Misty for Me*.
'It was a great experience all the way around and I intend
to do it again, but I'm not going to try to both act and
direct in the next one. I'd have to be insane to do both
again.' Rarely have words proved less prophetic.

9

Suspended Animation

A lone horseman charts an eerie course through a heat haze on the horizon. Where the sand meets the sky, the desert air is filled with swirling dust from the hooves. Dee Barton's neo-Morricone score fills the auditorium with jangling sound. As picked up by a long lens, the disembodied figure on the pale horse seems to float above the ground but as definition kicks in, he is revealed as Clint Eastwood, High Plains Drifter. No one who had seen the Leone films could mistake the purpose of the dramatically beautiful opening shot, as captured by Bruce Surtees at Winnemucca Dry Lake in Nevada, but anyone who hadn't soon receives enlightenment when the town dwarf says, 'What did you say your name was?' and the stranger replies stonily, 'I didn't.'

High Plains Drifter was an Eastwood film from conception to completion, a thoroughgoing attempt to fuse the best of Leone with the elements he liked in Dirty Harry. It was inspired by the case of Kitty Genovese, a girl who was murdered in front of thirty-eight indifferent witnesses. 'What if that happened to a marshal in a small town?' Eastwood enquired, and commissioned scriptwriter, Ernest Tidyman, to provide an answer. He came up with a ghost story in which the murdered marshal returns as the Stranger and creates his own form of hell for those who betrayed him. As Eastwood takes human shape, he rides into the small mining town of Lago, watched by a gallery of spectators. They look anxious, apprehensive even, as the scruffy, vaguely familiar figure stares icily ahead. Only the crack of a whip disturbs his equanimity.

His first stop is the saloon where three men menace him as he orders a drink. 'Flea-bitten range-bums don't usually stop in Lago. Life here's a little too quick for them. But maybe you think you're fast enough to keep up with us.' The challenge is unmistakable and the stranger has no hesitation in taking it up. 'I'm faster than you'll ever live to be.' A few minutes later, he proves it as he guns them down from under an all-embracing white sheet while taking a shave in the barber's shop next door. For the awestruck townsfolk, this display of expertise in dispatching their hired protectors suggests that the stranger is the best candidate to replace them, so he is offered the job of training them in self-defence.

The stranger agrees to their proposition only on condition that they promise to do exactly as he says, a rider he exploits to the full in a variety of mysterious ways. He insists on evicting all the other guests from the hotel so that he has sole occupancy, makes liberal sexual use of the town's women, and appoints the dwarf as mayor. He then commandeers food and drink for an elaborate picnic and orders a barn to be destroyed so that the wood can be made into tables for the feast. Finally he has the whole place painted red and, lest the significance of this should escape us, Lago on the town sign is replaced with Hell.

The background to these events unfolds in flashbacks that show the dead marshal, Jim Duncan, reporting the illegality of the mine on which Lago depends for its income to the proper authorities. When he is killed by three gunmen for taking away the town's livelihood, it is with the acquiescence of its citizens. Duncan now lies in an unmarked grave in a cemetery that includes tombstones that read 'Donald Siegel' and 'S. Leone'. 'A man lying in an unmarked grave can't lie easy,' the stranger comments cryptically. We also learn that the gunmen who were imprisoned for his murder are expected back any day to wreak revenge and claim their kingdom. When they arrive, the significance of the whip is dramatically revealed and the stranger is free to ride back into the haze, leaving the partially destroyed and severely depopulated town to its own perfidious devices.

As an actor, Eastwood holds all the aces in a film in which the rest of the cast are very much in the supporting mould. His stranger is both vengeful ghost and guardian angel, a combination that allows him to judge, sentence and execute at will. In another attempt to fuse the Old West with contemporary America, the stranger displays the intelligence of No Name and the brutal wit of Dirty Harry. However, Eastwood's wish to make the film into a metaphor for moral cowardice in the face of violence in the present day is confused by the stranger's overtly vigilante stance. As a rapist, a tormentor and a mercenary, there are many times when he seems better suited to hell than heaven.

As a director, Eastwood confirms the promise of *Play Misty for Me* with work that established goalposts that would not be moved in the future. By comparison with his first film, this was a large-scale production, with a six-week shooting schedule and extensive location building. Nearly fifty construction workers spent three weeks preparing the town of Lago on the shore of Mono Lake in the Californian Sierras. Fourteen houses and a two-storey hotel were complete buildings rather than façades so that Eastwood could shoot the interiors on site rather than at the studio. As half the town had to be burned down at the end, shooting was in sequence, which meant that the actors were hired for the whole production. Paying for idling time bugged the director, but he came to see that continuity filming speeded up the editing process, so allowing the film to start earning its money back sooner.

Eastwood had proved some of his theories on the advantage of on-site editing when he cut *Play Misty for Me* in a room above The Hog's Breath Inn in Carmel. 'From the first, I found I prefer editing on location as the picture is being shot, though I realise it's impossible to edit the total film that way. But it does give you enough of a head start so that it cuts down on post-production time.'

On *High Plains Drifter*, he broke more new ground by setting up shop for his editor, Ferris Webster, in a log cabin with spectacular views of Mono Lake's pine forests and snow-capped mountains in the belief that natural beauty would provide inspiration. 'In post-production, I learned the lesson of patience, going over film endlessly for hours at a time. Most cutting rooms are abysmally depressing, for no reason that I can figure out. Few of them have windows, or any relief from grey walls and racks of film cans. I've since discovered that if we set up cutting rooms with a little atmosphere, even if it consists of only one window, then everyone's creativity – the editor, the director and everyone involved – is heightened, and therefore the work is speeded up. Why be depressed when you don't have to?'

Despite the elaborate location and the number of special effects required, Eastwood brought *High Plains Drifter* in two days under its six-week schedule. 'I can't stand long production schedules,' he commented. 'Once you get moving, I don't see any reason to drag your feet. During production, I can function much more fully and efficiently if I move full blast. Maybe it's because I'm basically lazy but for me, there is no happy medium.'

Although *High Plains Drifter* established Eastwood as a director of some class, it won him few friends among the critics on either side of the Atlantic. 'The Leone trademarks are all well in evidence,' wrote the *Financial*

Times, 'the long, brooding pauses, the low-angle camera shots, the percussive score, the satirical treatment of the town's corrupt hierarchy.' Yet Leone himself didn't like the film, perhaps because it lays out a lot of background to justify the antihero's antisocial actions where the 'Dollar' films just presented him as an anarchic force. As justification is accompanied by the right to take revenge on the wrongdoers, *High Plains Drifter* brought Eastwood another batch of fascist accusations, especially in France. However, the American public loved it, no doubt for the very things the critics hated in it, and Eastwood hit the jackpot in the ratings for the first time.

The combination of Eastwood's political perspective and his belief that vigilante stories are good cinema made it inevitable that he would be called a fascist, especially as he both emphasised and eulogised the vengeful streak in the western hero. 'A period gone by, the pioneer, the loner, operating by himself, without the benefit of society. It usually has something to do with some sort of vengeance; he takes care of the vengeance himself, doesn't call the police. Like Robin Hood. It's the last masculine frontier. Romantic myth, I guess, though it's hard to think of anything romantic today. In a western, you can think, "Jesus, there was a time when a man was alone, on horseback, out there where man hasn't spoiled the land yet."'

This is clearly a statement of identification but, at a time when the left was creating social turbulence, few would have seen an Eastwood character as a Robin Hood figure. The Sherwood outlaw is a people's champion, best known for robbing the rich to feed the poor, whereas Eastwood's loners invariably put themselves at the head of the handout queue. Nor was Eastwood, the man, in the business for the fun of it. 'Working with Clint over lunch means getting your brains picked and then being charged

$3.95 for the club sandwich,' said a colleague who had the good sense to remain anonymous.

Another noticed changes that would intensify as his power base grew. 'He's become so serious this year,' said one, 'like he knows he's a corporation. And I don't mean an institution; he's been that since the spaghetti westerns. He's a multi millionaire conglomerate.' Even before he was rich, Eastwood was solidly Republican and he had no hesitation in voting for Richard Nixon in the 1972 Presidential election. Like many self-made men, his political stance was influenced at least as much by the wish to hang on to as much money as possible as by ideology. If Republicanism represented business advantage, then he would go with it all the way to the bank. 'I voted for Nixon like most everybody else did. You're voting for one philosophy against another. You vote for people with the limited knowledge you have at the time. That's about all you can do. I didn't like what the other guy was selling, so you take a choice. It turned out to be fucked up.'

Eastwood's first two films as a director established a pattern that he has repeated again and again over the past twenty years. Where *Play Misty for Me* was a cherished project, *High Plains Drifter* was overtly conceived as a breadwinner. *Play Misty* broke the mould of silent horsemen and trigger-happy cops who form the bottom line of the Malpaso production slate. Owing to good housekeeping and better directing, it was successful, but it wouldn't have mattered if it hadn't been because Eastwood always had certain moneymakers like *High Plains Drifter* to fall back on. In these too, he aspired to innovation, and sometimes achieved it, but again it didn't matter if he didn't because the film fulfilled its prime purpose of putting cash in the bank whether it was good or not. Many years would pass before Eastwood managed to combine these disparate elements in a single film, the multi-Oscar-winning *Unforgiven*, but meanwhile his two-pronged pragmatism served him well.

The next example of an oddball was *Breezy*, written like *Play Misty for Me* by Jo Heims. It is very much a woman's film, a sugary romance between a pompous middle-aged estate agent and a seventeen-year-old drop-out. Heims created Frank Harmon for Clint Eastwood, perhaps in the belief that a man approaching his forty-fifth birthday would enjoy the pleasures of young love. If so, she was disappointed, because he decided that screen sex was not for him. Maybe he'd learned his lessons from *The Beguiled*, when the public voted with their feet to tell him that vulnerability was unacceptable. Maybe he didn't want to expose himself to the kind of ridicule that lies in wait for an older man who falls in love with an adolescent girl. Maybe he just wanted to find out if he preferred being a director to an actor-director. Whatever the reason, his mind was made up. 'I've never done a love story so I'm staying behind the camera,' he said, and confirmed it by hiring an older man, William Holden, to play the male lead.

The casting of the female lead is mostly memorable for the presence of Sondra Locke among the hopefuls. 'I liked her but I didn't think she was right,' said Eastwood after his first meeting with the woman who would break up his marriage and drag his name through the mud in a bitter palimony dispute. Instead he cast Kay Lenz, the daughter of a San Francisco disc jockey, as Breezy. She was recommended by his editor, Ferris Webster, who'd worked on her most recent film, a Movie of the Week called *The Weekend Nun*. Webster did her a considerable favour by re-cutting some of the footage so that she appeared to be the central character before showing it to Robert Daley. Then he returned it to its original state, only to receive a request to see it from Eastwood. Obligingly, he re-cut it once again and, after an audition in which she described herself as 'terrible', Lenz got the part. 'You're joking,' she said when she heard.

Shooting took place on location on the streets of Encino, a prosperous Valley suburb in the northern part of Los Angeles. There is no disguising the lack of originality in a story that starts with the self-regarding Frank Harmon giving a lift to the hippie Breezy, not so much to help her as to get her off his immaculate suburban streets. After reluctantly agreeing to her demand that they should take an injured dog to the vet, he believes he's got shot of her for good, only to have her turn up on his doorstep claiming to have left her guitar in his car. Again, he sends her packing, but soon she's back, claiming to be his niece so as to avoid a vagrancy charge. And so it continues, an on-off romance that illustrates the mental angst and the physical advantages of trying to bridge the generation gap.

Clint Eastwood had little sympathy with the likes of Breezy, a scruffy unmotivated teenager of the kind he most despised. By making this clear, he further undermines an already weak scenario, but again, there is no mistaking the quality of his work as a director. 'I learned that it's a great deal easier to direct a picture with other actors than one in which you appear yourself. An actor-director is always thinking about two things at once when he's in front of the camera.'

With three films in the can, he'd developed a *modus operandi* that worked well for all concerned as William Holden confirmed. 'Why shouldn't I sound great?' he enquired on the last day of shooting. 'I am great. I'd forgotten what it was like to make pictures this agreeably. I'll work with Clint any time he asks. Besides, he can't pull any crap with me because he's an actor too. He's also even-tempered, a personality trait not much in evidence among directors. The crew is totally behind him and that really helps things go smoothly. There has been no temperament, no nothing. We all do our work and like it.'

One who didn't like it so much was the Encino resident who dared to demand a five-thousand-dollar fee for the right to shoot a corner of his property. Eastwood promptly turned his cameras elsewhere, only to have the neighbour line three cars up in his driveway, engines running and headlights blazing, in an attempt to ruin a night shoot. 'Really weird,' said Eastwood. 'I don't understand people like that. The headlights went right over us and were no problem at all. The running motors weren't picked up by our sound. In the middle of it, I sneaked up the hill and looked to see what he was doing. The guy was in his driveway pouring cans of gas into the cars! All he did was use up batteries and gas. I hope it made him feel better.'

As a general rule, Eastwood shot more takes than Siegel, but he also shot more quickly, so he reckoned the economic bottom line came out about the same. 'Don shoots leaner than I do. I admire him. I think it's best to make decisions while shooting and not to wait until editing. It gives you more energy and actually more room for improvisation because of not having wasted time and money. There are really two ways of directing. If it's a short scene, sometimes I have it exactly pre-planned. I know all the angles and exactly what is to happen. Other times, I'll rehearse the scene with the actors until it starts to come to life. If I'm acting as well, I use a stand-in to walk through it so we can work out the technical aspect. Then I can just go ahead and film it.'

He makes it sound so simple, but few actors have had such assurance behind the cameras from the outset. Ask Clint Eastwood for the magic formula and he has no hesitation in replying, 'Organisation. That's the vital necessity for a director, whether or not he's directing himself. In fact, two kinds of organisation. Obviously, directing is a demanding task that requires both mental and creative organisation on the director's part. He has to know what he's doing and what he intends to do. But even more important is that other kind of organisation made up of people who work with him. In this respect, I was particularly fortunate. I feel our production company is vigorous and growing because of the enthusiasm, dedication and qualifications of the people who make up Malpaso.'

He paid particular attention to Robert Daley, very much a hands-on producer on the three films, and to the crew of regulars they were building up step by step. 'When I stress the importance of organisation, I don't mean to imply that the old concept of dozens of people hanging around assists the director. On the contrary, when I went into directing, I brought to it the philosophy that a director needs a lean, creative, hand-picked crew, large enough to do the job, but small enough so everyone has a sense of participation and constant involvement. With the exception of a few "epic" types of films, pictures can be made just as cheaply in America as in Europe. It's true that labour and other costs are less than they are here in the United States, but after years of working outside America in Europe and Mexico I have learned how much faster and more efficient American crews are.'

By shooting for six labour-intensive weeks in America rather than ten languid ones in Spain, he reckoned he could bring in his pictures for the same price. In the future, he would only travel when the project specifically demanded it, and he has made sure that doesn't happen very often by establishing himself as the quintessential American screen presence and finding the projects to match it.

When he was making *Breezy*, he described it as a simple story which he hoped would be tasteful and effective. 'The term "dirty old man" is not allowed here,' he said, only half in jest. 'It's not that kind of movie.' When it was completed, the censor disagreed and gave it an R-rating, much to its maker's disgust. The cause was a brief shot of a bare breast. 'Twenty-some states in the Union have statutes that say showing a nipple on a woman's breast is obscene,' he commented bitterly, not least because he realised that the barring of the film to the majority of teenagers would do it no good at all at the box office. As the emotional problems of a privileged ageing estate agent lacked appeal in such a resolutely youth-oriented culture, *Breezy* found as little favour in the cinemas as it had with the critics. Most of them rightly concluded that Eastwood had too much contempt for a sponger like Breezy to allow her to come over as a real person. Spring–autumn romance is tricky to project movingly at the best of times, and never more so than when one character is unworthy of the other's love. Breezy was sustainable at best as a one-night stand so making her into half of an 'until death do us part' romance was over-ambitious from the outset.

Eastwood shrugged off what at most would have been a minor disappointment and turned eagerly to his next project, the resurrection and rehabilitation of Dirty Harry. When he looked at the uneven curve of his career in the three films since the San Francisco cop threw his badge into the swamp, he realised that Harry Callahan was too good a character to lose, especially if he could be re-fashioned to match the mood of the moment. As this was 1973, when the Watergate scandal was unfolding day by day, the word on everybody's lips was 'corruption'. Where better for Harry to find it than within the force whose rules he routinely broke whenever they impeded his personal vision of justice? It would be hard to imagine a more appropriate choice of a writer to dramatise Harry than the right-wing John Milius, and he duly wrote a story that emphasised the connection between the .44 Magnum and the penis. Looking around the world for contemporary images, he came up with the hijacking of aircraft and Brazilian-style death squads and incorporated both in a film that would be Eastwood's most violent yet.

Michael Cimino, then an inexperienced thirty-year-old scriptwriter with one credit to his name, was invited to meet Eastwood in Carmel in order to expand the Milius yarn into a screenplay. His brief included the humanising of Harry, who was given friends, invariably his colleagues and their families, and women friends. 'What's a girl have to do to go to bed with you?' one asks. 'Try knocking on the door,' he replies succinctly, an exchange designed to underline his sexual allure despite the stone-faced inhumanity he displays in almost every situation. He also has a hobby, though there are no prizes for guessing that it is target-shooting in competitions organised by a police benevolent association.

The start of the film finds the demoted Callahan carrying out routine surveillance at San Francisco airport, just the place for him to run into a couple of hijackers demanding a quarter of a million dollars and a pilot to fly an aircraft full of passengers to a place where they can spend them safely. Naturally, Harry volunteers to dress in the pilot's uniform and take the money to the plane, an offer that is accepted surprisingly readily, given the imminent arrival of the FBI. As fear of hijacking easily outpointed fear of flying in the climate of the times, this gave Harry a nicely non-controversial re-introduction, but it was not to last much beyond the credits.

The main action opens with the courts dismissing a union leader accused of manslaughter on a point of law, a verdict watched on television by an anonymous cop who dons a traffic patrolman's uniform, fires up his motorbike, accuses the newly released man of a violation, and guns him down at the wheel of his car. No, this is not Dirty Harry, but one of a gang of four of his colleagues, all young Vietnam veterans, who have become self-appointed angels of death.

As their illegal clean-up continues and gangsters die in a series of bloody massacres all over San Francisco, Harry Callahan is reinstated and ordered back to Homicide to assist Lieutenant Briggs – a characteristically slimeball role for Hal Holbrook – with his enquiries. Inevitably Harry is drawn to the gang of four as they ride tall through the streets on their high-powered bikes, but when they admit their responsibility and ask him to join them, he replies, 'I'm afraid you've misjudged me.'

As he assembles the evidence that will bring them to justice, he is confronted by his superior, who reveals himself as the motivating force behind the death squad. 'The legal process has broken down and somebody has to protect society,' he says, using the oldest argument for corruption in the police handbook. 'When the police start becoming their own executioners, where's it going to end, eh, Briggs?' Harry enquires. 'Pretty soon you start executing people for jaywalking and executing people for traffic violations. Then you end up executing your neighbour because his dog pisses on your lawn.' When Briggs scoffs at him for supporting an ineffective system, he replies, 'I hate the goddamn system but until someone comes along with some changes that make sense, I'll stick with it.'

This is a considerable volte-face for Harry Callahan. Where Dirty Harry spent his time shafting criminals illegally, Dirty Harry reborn dedicates himself to defending the rights of criminals to a fair trial rather than an impromptu execution. Although he admires his youthful Aryan colleagues, and especially the blond leader [played by David Soul in his pre-*Starsky and Hutch* days] who can shoot even better than he can, he displays totally uncharacteristic moral responsibility by taking them to task for their effective tearaway tactics. By any standards, this is blatant whitewashing, a fact that did not go unnoticed when the film came to be judged by the critics.

In the aftermath of the Watergate break-ins and the subsequent attempts at cover-up, Eastwood himself seems to have been a bit confused as to the degree of blame attributable to President Richard Nixon, a man he'd supported in the 1972 election because he was 'the tough man we need for where the world is going'. While he accepted that Watergate had to be exposed, he resented that it was not the scandal but America which became an object of global ridicule. Similarly, he failed to come to terms with the moral dilemmas faced by Callahan in *Magnum Force*, perhaps because he sees conflict between theory and practice when it comes to law enforcement.

'There is a reason for the rights of the accused,' he commented, 'and I think it's very important and one of the things that makes our system great. But there are also the rights of the victim. Most people who talk about the rights of the accused have never been victimised; most of them probably never got accosted in an alley. The symbol of justice is the scale, and yet the scale is never balanced. It falls to the left and then it swings too far back to the right. That's the whole basis of *Magnum Force*. These guys on the police force form their own élite, a tough inner group to combat what they see as opposition to law and order. It's remotely based on that Brazilian police death squad. It's frightening. And this was a film that showed the frustrations of the job, but at the same time it wasn't a glorification of police work.'

Inevitably Don Siegel was unavailable to direct the reinstatement of the man he believed should be relieved of his badge for good. In his place, Eastwood hired the more biddable Ted Post, the director who'd made money for him with *Hang 'Em High*. Wherever he could, Post backed away from the anomalies in the *Magnum Force* screenplay to emphasise the blood and guts glory of the adventure. Where *Dirty Harry* was character-led, at least to some degree, the sequel stitches incidents together with acts of extreme violence. Harry drives a car through a plate-glass window and engages in a waterfront motorcycle chase involving many hair's-breadth leaps over rapidly growing gaps, but the bulk of the murdering belongs to the avengers, and some of it is very bloody indeed.

'There's nothing wrong with glamorising the gun,' said Eastwood with conviction. 'I don't think that hurts anybody. I'm for gun legislation myself. I don't hunt. I love to shoot, but not animals. That turns me off. Besides, it's not the blood-letting or whatever that people come to see in the movies. It's vengeance. Getting even is a very important thing for the public. They go to work every day for some guy who's rude and they can't stand and they just have to take it. Then they go see me on the screen and I just kick the shit out of him. Everybody has that vengeance in him. It's a natural emotion. I feel that all this talk about violence in the movies is sort of overdone. Violence can be a catharsis for the audience. You might have, say, ninety people in a movie theatre and one nut and the violence might inspire this one nut to do something and everybody blames it on the movies. But we can't worry about that one nut.'

Of course, some people did, among them Pauline Kael, who added a note of personal animosity to her refusal to accept Harry Callahan's change of heart. 'Clint Eastwood isn't offensive; he isn't an actor so one could hardly call him a bad actor. He'd have to do something before we could consider him bad at it. And acting isn't required in *Magnum Force*, which takes its name from the giant's phallus – the long-barrelled .44 that Eastwood flourished. Acting might get in the way of what the movie is about – what a man and a big gun can do. Eastwood's wooden impassivity makes it possible for the brutality in his pictures to be ordinary, a matter of routine.'

Predictably, this was just what the public wanted. As a result of its increased lowest-common-denominator factor, *Magnum Force* far outstripped *Dirty Harry*, making nearly $7 million in its first week on release in 1973. When that figure rose rapidly to $40 million, another sequel became inevitable. And another, and another . . . but not yet.

Eastwood's next project was an extension of his work on *Breezy*, a study of the balance between youth and experience in a relationship that survives when all the odds are against it. In this respect, *Thunderbolt and Lightfoot* can be taken as further evidence that Eastwood was trying to water down his animosity to contemporary youth, which he usually portrayed as dirty and deviant cannon fodder. As the forum for the new film was the road, the ambiance criminal and the youth male, it can also be assumed that it was closer to Eastwood's heart than the incurably romantic *Breezy*.

Certainly it was close enough for him to play Thunderbolt, a bank robber who is threatened with death by his associates after he hides the proceeds of a heist for safety reasons. They are in the process of hunting him down when he accidentally hitches up with Lightfoot (Jeff Bridges), a drifter with a dream of paying cash for a new white Cadillac. When they learn that the building in which Thunderbolt hid the original money has been demolished, the odd couple convince their pursuers to join forces to re-stage the original raid on the Montana Armoury vault. Their success allows Lightfoot to fulfil his dream, but only fleetingly. 'We won, didn't we?' he says to his accomplice as they drive away, to which Thunderbolt replies, 'I guess we did. For the time being.'

If Eastwood was trying to clean up his attitude towards youth, hiring thirty-one-year-old Michael Cimino was a step in the right direction. 'He was a very good writer who'd written *Thunderbolt and Lightfoot*. I thought, "Why not give him a shot at directing it?" I hired all the crew. He directed it and came in on time and on budget and I thought he did a good job.' Cimino devised a superslick caper drama, with elements of comedy and some excellent set-pieces. The first comes right at the start as the camera pans over fields of Idaho wheat to pick out a homey white wooden church. Inside it, a pastor, with slicked-back hair and glasses, exhorts an earnest small-town congregation with a firebrand's zeal. 'The wolf shall dwell with the lamb, the leopard shall lie down with the kid,' Thunderbolt quotes prophetically, at which point Cimino cuts to Lightfoot as he feigns a wooden leg to lull a suspicious salesman into letting him try out a second-hand car.

Thunderbolt and Lightfoot is a buddy-buddy film that stems directly and powerfully out of an aspect of American life. Five years later, Cimino would receive much greater claim for a portrayal of male bonding under stress in *The Deerhunter*. Later still, he would prove that he hadn't absorbed the Eastwood creed on filming frugally by going massively over-budget on *Heaven's Gate*. Both films were savagely criticised on diverse fronts and yet received acclaim for the compelling way they are rooted in America, *The Deerhunter* among the furnaces of Pittsburgh and *Heaven's Gate* in the Old West. The same is true of *Thunderbolt and Lightfoot*, the film that established Cimino's ability to portray fairly routine action in arrestingly oddball ways.

This is not so much Hollywood as American independent cinema in which the mainstream of the action unfolds against bizarre vignettes of life as it might be lived in the boondocks. A drunken driver releases white rabbits on to the highway from a cage in his boot, only to blast them to perdition at point-blank range with a shotgun; a middle-aged woman poses naked for Lightfoot's benefit as he works as her temporary gardener; a younger, prettier woman attacks the side of his van with a baseball bat when he tries an easy come-on. The range of American mania is emphasised by the magnificence of its natural beauty, laid out as a surreal series of picture-postcard landscapes, each perfect in every opulent detail.

Against this vivid background, Eastwood and Bridges, the veteran and the rookie, establish bonds of trust accompanied by banter about the age and sexuality. Generously, it is Lightfoot who gets the best lines. 'We've got to stop meeting like this,' he tells Thunderbolt when the older man returns after initially rejecting his offer of friendship. 'People will talk.' Later, he dresses as a woman in order to divert a randy security guard. 'Oh, you sexy bitch,' he addresses himself in the mirror. 'I could go with you myself.' On another occasion, he pimps for Thunderbolt who has difficulty sustaining the rigours of a one-night stand. 'You stick with me, kid,' Lightfoot mocks him. 'You can live forever!'

Despite his youth, Bridges was something of a veteran in front of the cameras. The son of Lloyd Bridges, he had first appeared on screen at the age of four months as a crying baby held by Jane Greer in *The Company She Keeps* back in 1949. He'd also done some pre-teen guest cameos with his father in the television series *Sea Hunt*, before getting an Oscar nomination for Best Supporting Actor for his role opposite Cybill Shepherd in Peter Bogdanovich's *Last Picture Show* in 1971. This experience combined with his amiable screen persona made it easy for him to dominate an Eastwood who seemed inhibited opposite an established male star, even one less than half his age and lacking his box-office clout.

The key to their different levels of success may lie in the fact that over the intervening twenty years, Bridges has emerged as one of the best all-purpose character actors of his generation, whereas Clint Eastwood has established himself as the outstanding star of his. As the characters they play in *Thunderbolt and Lightfoot* are not Hollywood ciphers but flesh-and-blood folk, it is Bridges who is best equipped to capitalise on his particular skills. Eastwood holds his own in the action sequences but buddies are there to relate to one another rather than squint enigmatically into the sun, and this proves to be beyond him.

After three films in twelve months, each a showcase for some aspect of his talent but none a complete artistic success, Eastwood decided that what he needed most was time out from the daily grind to re-charge his batteries. Not that he would give up work altogether. Rather the reverse, in fact, because he'd decided that Malpaso's next production should be *The Eiger Sanction* and his next character a government hitman turned art historian called Jonathan Hemlock. When he is offered the money he needs to enhance his illegal art collection, he agrees to rejoin the service for two final assassinations, one of them on Switzerland's deadliest mountain. His qualifications for the assignment included climbing expertise but Eastwood's didn't, so he took a three-day course in Yosemite National Park. 'I went through all the techniques with a group of professionals and then practised them three, maybe four days a week for a couple of months at home in Carmel. I'd fooled around a little as a boy. A friend of mine and I climbed rocks maybe forty feet high. But you know, there isn't much difference whether you're looking down forty feet or four thousand feet.'

Don Siegel disagreed and declined to join him on the Eiger or any other mountain. This was partly because he had no affinity for the screenplay, a typical three-way Hollywood collaboration based on a novel by Trevanian. The high-rise adventure had been a best-seller when it was published in 1973, which gave Eastwood cause to believe that it had the makings of a Bondian blockbuster. Siegel disagreed with that too and, at the age of sixty-two, he had no intention of directing at ten thousand feet. Nor did anyone else, which left Eastwood with a straight choice between abandoning what had become a cherished project and directing it himself. 'I couldn't find another director willing to climb up and down mountains and dangle several thousand feet above the valley floor. The only way you can direct mountain-climbing sequences is by being right there with the actors.'

With hindsight, he would probably have opted for abandonment but, carried forward on a tide of enthusiasm, he hired a team of British climbers as consultants and instructed them to meet him in Wengen, the resort town at the foot of the mountain, in August 1974. The Eiger didn't come by its name – it translates as the Ogre – for nothing, and it was quick to strike back at such temerity. On 13 August, the second day of filming, Dave Knowles, the middle man on a rope of three, was edging back to safety when he was killed by falling rocks. Eastwood, who had been in the same spot a few minutes earlier, vividly recalls the accident. 'One of our mountaineers was dangling on a rope several thousand feet above the valley floor. We'd finished shooting for the day and he was getting back on the ledge when someone yelled, "Rocks!" He looked up and was hit by a huge rock. Killed instantly.'

Mike Hoover, the film's specialist mountaineer-cameraman, was struck by a rock in the same fall but survived with a fractured pelvis. 'Clint always comes off as very callous and pragmatic,' he later commented, 'but inside he's mush. He was shaken by the accident. He even started to cry. And he was ready to shut down production of the film. He's the first guy to do the dirtiest job and not in a show-off way. Clint seemed so simple I thought he was phoney, but after a while, I realised how sharp he was. He isn't verbal, but he's one sharp mother.'

After the tragedy, Eastwood's faith in *The Eiger Sanction* gradually drained away, but he kept going in the belief that its climbing footage would be a fitting tribute to Knowles. 'It didn't have the kind of story you could tell with *Play Misty*'s kind of impact and excitement. The only excitement you could do was on a visual level and that is the way it was written.' As the days passed, he learned why the Eiger is a killer, something anyone who lives in Wengen could have told him at the outset. 'It's partly the weather – it keeps changing – and partly the angles – straight up. Most of all, it's a dirty mountain. It keeps crumbling. Yosemite is different. It's hard rock. The pitons stay in the mountain and you don't have to wear a helmet. The Eiger is like a combat zone. There are constant avalanches and rockslides. The other day, an avalanche went over where we were supposed to work. If we had been there, we'd have been wiped out.'

Even when the hazards became increasingly self-evident, Eastwood refused to give up, doing all the close-ups and many of the long shots himself. On the only occasion when he agreed the stunt was too dangerous because it involved a 2,500-foot fall, he was replaced with a dummy. 'There were times when I was petrified, a couple of times when I had the feeling I was going to get into trouble, but I just got myself involved deeper and deeper. There was no turning back. At first, I was going to use a double, but a double can only think of the stunt. He can't think of the characterisation. It just wouldn't have worked with a double.'

It is fortunate that filming in high places is so complicated that he had little time to fret over his own mortality. Equipment had to be taken up the mountain by train via the Jungfrau Joch, then put in place by helicopters. For Eastwood, it was the start of a long love affair with the whirlybird that persists today. 'The helicopters are the most exciting part of filming on the Eiger. That's how we get to the cliffs where we can't get equipment up any other way. We're winched down on to a ledge, and up again when we leave. One climber was dangling from the rope all the way from the top of the mountain down to the Kleine Scheidegg where we are staying. But usually they winch us up so fast, it's all over in thirty seconds. In fact, the helicopter pilot usually pulls up and away while you're still being pulled up, which means you're dangling over nowhere.' Although the professional mountaineers assured him that he would get used to hanging in space, he says that he never did, and he has not made a climbing film since. 'I don't take chances if I can help it, but I guess I'm what you would call a fatalist.'

Although there was some praise for the climbing footage, fatalism was the most useful response to the sustained contempt the critics unleashed on *The Eiger Sanction*. 'All the villains have been constructed pre-fabricated from Bond models,' wrote Richard Combs in *Monthly Film Bulletin*. 'Most depressing, Eastwood directs in a bland, blunt and boorish fashion, alternating panoramic views of the landscape and equally broad tributes to his macho presence. Where *Play Misty for Me* and *High Plains Drifter* suggested he was capable of bringing a degree of irony to his own image, here Eastwood the director asks of Eastwood the actor only the faint curling of the lip as every female character topples before him, and the more energetic clenching of the teeth through which he can promise "something massive" for the film's regular bursts of retaliatory violence.'

In the face of this and other well-justified criticism, Eastwood shrugged and waited for the audience to vote with their wallets. As usual, they didn't let him down. 'If we are honest with ourselves, we enjoy those sort of films,' he concluded. 'Look at the front page of any newspaper, if you can bear it. That's the world as it is, not as we would like it to be. Man is a very violent animal. What's wrong with showing it?'

10

A Fragile Happiness

When Clint Eastwood returned from Switzerland in the autumn of 1974, he was a man who seemed to have everything. His eldest child, Kimber Tunis, was ten years old, yet his marriage to Maggie had survived, even blossomed in the decade since she'd been born. The legitimate Eastwood family now numbered four, following the birth of Alison on 22 May 1972, at St John's Hospital in Santa Monica. She arrived fifteen days prematurely, pre-empting her father and brother Kyle, who were on the long drive south from Carmel to Los Angeles. 'Are you sure it's a girl?' Maggie asked when she heard she had the daughter she wanted. Later, she said that Clint looked like 'the cat that ate the canary' when she broke the good news to him.

In October 1972, he led his mother, dressed in a full-length aqua-knit crêpe gown, down the aisle of the Erdman Memorial Chapel near his home in Pebble Beach outside Carmel for her marriage to John Belden Wood. A widow since 1970 when Clinton Eastwood died following a stroke, she'd met her second husband a few months earlier during a holiday in Mauna Kea, Hawaii. Despite his turbulent sex life, Eastwood has always tried to instil his parents' values in his own children. 'I was lucky to have parents like my father who knew who he was on the planet and my mother who knew who she was, and they liked where they were. I had terrific parents. There were never any doubts. I saw the way doubts built up in other kids I knew. It destroyed them.'

In line with Clint's thinking on parenthood, Maggie Eastwood now spent more time in the fan-shaped house in Pebble Beach with their children and rather less on location with her increasingly preoccupied husband. She was a fanatical tennis player, even to the extent of turning out for the Celebrity Tennis Tournament when Alison was six weeks old. This was an annual charity event, lavishly hosted for the likes of Charlton Heston and John Wayne by the Eastwoods and their neighbours, the Gawthrops. 'Maggie doesn't care what I do so long as I can keep her in tennis racquets,' Eastwood once joked. Whether or not she cared about her husband's second family, Maggie certainly condoned it, even to the point of chatting amiably with Roxanne when the two women met during the shooting of *Breezy*. Maggie has always refused to answer specific questions about Roxanne, but she has responded to general ones about her husband's extra-marital affairs with dignified stoicism. 'I used always to hope for the best. I wanted to protect myself. I wondered about it but I didn't dwell on it because it would probably have driven me insane. I just preferred to hang in there and not worry too much about it.'

She gave her husband the freedom to spend time with Roxanne and Kimber. Until 1975, when she deliberately broke the mould by moving to Europe, the statuesque actress hoped that Eastwood would leave Maggie and move in with her. Kimber recalls that he came to visit for one night approximately four times a year, a family occasion marked by a special supper cooked by Roxanne. He always brought presents and Kimber called him 'Daddy' from the start, but only in private. When she tried to claim his as her father in front of her friends, they thought she was boasting. On the one occasion he took Roxanne and Kimber skiing in

Vail, he booked them into a separate suite and introduced them as friends rather than relatives. Although the visits were rare, he didn't hesitate to use them to peddle his good-housekeeping message. 'Sometimes he was mean with money, or at least that's how it seemed to me,' Kimber has said. 'He would sit down at the table and say, "I have got where I am by working hard for myself."'

In public, Maggie supported her husband with style and loyalty, and never more so than at the Oscar festivities in 1973 when he was unceremoniously drafted on to the stage after the scheduled presenter, Charlton Heston, got stuck in traffic. When Clint demurred at Howard Koch's request that he should replace him, Maggie was the first to urge her husband to save the night. Heston's cue cards were already in place and his replacement stumbled through inappropriate sentiments relating to Cecil B. De Mille and *The Ten Commandments* with mounting embarrassment under the gaze of eight million television viewers. 'It was a parody of Moses, thou shalt not be this and that all relating to movies. Bad material, even for Moses. I said, "You gotta be kidding. Never invite me again." "Will you come back if you're nominated?" Koch asked. "Yeah, I'll do that," Eastwood replied. "Then I don't have to worry," said Koch.'

When the ordeal was over, Eastwood headed for the press bar where he knocked off four beers in quick succession before joining his wife in the audience. 'Clint Eastwood did a pretty good job for somebody who never talked before,' Johnny Carson summarised the next night in response to Eastwood's own impromptu joke, 'Why pick on a feller who has said only eight lines in his last three pictures?'

When he wasn't working, he tried to lead as normal a life as possible. If he wanted to go to the movies, he'd disguise himself in hat and sunglasses and take Maggie to the local cinema, rather than set up a screening in a private viewing theatre. As soon as 'the squirts', as he called his children, were old enough to recognise his fame, he encouraged them to treat him as a regular dad. 'I first saw the "star" thing in my son. He'd see people coming up to me, paying attention or asking for autographs and he'd ask me, "How come people ask you to sign papers?" I said, "Well, the nature of business I'm in . . . they see me in the theatre and it's sort of a custom that some jerk invented years ago . . . they take the paper home and say, 'This is who I saw'." He knows his dad's an actor and so what? Alison's the same way. She couldn't care less. She sees me on TV and gets all excited, then five seconds later, I could be in an important scene and she's off playing.'

On the question of whether his son would model himself on his father's gun-toting image, Clint bowed to the inevitability of the trigger-happy spirit within any boy. 'Maggie and I let him play with toy guns because we found that if we take away the gun, he just uses a stick and pretends it's a gun.'

Eastwood might well have continued to intersperse a well-balanced family life with a fairly overt extra-marital one if it had not been for Sondra Locke, the girl from Shelbyville, Tennessee, whose tiny frame concealed a lively intelligence and an iron will. 'Sondra, not Sandra,' she said sharply when she was making her first film, *The Heart Is a Lonely Hunter*. 'Then I'd be called Sandy and I'd hate that. I don't like any nicknames or abbreviations. I'm not a kid just because I'm seventeen. I take what I'm doing seriously and I want to be taken seriously as an actress.' On the surface, the kid grew up into the kind of woman Eastwood might have believed he could dominate. By comparison with Maggie and Roxanne, she was a waif, five feet four inches tall and weighing just 101 pounds. However, her Southern upbringing had spawned ambitions as an actress, a director and a woman that would result in fierce passion followed by bitter pain.

It was typical of Sondra, a small-town girl who would realise a variety of high-flying dreams against all the odds, that her chosen career should come about by chance. The trigger was an article in the *Nashville Tennessean* about the search for a girl to play in the movie adaptation of Carson McCullers's *The Heart Is a Lonely Hunter*. It appeared in August 1967 and Sondra joined the queue of two thousand hopefuls who responded to it. It was also typical that she didn't join it unprepared. Once she'd acquired a copy of the book, she learned that Mick Kelly, the girl who has an affinity with a deaf-mute, was three years younger than she was, so she set about making the necessary adjustments. In this, as in most things, she was helped by a fellow dreamer, Gordon Anderson, who'd won a state award for directing her in a play called *The Monkey's Paw* in 1965. He gave her advice on what to wear for the audition and suggested binding her bosom. 'I'd been worried about looking too old so Gordon sprayed my nose with some chemical he uses for his painting. When it dried, we pulled it off so that my nose looked skinned, the way a tomboy's would. Gordon also gave me a set of freckles with a brown marker! I didn't know what these things were going to do to my skin, but I figured it was worth the effort.'

And it was, because she not only got the role, but an Oscar nomination for Best Supporting Actress. In July 1967, when they were both nineteen, she married Gordon and they moved in with his parents, sleeping in his old room surrounded by the movie posters that had triggered Sondra's ambitions. 'I dated other boys my own age, but I usually felt older than they were and never had too many things to talk to them about. My parents weren't too happy about my getting married so young, but we've never been very close. They've never really understood anything about me. When I would figure out what to do to become an actress when you live in Shelbyville, population ten to fifteen thousand, they thought it was pretty ridiculous and wanted me to go to school or go to work.'

Once the film was completed, the newlyweds moved to Hollywood in the belief that Sondra's career was made. 'We're like one person,' she said of the husband who had stood by her through every kind of triumph and humiliation. 'He paints and carves little figures out of balsa wood but basically he's an actor too.' Anderson turned out to be more sculptor than actor, but either way his artistic aspirations were an anathema to Sondra's strait-laced parents. They also believed that Gordon and Sondra, who had known each other since they were ten, were friends rather than lovers, an objection that has some justification in the light of persistent reports that their marriage had never been consummated.

By the time Sondra Locke met Clint Eastwood for the second time, she'd been married to Anderson for eight years. The couple lived comfortably in what has been described as a Gothic townhouse in West Hollywood which once belonged to Marlon Brando. It contained Sondra's collection of fairy tales and fables, art nouveau furnishings, and Gordon's figurines, meticulously crafted pieces that sold for one thousand dollars and more. Their marriage worked, on one level at least, because each was prepared to allow the other to run on a long leash. When they were together, they were good friends; when they weren't, they didn't waste their time on jealous resentments. 'We are very independent and have a strong direction of our own. Gordon is very committed to his interests and his work.'

During her early days in Hollywood, Sondra's career had fallen rather short of her expectations. True, she'd made a film a year, but the youthful nature of her first role had stamped her as a perpetual adolescent. 'I was afraid *Heart* had put me into some kind of sexual oblivion. I played a practically pre-puberty tomboy and some producers thought I was a boy,' she commented, after a string of commercial and critical disappointments. The only exception was *Willard*, a rat-infestation genre thriller, in which she had fourth billing to Bruce Davison, Ernest Borgnine and Elsa Lanchester.

By 1975, she was neither a child-woman nor a hot-property, a double that had sapped her will to work at all. 'The trouble with me is that I like to sleep till noon. I'm not in a hurry to find work so I don't panic when the telephone isn't ringing. I don't really do much when I'm at home. I think a lot and I like to be alone a lot. I've been told that you have to go to the right parties to get work, that maybe my name should be more of a household word, but I've never gone around with the Beverly Hills crowd, so I never have any idea who is saying what about me anyway. To be honest, one film a year is quite enough for me and I only like to work when it's something interesting. I go crazy working on something I'm not wild about.'

One of the things she was prepared to be wild about was Clint Eastwood. 'I'd admired him for quite some time. I felt his screen presence was something unique, direct and strong, and I'd admired his work as a director, particularly on *Play Misty for Me* and *Breezy*.' And so it came to pass that Clint Eastwood cast Sondra Locke as his love interest in *The Outlaw Josey Wales*, arguably the best western he would ever make, up to and including *Unforgiven*. It was based on a book called *Gone to Texas* by Forrest Carter, a half-Cherokee oral poet and historian who was persuaded to put his gift for storytelling into print. The results were published privately in Arkansas in an edition limited to seventy-five copies, one of which arrived unsolicited on Robert Daley's desk at Malpaso. Daley read, enjoyed and summarised it for his boss who read and 'fell in love with it'.

By his own account, he was coming to rely more and more on his instinctive responses. Where many directors started out loving a project, only to mull it over so thoroughly that they came to hate it, Eastwood allowed himself minimal introspection, so leaving himself with plenty of energy for getting the show on the road. 'You have to go with the thought you had when you first got into it. You have to trust that motor inside, whatever it's telling you. It's put me where I am. I'm moderately educated, not a scholar. I just work more and more from the motor inside me.'

It is not surprising that he liked *Gone to Texas*, a tale of retribution before and after the Civil War. For a start, it was right for the middle seventies, an American low ebb when the self-styled world's policeman was licking its wounds externally and internally after military defeat in Vietnam and moral opprobrium over Watergate. In the heyday of the western in the thirties, forties and fifties, the genre persistently celebrated America's muscular heroism on the world stage. Audiences were able to cheer Gary Cooper, Henry Fonda and John Wayne as they flashed their sheriff's badges and gunned down the enemies of the state in the interests of the great American way. As the national confidence waned, so too did the popularity of the western. When they were made, which was rarely, gung-ho superiority was replaced by insidious doubt. Progressive independents like Arthur Penn and Robert Altman registered the contemporary malaise in *The Missouri Breaks* and *Buffalo Bill and the Indians*. In this, they were assisted by the more radical stars in the Hollywood firmament – Marlon Brando, Jack Nicholson, and Paul Newman.

Eastwood had been looking for a project that would allow him to join them for some time. Not that he had any wish to put over a radical perspective, but he believed that he had not reached, or even approached, the limits of his potential in the genre that was undeniably the most effective showcase for his talents. Forrest Carter's protagonist was a rebel with a justifiable cause caught up in a war that was not his own. Unlike the ghostly retaliator of *High Plains Drifter*, Josey Wales was deeply rooted in land and family. The Civil War, with its in-built acrimony as American faced American over issues of race, slavery and dominance, was a fitting metaphor for the political chaos of the mid seventies. The precise location, the borders between Missouri, which favoured slavery and the Confederate cause, and Kansas, which was bitterly factionalised over emancipation and the possible financial advantages of Union membership, was appropriately Middle American.

The story's resolution, in a pastoral, multiracial community on the Mexican border, conjured up images of hippie freedoms that were usually an anathema to Eastwood, but he put his doubts aside when he bought the rights to the book. He commissioned Philip Kaufman, a director with western cred after his witty debut, *The Great Northfield Minnesota Raid* in 1971, to write a screenplay. Fresh from the hazards of *The Eiger Sanction*, he asked Kaufman to direct as well, but the arrangement didn't survive the discovery that Kaufman didn't share his vision. By the end of the first week, he'd taken over himself.

In the pre-credit sequence, Josey Wales is watched by his young son, played by seven-year-old Kyle Eastwood, as he engages in honest ploughing. When his wife calls the boy back to the homestead, there is a frisson as we realise that the peace is illusory and the family dangerously exposed. A few more moments of false calm pass before smoke rises from the house and Josey Wales dashes back to find it surrounded by Kansas 'Red Legs', pro-Union vigilantes whose immediate concerns are not so much political as murderous and rapacious. When Josey Wales comes round after a knockout blow, his wife and son are dead, his home burned to the ground, so we know that he will never sleep peacefully until he has had his revenge. A crime of this magnitude is an excellent starting point for a western, and Josey Wales barely has time to bury his dead before he meets up with an opposing band of pro-slavery vigilantes from Missouri who identify the killer of his family and sign him on for their own crusade.

The story proper starts seven years later, when hostilities officially cease in an on-going climate of bitter back-stabbing. With no home to go to, the outlawed Josey Wales heads south with a five-thousand-dollar price on his head, an odyssey that attracts an assortment of like-minded misfits. In Indian territory, he hooks up with a fellow victim of Unionist brutality, a Cherokee chief played by Chief Dan George, already something of a mythical character after his Oscar nomination for Best Supporting Actor for *Little Big Man*. They are joined by a Navajo squaw, who has been rejected by her tribe for not resisting rape by rival Arapahos with sufficient force, and then by Grandma Sarah, whose son had died fighting for the Unionists, and her granddaughter, Laura Lee. Fortunately, Grandma Sarah has a farm outside a derelict ex-silver-mining town on the Mexican border to provide both a refuge and a means of earning a livelihood. Less fortunately, it falls within the territory of a Comanche chief who will brook no intruders.

The clash of wills between Josey Wales and this just but far from gentle giant – he is played by Will Sampson, Nicholson's mighty pal in *One Flew over the Cuckoo's Nest* – is the turning-point in a story that ends with unexpected optimism. Admittedly, Josey Wales gets his revenge on the killers of his wife, but on all other fronts he learns to compromise and so earns the right to farm the land happily ever after with Laura Lee, alias Sondra Locke. Like *High Plains Drifter*, *The Outlaw Josey Wales* comes full circle, but in a much more positive way. Where the antihero in the earlier film starts and finishes as a dispossessed apparition, with a short period of rather low-quality life in between, Josey Wales starts and finishes as an honest son of the soil, with a period of living death in between.

This life-affirming statement is reinforced by a more positive presentation of his minority countrymen, the Indians and Mexicans, who had previously appeared in his films as junkies and killers, and the women, who were generally little more than sex objects. In this respect, Eastwood believed that *The Outlaw Josey Wales* was an effective counterbalance to Pauline Kael's on-going accusations of right-wing machismo. 'I agree with a lot of things she says about the country's reaction to the experience in Vietnam and Watergate,' he told *Village Voice* when *The Outlaw Josey Wales* was in post-production, 'and that there's a great feeling of impotence and guilt as a result. It bothers me that she seems so pleased by it. I think Kael's opinion of what a man is isn't shared by everybody. She's obsessed with the male weakness thing, and I'm not saying that there isn't room for all the things she's talking about, but there's definitely room for others. Kael just seems to like men as losers. She likes the Altman kind of things. I don't think that women in general or audiences in general agree with her. I think that women are intrigued by a certain masculinity.'

Eastwood took exception to Kael's description of him as 'empty', especially in his screen handling of women, and he deeply resented the way she promoted Marlon Brando, Robert De Niro and Jack Nicholson as superior screen males because they expressed human doubts rather than Olympian superiority. He cited Bernardo Bertolucci's *Last Tango in Paris* as an illustration of ideological differences between them. For her, it was romantic; for him, it was an affront to women. 'If I were a feminist, I'd think that the portrayal and treatment of women in that movie was terrible. I mean, if buttering up a girl's ass and giving her a poke-job is romantic sex, or represents male tenderness, then, I'm sorry, but I'm on a different plane than she is. Higher or lower, depending on whose opinion. Jesus, how can she not see that as violent? Obviously she's never been on the other end of that.'

As for acting, he believed that the proof of the pudding was in the eating. If he could hold an audience for two hours, then he was doing a good job, and if having a lot of imitators was the sincerest form of flattery, then he was well ahead of the game. 'What I do, I do the best. Maybe I'm not as versatile as other actors but for the type of thing I do, I do it well. I'm not alone in that. Nicholson and all the others do what they do best. The kind of thing I do is glorify competence. I think that bothers people like Kael most of all.'

As the intellectual left has always held glorification of competence in particularly low esteem, the Kael-Eastwood divide was not for easy healing. It seems unlikely that Eastwood, with his deep-seated certainty in male superiority, needed bolstering after these attacks, but if he did, solace was ready to hand. After her fragile portrayal of the wispy Laura, Sondra Locke was more than ever a dedicated fan. Even a glimpse of the legendary temper, unleashed momentarily when he smashed a recalcitrant horse in the jaw, didn't put her off. 'He's one of the most sensitive, gentlest men in the world. I have the greatest amount of respect and fondness for Eastwood as a person and a talent, and I think it's mutual.' She was right. 'I think she's marvellous – she has good spontaneity. She's one of the best in the business,' came the reply.

However, nothing she had done before had prepared her for the lack of star treatment on *The Outlaw Josey Wales*. When she asked how she was to do her close-ups after losing her eyelashes in an encounter with a bonfire, Eastwood said dismissively, 'Oh, the stumps look fine.' At other times, she would sneak back to her dressing room to tidy up between takes, much to the director's disgust. 'I'd think, "If I looked like you, I wouldn't go back to my dressing room either",' Locke recalled drily. 'Clint doesn't bother about glamour. An actress geared to certain shots that make her look good simply couldn't work with him. He likes everyone to look natural and he kept telling the make-up man, "Get away from her. What are you doing?" I didn't care that much. I just thought, "Oh well, Sondra, there'll be another shot and with luck you'll get your good side in it."'

On a professional level, she was impressed by his unselfishness. 'I went into the film a little in awe of Clint Eastwood, top star,' she told the *Hollywood Reporter*. 'I finished it in awe of Eastwood, the total talent. When he directs other actors, he's generous. He gives actors the freedom creative people need in order to perform best. In addition, he's so totally generous to his co-workers. He kept throwing more and more footage to Chief Dan George because it was going so well, and Clint was just delighted.'

So too were Warner Bros, the studio that now established itself as an integral element in the Eastwood career. They had already financed *Dirty Harry* and *Magnum Force* for considerable corporate gain. Now Malpaso raised the $3.7 million budget for *The Outlaw Josey Wales*, then sold the film to Warners for distribution long before it was finished. When Eastwood had brought it in on time and on budget, he edited it and showed it to the studio. Once the print had been handed over, the deal required Warners to consult with Malpaso as regards advertising, promotion, choice of cinemas and the timing of the release. Effectively this gave Clint Eastwood total control with no financial liability from conception to delivery, as he was quick to recognise. 'I have a voice in what happens to my film. Let's just say that there is a constant exchange of dialogue between the studio and myself. The pros of being an actor-star are that I get to make the film I want without interference. The cons are that I'm doing two jobs and that's very difficult – fun, but difficult. When I direct, I picture the whole story in my mind, frame by frame, and I want the film to reflect the way I see it.'

As far as the critics were concerned, this new vision was much more acceptable than the old. Dilys Powell, who would become one of his warmest supporters, wrote in the *Sunday Times*, 'It's a very different image and very promising. I think it's a very, very good western.' Pauline Kael was not ready to go anything like that far, but she did condescend to dip a toe in the water. 'Perhaps an improvement' may not be a warm endorsement, but it was a lot better than anything that had come before.

I I

Freedom of Choice

'The essential American soul is hard, stoic, isolate and a killer.' Of course, D.H. Lawrence didn't write these words about Clint Eastwood, but they strike a chord in relation to his screen persona, especially as perceived by those who responded most warmly to his films. As an actor, he had suffered gibes along the lines of 'a founder member of the Mount Rushmore school' or 'a man with four grimaces and two glances' for years. Yet there were those who thought that by deliberately restricting himself to descendants of The Man with No Name, he was not being true to his talent. 'It surprises me that he is not more interested in a greater variety of roles,' said Don Siegel. Eastwood's response was characteristically laconic. 'A lot of actors who play Henry V can't play my character. They'd be ludicrous.'

In his opinion, this was sufficient justification for not sticking his neck out after *The Outlaw Josey Wales*, a right time if there ever was one to search for new horizons. Not only did the film make money, but it had a hard-edged quality that would have earned Oscar nominations in another climate. As it was, neither a western nor a Clint Eastwood movie could be considered, so that was that. However, by his own account, the director-star had achieved his goal of total control over his empire. 'Financially I'm in a position to do any kind of film I want,' he said in February 1976, even before *The Outlaw Josey Wales* opened. 'People always ask me if I'd do another *Beguiled*, which did not make money. And I say, "Sure, I'd like to do another film like that."'

But he didn't. Instead he reverted to Harry Callahan III, better known as The Enforcer, a choice guaranteed to alienate all the new friends he'd made with Josey Wales. Was this perversity, money-grubbing, or fear of flying too close to the sun? Probably a bit of all three. It must be remembered that Clint Eastwood comes from a generation, perhaps the last generation of the present century, that takes its dignity very seriously. By the standards of his time, he is exceptionally relaxed, preferring first names and casual clothes to the formalities many of his contemporaries insist on, but his easy-going attitudes stop well short of making a spectacle of himself in classical roles. And not only a spectacle, perhaps, but a loss.

Besides, he not only liked Dirty Harry, the lone isolate American killer, but approved of him. He recalls watching the original film with a regular audience in a cinema in San Francisco. When Harry threw his badge into the swamp at the end, his black neighbour turned to him not knowing that he was Clint Eastwood and said, 'Man, San Francisco just lost one damn good cop.' It was a viewpoint Eastwood endorsed wholeheartedly. How come, he enquired, he was accused of being a racist for showing Harry gunning down black bank robbers? 'Well, shit, blacks rob banks too. This film gave four black stuntmen work. Nobody talked about that.'

So *The Enforcer* it would be. In mitigation, it should be said that he'd decided to re-establish Malpaso under the Warner Bros umbrella. This involved moving his offices from the Universal lot to new premises, known as Taco Bell because they resembled the fast-food chain, on the Burbank lot up the road. The reason for the change was the introduction of the Universal tour. 'I had a really nice bungalow, a very comfortable place to work, but

I'd walk out of my office and the bus would be there with people yelling. So finally I called Frank Wells [at Warners] and said, "I'll move over there if you've got a space for me, but if you ever have a tour, I'm leaving." He said, "We're not in the tour business." ' The company was run so tightly that moving meant little more than shifting a few files. 'If I've got a six-pack under my arm, a few pieces of paper and a couple of pencils, I'm in business,' said the master of frugality proudly.

A quid pro quo deal with Warners guaranteed Eastwood the freedom to make films without studio interference. In return, he would resuscitate Harry Callahan. Third time around, his exploits were masterminded by Stirling Silliphant and Dean Riesner. Unlike the *Magnum Force* team of Milius and Cimino, they held no particular torch for Dirty Harry's *modus operandi*, so they contented themselves with constructing a series of adventures that would showcase the aspects of the character the public liked best. 'We feel we know what the Eastwood fans want and expect,' said Robert Daley. Accordingly, the writers' blueprint included Harry incurring the wrath of his immediate superior by overreacting and subsequently getting demoted to a job not worthy of his talents. In the course of unacceptable duties, he finds, trains and loses another partner and tracks down a psychopathic killer for the greater good of the city of San Francisco.

Once the formula was agreed, Silliphant and Riesner looked around them for pegs. Two issues that were frequently in the news in the mid seventies were the increasing number of women detectives and violent action by the Symbionese Liberation Front. Accordingly, the writers created the rookie police officer Kate Moore as Harry's new partner and the People's Revolutionary Strike Force (PRSF) as his callous adversary. The first set-piece shows Callahan responding to a demand for a getaway car from four gunmen holding up a liquor store by driving straight through the shop window and picking them off with his trusty Magnum. As you might predict, his prissy bureacratic boss, Captain McKay, sidelines him in Personnel, an assignment that gives him his first chance to pour scorn on Kate.

When his existing partner is killed by the PRSF leader, Bobby Maxwell, Harry is sent after him with a substitute partner: Inspector Moore. 'Oh shit,' he says economically. 'Don't concern yourself,' she replies coolly, but she soon works up a sweat when he strides manfully into the distance and she has to teeter after him in pencil skirt and stiletto heels. The pace hots up when Maxwell and his revolutionary forces kidnap the mayor and demand a five-million-dollar ransom. Pay it, says McKay, but Callahan has other ideas and implements them with increasingly effective assistance from Kate.

In an attempt to boost sales in the blood-lusting youth sector, *The Enforcer* was billed as 'the dirtiest Harry of them all', a tag that was correct only in that it was the most robotic and the least well made. It was officially directed by James Fargo, an assistant on *The Eiger Sanction*, but with continuous input from Clint Eastwood. As an actor, he appeared to be going through the motions as if more than a little bored by Harry's knee-jerk reactions to the pinpricks of his trade. Harry is at his most animated in his scenes with Kate, played by Tyne Daly in her first major screen role. Eastwood chose her because he thought she looked like a policewoman rather than a starlet, an opinion that was reinforced when she was cast as Lacey in the ground-breaking female TV cop show *Cagney and Lacey*.

Kate Moore, the most rounded woman's role to date in an Eastwood shoot-'em-up, allowed Daly to mix it with Eastwood in scenes ranging from confrontation to buddy-buddy affection, with a touch of mutual attraction thrown in for good measure. In a convincing performance, Daly is acerbic, witty and moving, albeit a bit unlucky that Kate's promotion from uniformed policewoman to plain-clothes detective should command such an impractical wardrobe. Daly, who worked hard to express the emotional strains, and above all the loneliness, of being a female cop, admitted that the role made her career. 'I've been earning big fat money ever since.'

After the racist outcries over *Dirty Harry*, Eastwood always provided the disruptive inspector with a quota of opponents as pale-skinned as himself. In *Magnum Force*, they are neo-Nazi motorcyclists clad in black leather; in *The Enforcer*, they are multiracial self-styled revolutionaries, but led by pretty-boy Maxwell, a blond, blue-eyed sadist. Although his behaviour never establishes him as a homosexual, Harry assumes that he is when he blasts him to eternity with a miniature bazooka and the words 'you fucking fruit'. 'Is this the last outpost of the western hero, killing homosexuals to purify the cities?' asked Pauline Kael, perhaps regretting her moment of leniency over Josey Wales.

As pale-shadow repetition has always appealed to mass audiences, it was no surprise that *The Enforcer* shot up the charts. Earnings of twenty-four million dollars in the United States and Canada made it the third-most successful Eastwood film up until 1980, behind the *Any Which Way* comedies. At the time, Eastwood believed that he'd gone the distance with Harry Callahan, little knowing that his most profitable hour – and his trademark phrase – were yet to come.

Eastwood's next film explores the notion that the antidote to the achiever, as represented by Harry, is the bungler, as represented by Ben Shockley in *The Gauntlet*. It was Barbra Streisand who first alerted him to the existence of this inept Phoenix detective. She had the rights to the screenplay and the powers-that-be at Warners believed, with good reason, that an Eastwood–Streisand double act would be a licence to print money. Eastwood may have remembered his lessons regarding dominant female co-stars from *Two Mules for Sister Sara*, or he may merely have been looking to further his relationship with Sondra Locke, but, either way, he ducked the challenge. Instead he acquired the Michael Butler–Dennis Shyrak script from Streisand, hired Locke to play opposite him, and set up the most expensive Malpaso production ever in the Arizona desert. As the name Sondra Locke appeared alongside Clint Eastwood, she became the first person to get co-star billing on one of his own films.

When he first emerges from an all-night poker game, Ben Shockley is as unshaven and red-eyed as any of the Eastwood antiheroes who have come before him. When he arrives at the police station, he stumbles out of his car and tosses an empty whisky bottle into the gutter. Inside, the new police commissioner sends him to Las Vegas to extradite a trial witness called Gus Mally. 'He's a man who gets the job done,' the Commissioner says of Shockley, adding, 'It's a nothing witness for a nothing trial.' This is enough to alert the viewer to the fact that Shockley has been chosen for his ineptitude and that the Commissioner is not only hoping he will fail, but will ensure he does if he should ever look like succeeding.

The scene is now set for a voyage of redemption that takes on a much more interesting note when Ben learns that Gus is short for Augusta and that his charge is a lippy young hooker under a death threat from the Mob. 'On a scale of ten, I'd have to give her a two,' he tells the guard as they wait for her release papers to come through, 'but that's only because I've never seen a one before.' This is the start of an engagingly confrontational relationship between the two, with Gus sceptical of Ben's ability to save her and scornful both of his lack of education and his Neanderthal attitude to women. Sadly the inspiration is all too brief and a promising scenario is systematically reduced to a riot of crowd-pleasing special effects that accounted for a fifth of the $5.5 million budget.

In one of them, Ben and Gus are chased through the desert by a helicopter that gets a $250,000 come-uppance when it explodes against an eighty-five foot tower erected for the purpose. In another, the police fire eight thousand rounds of ammunition into a house, razing it to the ground. The house cost another $250,000, the bill for a month's construction and the drilling of seven thousand holes, each fitted with an explosive squib so that it would fold from the inside as if 'eaten away by a gigantic mass of termites'. Most absurd of all is the climactic sequence in which Ben drives a heavily armoured coach through a hail of police bullets up to the City Hall where the trial is being heard. Completing his mission against all the odds has transformed him into a quintessential Eastwood character, riding high on the self-respect that comes with cracking a big case after years of disappointments. Unfortunately, by surviving hail after hail of bullets, he has also become immortal, which makes it hard to believe either in his survival or his redemption.

For Locke, the role of the uncompromising Gus was a great improvement on the flaky Laura Lee. For a start, the prostitute is a good deal smarter than her protector and both of them know it. Where he is a burned-out hulk, she is a lithe viper, capable both of constructive analysis and dynamic action. When she is sexually abused by the police commissioner, she doesn't wait for Shockley to avenge her, she does it herself. *The Gauntlet* attempts to analyse machismo, with Gus comparing a whore to a cop, the essential difference being that the whore washes clean each night while the cop is stuck with being a flunky so long as he serves in the police force. For most of the film,

Locke gets the best lines while Eastwood plods in her wake reiterating his catch-phrase, 'I reckon so'. The balance can only be restored by her falling in love with him.

It was at this point that the world sat up and took note of the fact that life was imitating art, though the likelihood is that the Locke–Eastwood affair was already well set in its ways before shooting on *The Gauntlet* began. When Clint cast Locke against the way the part was written, at least in a physical sense, he described her as an 'outstanding' actress and very intuitive. He particularly liked the way she picked up on his suggestions and pitched in with her own without fuss or overintellectualising. 'For the most part, I like to go for a first take without too much rehearsal. If it's working and everyone feels good about it, then why not go? The great thing about film is that you can always go back to the drawing board and do it again if your first attempt doesn't pay off the way you thought it would. With Sondra, you can do that because she doesn't work by talking everything out in heavy detail.'

On location for *The Gauntlet*, Locke and Eastwood came out as a couple in a way they hadn't on *The Outlaw Josey Wales*, though both insisted they were perfectly happy with their respective spouses. 'Sure, I love working with him but there's nothing specific in the works. Everybody would love us to say, "It's true, we're madly in love." There's no point in my saying that I like the man a lot, I enjoy working with him and few other directors have given me the chances Clint has. We have similar ideas about the movies, we both believe they should entertain people. Basically, I love good, old-fashioned entertainment. I think a lot of people are ashamed to say that nowadays.'

It is not difficult to see where the attraction between them lay. Locke saw Eastwood as a demi-god, which must have been all the more flattering because she was so bright herself. He saw her as a companion who shared both his contempt for the Hollywood social scene and his liking for derring-do. On *The Gauntlet*, she eagerly joined in an assortment of stunts that would have had most actresses calling for a double. 'When I read the script, I saw all these great dramatic scenes,' she recalls. 'It wasn't until we were out there in the Arizona desert and I had to fall out of a fast-moving ambulance door with Clint inside hanging on to one of my feet that I suddenly thought, "My God, this is a really physical film and I have been tricked into the whole bloody thing."'

If their behaviour hadn't been an accurate barometer of their feelings, then her comments on his professional skills would surely have given the game away. 'There's no way you are going to overpower him,' she stated, with what sounds like breathless admiration. 'He practically gives scenes to other actors. He has a smart business head and a creative talent and he just doesn't see himself as a sex symbol, no matter what other people say. I remember saying to him, "How does it feel to know so many people pay money to see you?" But his ego is so low, he can't really relate to that kind of question. Clint is a throwback to an era in the movies which had huge stars.'

At this point, the Eastwood–Locke combo took the bizarre decision to turn to slapstick comedy in *Every Which Way But Loose*. From the outset, employees at Malpaso and advisers elsewhere gave an emphatic thumbs-down to the puerile script about a barroom brawler who falls in love with a country and western singer but, as usual, Eastwood was adamant. If he wanted to do it, do it he would. Throughout the seventies, he and Burt Reynolds had swapped places at the top of the American popularity charts with a selection of shoot-'em-ups that had immense public appeal. Then Reynolds modified his tough-it-out image to star in *Smokey and The Bandit*, arguably one of the silliest movies ever made. When, despite this, it pulled over one

hundred million dollars at the box office, Eastwood sat up
and took note of the lucrative drive-in market that formed
the bulk of the audience for this kind of fare.

Finding a means of tapping into lowest-common-
denominator filmmaking was not to prove too difficult.
Essentially, *Every Which Way But Loose* transfers the
extended family from *The Outlaw Josey Wales* to the San
Fernando Valley. Instead of coping with tragedy, its members deal with the day-to-day pitfalls – or more usually
pratfalls – of an itinerant existence. The protagonist, Philo
Beddoe, is a blue-collar icon, a trucker who spends his
off-duty hours drinking beer and listening to country and
western music in a selection of run-down bars. His reputation as the best barroom brawler in his territory is
carefully nurtured to attract a string of challengers. As each
lines up to prove it wrong, Philo strips to the waist and un-
leashes his fists while his chosen companions, Orville and
Clyde, clean up by betting on the result. Orville is a regular
sidekick, an easy-going mechanic who salvages wrecked cars
when he's not fixing fights for Philo. Clyde is an orang-utan,
released from a desert zoo after Philo won him in a fight and
now gainfully employed as his sparring partner.

If this sounds bad, the development of the so-called plot
is even worse. Philo falls in love with a country and western
singer, Lynne Halsey-Taylor, and pursues her across the
country with doting devotion, lavishing his hard-earned
money on her so that she can set up a bar with her lover.
Where he is stupid and feckless, she is smart, ruthless,
promiscuous and feckless. She lets him into her bed but
never into her stony little heart. Meanwhile he spells out his
raison d'être to Clyde, secure in the knowledge that he can't
treat his sanctimonious maunderings with the contempt
they deserve. 'I suppose you think I'm crazy traipsing across
the country after a girl I hardly even know,' he says as they
sit together in front of a campfire beside a babbling brook.

'Hell, I'm not like Orville. Takes me a long time to get to know a girl, even longer to let her know me. I'm not afraid of any man, but when it comes to sharing my feelings with a woman, my stomach just turns to Royal gelatin.'

Ouch! The men he is not afraid of are the Black Widows, twelve elderly bikers who are eventually dispatched en masse to the accompaniment of Morricone's score from *The Good, The Bad and The Ugly*. The women he is afraid of include Orville's mother, a whining shrew who is capable of turning a shotgun on anyone when the need arises. She is played for maximum irritation by Ruth Gordon, with Geoffrey Lewis as Orville and Beverly D'Angelo as the girlfriend he picks up along the way. As for Clyde, he is an eleven-year-old 170lb orang-utan called Manis who was discovered in a Las Vegas show. Trained as a stunt ape since the age of two, he walked confidently on his hind legs and improvised with the other performers with the instinctive skill that comes with years of crowd-pleasing. And, of course, he stole the show.

Like *The Enforcer*, *Every Which Way But Loose* was directed by the Eastwood protégé James Fargo, leaving the actor free to work with Clyde within the limits set by his trainers, Bobby and Joan Berosini. They described their charge as 'naturally timid' and insisted that the understanding they'd built up with him over the years should not be abused during shooting. According to them, it was love at first sight, with Clint putting Clyde at his ease with his own natural calm and poise. 'We took a big chance with this film, but Clint made it simple, and we're very pleased with the results.'

'Orang-utans are shy and stand-offish,' Eastwood confirmed. 'With Clyde what we'd do was simple. I'd give him half a can of beer, he'd relax and we'd do the scene. We had to get it right first time, though, because Clyde didn't have much patience. His boredom threshold was

very low.' A one-take actor, and for the knock-down price
of half a can of beer? No wonder Eastwood, the master of
home economics, was prepared to kiss him on the lips.
'You've got to understand that people get sort of attached
to Clyde. Besides, Clyde is a very warm-lipped primate,'
he said in tribute to his co-star.

When he wasn't bonding with Clyde, Eastwood was
learning the rudiments of prize fighting from Al Silvani,
one-time coach to Jake LaMotta and Floyd Patterson. In
recent years, he'd switched from real to fake in order to
prepare Sylvester Stallone for Rocky. Now he performed
the same service for Eastwood. In his opinion, Eastwood
was a natural upright boxer with a long reach and an
aptitude for copying the punches with conviction. His job
was not to teach the actor to box but to make him look
like a boxer, more a matter of balance, movement and
attitude than delivering the goods. His verdict was that
Eastwood was a real craftsman, with a capacity to absorb
information rapidly and put it to effective use. 'The guy
knows what he's doing and he's got a nice boxing style.
When he puts together some of those combinations, well,
it's something beautiful to see.'

Meanwhile Locke was going through a learning curve of
her own. In order to convince as Lynne Halsey-Taylor, she
had to master some basic guitar chords and sing in front
of a live audience. 'Scary,' she said at first, but as filming
progressed and her massive self-confidence kicked in, she
began to look forward to her moments in the limelight and
even to consider a future career as a singer.

If the serious critics had liked *Every Which Way But
Loose*, Eastwood would probably have been disappointed.
His stated aim was to make a mass-market comedy with
action-adventure elements that wouldn't 'alienate the bare-
knuckle sub-culture'. 'I had done a lot of hard R [restricted]
films, geared primarily to an adult audience. When I read

this script, I saw it as an opportunity to reach down into the next generation. This story had a hip twist that would keep adults satisfied, and the animal works well with the kids.'

Release-wise, the fly in the ointment was that Warner Bros were also in charge of *Superman*, much hyped, eagerly awaited and very highly budgeted. 'We knew we were a five-million-dollar budget picture going out against one of the most expensive films of all time,' Eastwood told *Variety* in January 1979. 'We were wondering if Warner Bros would expend its biggest push on *Superman*. We kept our wheels squeaking to make sure we had the treatment necessary to push this film.'

Warners got the message and came up with a detailed and, as it turned out, highly sophisticated strategy for keeping their money-spinner happy. While *Superman* mopped up in the big cities, *Every Which Way But Loose* opened wide over Christmas 1978 in small rural places that didn't expect to see an Eastwood movie until it had been showing for weeks in more favoured locations. Under normal circumstances, an Eastwood R-movie was dead in suburban cinemas after two to three weeks, but this modest PG-rated comedy was still pulling in the redneck crowds in 1,170 of its original 1,246 rural cinemas five weeks later. What's more, it was still building, and there was a second advertising campaign to come for the film's soundtrack featuring popular country and western stars Charlie Rich, Eddie Rabbitt, and Mel Tillis. Small wonder that it took forty-eight million dollars in North America, making it the second-highest grosser of 1978 after *Superman*.

What matter, then, that *Time* Magazine's Frank Rich wrote that it was 'almost impossible to sit through', while *Newsweek* ingeniously decided that 'James Fargo directed every which way but well'. 'One can forgive the orang-utan's participation,' the reviewer added, 'he couldn't read the script. But what is Eastwood's excuse?' As his current

deal with Warners was no salary and forty-two per cent of
the gross, it is unlikely that he felt he needed one.

When Don Siegel called Malpaso with a proposal early
in 1978, Eastwood was in a mood to listen. The project
was *Escape from Alcatraz*, a grim prison drama set on the
bleak penal colony in San Francisco Bay. As there were no
women, no apes and no silly japes, it was the perfect antidote to *Every Which Way But Loose* and wildfire rumours
about Eastwood and Locke. Siegel had been involved in the
development of the partially true story of Frank Morris, a
bank robber who escaped from a number of prisons before
he was sent to Alcatraz for a long time.

Once Morris was locked up in what the authorities
claimed was an escape-proof prison, he dedicated himself to
achieving the impossible with considerable ingenuity. When
he noticed that the plaster round the grille from his cell into
a ventilator shaft was crumbling, he helped it on its way, first
making a lookalike grille in papier mâché to replace it with
after his escape. He also made fake plaster heads complete
with hair stolen from the prison barber's to leave in the
beds so as to avoid detection for as long as possible. After
a seamless escape over the wire on 11 June 1962, Morris
and his two companions, Clarence and John Anglin, headed
away from the city towards distant Sausalito, using rafts
made from rubber raincoats. They had a nine-and-a-half-
hour start, but no one ever knew for certain if they survived
the notorious currents in San Francisco Bay.

'The case is still open seventeen years after they made
their escape,' said Eastwood. 'The FBI thinks they're dead.
They think they all died, drowned in the water. But that's
just their opinion. Nobody really knows. They figure that
out of the three convicts that got away, at least one of them
would try to contact old friends or family; that's the nature
of convicts, but nobody's ever heard from them.' As the
bodies were never found, the escape has kept its place in

the history books as the only unsolved incident in a prison that was closed within the year.

Siegel had written a treatment of the Frank Morris story based on J. Campbell Bruce's book, *The Rock*, in 1963, but it was journalist Richard Tuggle who provided the impetus needed to develop it for the screen. When he lost his job as editor of a San Francisco health magazine, he acquired the rights to the story from publishers McGraw-Hill, and turned it into a screenplay. Hearing that Siegel had once been interested, he sent his first-ever script to the veteran director. Siegel bought it immediately and tempted Paramount into the arena with the lure of Clint Eastwood as Frank Morris. The bait was sufficient, and the film went before the cameras in the early months of 1979.

If anyone was born to play Frank Morris, a loner since he'd been abandoned by his chorus-girl mother at the age of three, it was Eastwood. Tuggle's screenplay packaged him as a supremely competent individualist with a withering scorn both for his fellow prisoners' attempts to dominate him and for the state's efforts to contain him. 'Morris was a reclusive-type guy,' the actor explained. 'He had no education but, according to prison records, he had an IQ of 148. He could have been a success in life if he'd channelled his pursuits a little differently. He was extremely inventive; he showed the other two cons how to make drills out of twisted pieces of metal and rafts out of raincoats.' The film develops into a symbolic contest between Morris, the free spirit, and the Warden, representing the sadistic face of authoritarianism. He was played by Patrick McGoohan, a complete casting turnaround as his main claim to fame was the title role in the popular sixties television series *The Prisoner*.

Unusually for an Eastwood picture, much of *Escape from Alcatraz* was shot at Paramount Studios on intricate sets representing the narrow shafts and passages used by the prisoners during their escape. However, the flight from the island could only be shot realistically on the rock itself, now a tourist attraction by day but empty by night. The first step was to re-connect the prison to the city's electrical supply with fifteen miles of cable. The next was for Eastwood and Siegel to come to some accommodation over the dramatically dangerous details of the swimming sequences. Since the pair had last worked together on *Dirty Harry*, the balance of power had tilted in Eastwood's favour. Although he had never been the pupil sitting at the feet of the master, he had started out with considerable respect for the older man. However, their recent track records had reversed their positions in the pecking order. While Eastwood had become, in Siegel's words, 'a powerful man and the wealthiest actor in the world', the director had compromised his talent with failures like *The Black Windmill*, starring Michael Caine, and *Telefon*, starring Charles Bronson.

'I was forced into the action mould because of a series of circumstances over which I had no control and I had to go with it because there was nothing else around,' he commented bitterly at the end of *Telefon*. 'By the time the Committee noticed me, they couldn't see me do anything but action. I can't re-write my past which, all things considered, wasn't that bad but I haven't had the options I might have wanted. *Telefon* was a cockamamy idea, with a bad script, but it was worked on and worked on, and then I went to work on it, and I think we've come up with a good picture. Nothing that will win Oscars, but it'll please the audience and that's something that's very important to me. When I started out, if I imagined people watching my movies, I think I pictured entire theatres either doubled up in tearful agony or else shrieking with joy. It didn't quite work out that way, I'm sorry to say, and it's a sorrow much deeper than most people imagine.'

Instead of comedy and romance, he got Clint Eastwood, man of granite and, by 1979, in a position to implement a will of iron. As a result of Siegel's disillusion and Eastwood's buoyancy, *Escape from Alcatraz* did not always go smoothly. In a situation in which the actor controlled the money and the director owned the script, each felt free to impose their ideas on the other, often with stormy results. 'When you work with a top star you have to accept that it's going to be that way but I don't like that kind of burden,' said Siegel guardedly. 'Clint always comes up with lots of ideas, and when they've been good, I've welcomed them. But when I didn't agree with him, if I didn't think his idea was as good as mine, then I did it my way. When his idea was no better than mine, it stimulated me into a new way of thinking. That's a pretty healthy way to work. And I've changed too. I'm a little feistier, more self-conscious of my position in the film industry.'

One area of conflict was over the use of doubles for the escape down the walls of Alcatraz into San Francisco Bay. Siegel thought that a fall-and-you-die descent unprotected by nets was too dangerous for Clint and his fellow fugitives, played by Fred Ward and Jack Thibeau. However, they'd been cast as much for their athleticism as for their acting skills and they agreed with Eastwood that doubles would seriously lessen the film's impact. On the night in question, the trio climbed up through a shaft to the prison roof, then slid three storeys down a drainpipe and so into the water where they had to swim until the current swept them out of shot to a waiting boat. 'I can tell you right now that none of us could have made it if we were really escaping,' Eastwood informed Siegel over the radio as a savage current drove him towards the Golden Gate Bridge. 'Twice, I almost thought we'd lost him,' said Siegel. 'It was a really tough fight for them to make it in the darkness; the boat was four hundred yards away.'

By Eastwood standards at the time, *Escape from Alcatraz* was a modest critical success but, with around a fifth of the gross of *Every Which Way But Loose*, a relative commercial failure. No matter, said the star. 'This is the best era for actors. Any actor today who's doing well can have a certain amount of control. The old days seem like they were better for stars, but in spite of all the glamour, it was still, "Here's your next picture, Mr Bogart." Today, you're a free agent. If somebody doesn't want to do what you want to do, you can leave 'em for another outfit.'

Although Eastwood and Siegel had grown too far apart to work together again, the director spoke of his performance in *Escape from Alcatraz* with unrestrained admiration. 'He's not showy as an actor, but rather reserved, which is why he is so underrated. *Alcatraz* was his first real character study, and I don't think he quite believed me when I told him how good he was. He's modest and doesn't like to hear it. But I thought he was incredible. Even the critics said so. I think he's getting better, more assured. And he's more likely to gamble than he was a few years ago. Within limits, which he's aware of, he's as good as anybody.' As a tribute to a star who had outgrown his mentor, it could hardly have been more generous and Eastwood would prove that, in many respects, it was well deserved.

12

Stormy Weather

On New Year's Day 1979, Eastwood's fiftieth birthday was a year and a half away, but his male menopause was well into its cycle. In Locke, he had a trophy mistress, and one he increasingly liked being seen around with. In winter, they'd visit the ski slopes of Vail and Sun Valley. In summer, they'd head north to the wild country, the Fraser River Canyon in British Columbia or the San Juan islands to the north of Vancouver, where they caught their own food – salmon, clams and crabs – which they washed down with white wine. 'You can't beat that for eats,' said Clint, whose chosen recipe for the *Sun Valley Celebrity and Local Heroes Cookbook* combines these exotic seafood ingredients in a dish called Spaghetti Western.

In 1978, he'd gone further down the rich man's path by buying a $100,000 red competition Ferrari. As it is not in his character to be reckless, he took professional instruction, a five-day course at the Bob Bondurant School of High Performance Driving in Northern California. His co-pupils were his fellow Hollywood hard men, Gene Hackman and James Brolin. Some years later, a Bondurant instructor revealed that his distinguished pupil was a clever, careful driver who was not afraid to take risks. By the spring of 1979, he was taking them alongside Paul Newman, a much more dedicated race driver, in celebrity contests on the Riverside Raceway. As the box-office returns mounted on *The Gauntlet* and *Every Which Way But Loose*, it was

white-knuckle time for Warner Bros, but they really had
no option but to keep their fingers crossed and sit it out.

Maggie Eastwood, on the other hand, had finally decided
that sitting it out had no future. For years, she had behaved
circumspectly in the face of extreme provocation, but now
America's gutter press was dedicating itself to bringing her
private pain into the public domain. It is not easy to live
with headlines like 'Clint Eastwood's death-defying new
life with fast cars and a beautiful girl', and Maggie decided
that enough was enough. 'It was my decision to leave
him but now we both have a lot of decisions to make. I
don't know what is going to happen,' she said when they
were legally separated in February 1979 after twenty-six
years together. 'We're all pals,' she added bravely, but also
prophetically, because they've remained so ever since.

She still lives in the house at Pebble Beach, a five-million-
dollar property in those days but worth double that now,
even in recessionary times. Her husband moved closer to
Carmel into a more modest redwood house concealed behind a high fence on San Antonio across the road from the
beach. The thing he missed most was his state-of-the-art
gym, with its floor-to-ceiling picture windows looking out
over the Pacific. No man who prides himself on his physique
finds it easy to grow older without trying to turn back the
clock. In Eastwood's case, exercise had been part of his
daily routine for so long that increasing it could do nothing
to delay the ageing process. 'I try to do a few gut exercises
in the morning, something for the neck. I try to run early in
the day. Then in the afternoon, I press a little iron. It's just
something I've been doing for as long as I can remember.
You have to run to get real speed, but weights give you
strength.' As he spoke, he waved away coffee – bad for the
nervous system – and pastries.

His custom was to put jazz or Bach on the tape deck
while he worked out on parallel bars, a slantboard, a

punchbag and a huge black and chrome Universal exercise machine. His weights 'looked as if they could easily tip the scales at a couple of hundredweight,' according to the Hollywood-based British journalist Barbara Paskin. This diligent hyperactivity ensured that the body remained beautiful, but what about the face? No lifts, Clint insisted. The rumours were lies. 'Kyle has dimples, I have pleats,' he joked. 'If I had a facelift, I'd ruin all these lines. Anyone who knows anything about facelifts knows that if this were one, it would be the worst one in history!'

As Eastwood was well accustomed to Maggie's complicity in his unfaithfulness, her decision to separate came as a shock. He'd frequently told Roxanne Tunis, and probably many of her successors including Sondra Locke, that he would never leave his wife and the indications are that he meant it. As a married man running on a long leash, he knew he had the best of all possible worlds. As late in his marriage as 1978 he said, 'Maggie doesn't chain me. She knows me well enough by now and she knows what to expect. Who do you know who can't wait to rush off home to his wife? I like to get lost when the mood strikes. I'm either doing a picture or cutting one or running on a beach or hiding away or standing on top of a mountain.'

Nothing else? 'I've misbehaved but I have always tried to make it up. Maggie knows I'm working with gorgeous women most of the time. If she thought I couldn't keep my hands off every lady I worked with, she'd have a problem, but she knows what I'm about and she accepts me. Maggie is my wife, but she's more than that. She's my friend. It's easy to be romantic. Everyone talks about love; no one talks about like. There's an old joke about sex. What do you talk about afterwards? There's very little during but an awful lot of afterwards.'

When he was quizzed by Barbara Walters on networked television a few weeks later, he filled in the answers even before she asked the questions. 'I'm legally separated, if that's what you mean,' he said pre-emptively. 'People have problems within marriages. Everybody has them and some people manage to resolve them or work them out and others don't. Whether she helped me or I helped her – I mean, we have a very good relationship. She and I are probably better friends and having much more amiable conversations, more sensible conversations about philosophical differences or agreements now than we ever have.'

'Is Sondra Locke the number-one relationship in your life?' Walters probed. 'She's an extraordinary girl,' he replied, 'a very intelligent girl, very smart. I enjoy her very much as an actress and personally. She's one of my number-one friends.' And that was that. When *People* magazine reported that he was 'seemingly under Locke and key', they received a warning letter from the star accusing them of 'adolescent titillation'. Nor would he be drawn on the subject of re-marriage. Pre-planning films and his children's education were priorities, but the rest of his life was his own affair. 'The formality of matrimony is more important to the female of the species. If I were starting out now, at my present age and income – and this is totally hypothetical – perhaps I wouldn't get married at all. The only reason today is for the children. It makes their lives a little less complicated.'

After the separation, Kyle and Alison lived with their mother, but their father picked them up from school whenever he was in Carmel. 'What I like to do best when I'm not working,' he told *Cosmopolitan*'s John Love, 'is store up big chunks of time to spend with my kids. I'd like to see them more, but unfortunately I have my job and they have to go to school. I'm gone for long periods and they understand it's the nature of my work.'

As they grew older, he introduced them to the things he loved, especially jazz and skiing. 'Sondra skis a little more conservatively than me,' he commented, 'but Kyle is fearless like his father. He just gets out there and rolls.' During what was inevitably a testing period in their relationship, he put himself out for his children, especially for his son, disguising himself in beard and moustache on occasion to take him to the rodeo and the cinema. 'After a while you begin to understand your father, how he was tired that night he yelled at you. I haven't yelled at my kids in a while. I notice traits in my son that were once mine. He can entertain himself, make up characters and play with himself all day long. Keep himself happy. I don't want to ask him about his characters because I don't want him to feel self-conscious when I'm around. "Uh oh, Dad's here. I better act normal." If you've got secrets, they don't belong to anybody else. Unless you want to tell.'

Although Maggie Eastwood has always refused to be drawn on the role of Sondra Locke in the break-up of her marriage, her decision to separate left him free to romance his winsome co-star on his next two pictures, the disparate comedies *Bronco Billy* and *Any Which Way You Can*. When the script for *Bronco Billy* arrived unsolicited from writer Dennis Hackin, Eastwood was on the verge of sending it back when he was caught by the title. 'My first thought was that Frank Capra or Preston Sturges might have done it in their heyday. It had some values that were interesting to explore in contrast to the sixties, Vietnam and Watergate and so on. Here was a guy who was a loser but who wouldn't acknowledge it and who was a hold-out against cynicism. It wasn't old-fashioned but in a way it was. The guy was fun to play because he had to be stripped bare of all his dignity.'

Although Eastwood knew the script didn't have much commercial potential, he stayed true to the author's intention by resisting suggestions that he should beef it up with action and sex. The film took him as far down the line of self-parody as he would ever go. The characters he'd played since The Man with No Name were in direct descent as far as their competence was concerned. They might be criminals or law enforcers, ancient or modern, moral or immoral, but they shared an ability to cope with whatever fate threw at them. Even the most human of them, the self-doubting Ben Shockley from *The Gauntlet* and the idiotic Philo Beddoe from *Every Which Way But Loose*, find some kind of salvation through expertise. Shockley earns the love of a woman when he finally cracks a case, while Beddoe always has one area – the barroom brawl – in which he reigns supreme.

   Bronco Billy is not so lucky. For a start, he is a fraud, a New Jersey shoe salesman with dreams of being a cowboy which he doesn't even start to realise until he's over thirty. When he does head west, it is after spending seven years in prison for the attempted murder of his adulterous wife. Like Josey Wales and Philo Beddoe, he feels responsible for a multiracial 'family' culled from among society's castoffs, sub-criminals including Doc Lynch, once warned off for practising medicine without a licence, Two Gun Left Le Bow, a corrupt former bank teller, Chief Big Eagle, an armed robber turned author, and Lasso Leonard James, a Vietnam draft dodger. Under Billy's guidance, these losers take part in a low-grade Wild West road show, playing small towns in desperate places in and around Boise, Idaho. All they lack is a female assistant to form the target in the grand finale, the Wheel of Fortune Shoot Out in which a blindfolded Billy throws knives and bullets at balloons arranged strategically around the spinning woman.

   The tone for the show is set by Billy, dressed in tight brown jeans and a white rodeo shirt with prancing stallions embroidered on the cuffs, waving his silver-medallioned

Stetson to the crowd as he sits astride his rearing palomino. Soon this upbeat moment dissolves into farce as Chief Big Eagle, alleged master of the 'legendary rattlesnake dance that no white man has ever seen before', gets bitten by his co-stars while Billy wings the assistant of the moment with one of his throwing knives. Her resignation makes way for Locke as Antoinette Lily, a cynical New York heiress on the run from a detested marriage of convenience, to replace her on the wheel.

As in all their screen associations, Eastwood and Locke are constantly at loggerheads. She is the quick-witted city slicker with the verbal skills to destroy the redneck she despises. He is the no-hoper with a heart of gold and a head full of old saws to support it. 'He's just a guy trying to make things work,' Eastwood explained. 'He's more open and vocal, and being expressive of his feelings, he's vulnerable. He believes in God and country, and goes around preaching old-fashioned ethics to kids like, "Say your prayers before you go to bed." And yet, he's an ex-convict. He's also like a messiah to this little ragtag band of losers. It's almost a statement of loyalty in the way he keeps them from giving up.'

Eastwood directed *Bronco Billy* himself, displaying an unexpected flair for self-mockery in a culture-clash movie that shows the intrinsic worth of grassroots decency, especially when compared to more showy but essentially empty urban values. Some of the French critics accused him of promoting Reaganite principles in the run-up to the 1980 Presidential election, but the American and British ones recognised the film as a watershed. 'From his days in spaghetti westerns, Eastwood has retained the strong silent mirthless macho image,' wrote David Robinson in *The Times*, 'but *Bronco Billy* clearly demonstrates his reluctance to be trapped forever in that image. Only the autocracy and independence conferred by such supreme stardom and command of the box office could permit him to make such an odd, unfashionable, self-deprecating and wholly attractive film.'

Although Eastwood's working practices weren't affected artistically by the break-up of his marriage, the prospect of divorce resulted in the setting-up of a new company, Robert Daley Productions. All the films made by Malpaso while the Eastwoods were co-habiting would be taken into the final accounting, but the actor had no intention of giving his ex-wife any financial call on future profits. His resolve had been strengthened in this respect by *Every Which Way But Loose*, which had earned most of its money after the split in February 1979 and yet would still be included in the divorce settlement because the couple were not legally separated while it was being made.

Otherwise it was business as usual, with *Bronco Billy* coming in $830,000 under its five-million-dollar budget and thirteen days ahead of schedule. 'It's not because we over-skedded it,' said executive producer Daley. 'The studio would catch on. I've known Clint for twenty-five years, since he was digging pools and I was in the budget department at Universal. We talked efficiency all the time. When he got on *Rawhide*, he never went to his dressing room but stayed on the set and observed.'

The Outlaw Josey Wales was the only film Eastwood had ever gone over budget on, and that only by $200,000 owing to bad weather, a record that was all the more impressive in an era of costly turkeys like *Apocalypse Now* and *Heaven's Gate*, and hugely expensive special-effects movies like *Superman*. 'Some of these new directors will shoot thirty takes of a scene just because they don't know what they want,' Eastwood commented. 'Then every night they sit around smoking dope and looking at the dailies, saying, "Wow, ain't it great." Then they wind up with thousands of feet of film and have to cry for some editor

A lovelorn urban cowboy: bare-knuckle brawler Philo Beddoe sizes up the opposition in *Every Which Way But Loose* (1977).

Alison and Kyle Eastwood may take after their dad but it's Clyde, the orangutan who shares the action in *Every Which Way But Loose,* who has what it takes to steal the show.

Clint and Sondra share a moment of mutual assessment in *Bronco Billy* (1980).

This sporting life: Clint Eastwood demonstrates a natural swing, an unflatteringly high start number and a steady hand on the wheel.

Stepping out with Frances Fisher, his new love and the mother of his baby daughter, Francesca, at the 1992 Deauville Film Festival.

Wolfgang Petersen explains the best way forward to Secret Service Agent Frank Horrigan in the thriller, *In the Line of Fire* (1993).

Dressed to impress: a smile and handshake for Charles and Di during a visit to London but it's Kyle who gets the ultimate seal of approval.

Glittering prizes: a mayor in the making addresses the party faithful during the run-up to the 1986 election; *Unforgiven* takes top honours at the 1993 Oscar ceremony, with a little help from presenters Jack Nicholson and Barbra Streisand.

Still seeking new horizons: Clint Eastwood directs himself as Texas Ranger Red Garnett in *A Perfect World* (1993).

to come in and save their butts. If you can't see it yourself, you shouldn't be a director.'

At the time, he was in self-congratulatory mood over his good sense in turning down big bucks to play Willard in Francis Coppola's Vietnam epic. The initial approach had come from Steve McQueen. He'd been cast by Coppola as Willard, but hoped to persuade Eastwood to take his place so that he could be Kurtz. When Eastwood asked him why, he said, 'Because I can do it in two weeks.' Later Coppola approached Eastwood himself. 'He said they were going to the Philippines for sixteen weeks. It was just too long. If it had been eight weeks, I would have done it. I also said that the story didn't make sense to me, particularly the ending. Two years later they were still shooting and Martin Sheen [who took over as Willard] had had a heart attack. I thought "Goddamn! That could have been me." Anyhow, who wants to spend a year and a half in the jungle making a movie? I like to get in, do a film, go edit it, and then relax. With that kind of budget, I could have invaded a whole continent.'

Like Josey Wales and Bronco Billy, Eastwood has an endearing loyalty to his professional family, the people who work for him on film after film, behind and in front of the cameras. Although pleasure always comes second to efficiency, the actor-director's ability to relax in the most stressful circumstances ensures that everyone has a good time. 'Why not use strong characters who work well together?' he enquired. 'These people are the best – talented, flexible, and they like to work hard with no bellyaching.' *Bronco Billy* reunited him with several regulars, among them Geoffrey Lewis, father of the young actress Juliette, Bill McKinney and Scatman Crothers. 'Clint's the captain of the ship round here,' said McKinney. 'You don't see no shoutin' or hasslin' round here, do ya? That's cuz Clint's so low-key. He's got a hell of a lot of native intelligence. Look how he's threadin' the needle with this picture – the comedy's here, but not too broad. He's got an uncanny sense of what the audience wants to see.' Crothers' tribute was more succinct but equally warm: 'Mr Clint Eastwood, he's the man with the lens. Every picture he does, it always wins.'

These comments suggest that men were primarily attracted to Clint's calm competence. However, women placed no such limitations on their expectations. 'He's not at all like the tough guy I imagined,' said Tessa Richarde, briefly a bosomy blonde on Billy's Wheel of Fortune. 'He's got a rugged body, but in his face, he's very sensitive. He can look fierce one minute and loving the next. He's so overwhelming you can actually be afraid of him, yet you immediately feel you can trust him. He makes you feel like part of the family right away.' For Sierra Pecheur, who played Chief Big Eagle's wife, Running Water, the sexual charge was even more overt. 'I had no idea how rascally he is. He has this little air of devilry right behind his eyes. He's very playful, a real charmer. Macho doesn't really apply to Clint. He's actually very delicate. There's a fineness about him. I don't mean effete. And he's definitely sexy, though maybe magnetic is a better word. Not a cold kind of magnetism, but a playful, pleasure-filled, delicious kind of life energy.'

If all this breathless admiration for the man she loved was trying for Locke, she managed to conceal it during the making of *Bronco Billy*. Indeed, the shoot had a somewhat festive feel to it, with Clint and Sondra free to behave as a loving couple among people who'd loyally kept silent during the earlier collaborations. Kyle and Alison were invited to join the party – and to play small parts in the movie.

In this relaxed mood, Locke was prepared to expand on the forces that had drawn them together. 'I always saw something underneath those tough-guy roles that made him interesting, a hint of vulnerability, a certain boyishness and humour within the superman image. When we got to know each other, the boyishness became even more apparent. I've always been surprised that people don't pick up on it straight away. That, and Clint's great sense of humour. Clint is a rascal, but the people I've enjoyed on screen over the years have always had that element. Off the screen, people can know him for years and never be sure of what he's thinking. He's one of the warmest people in the world, but there's a certain distance, a certain mystery to him. He's always unapproachable to some degree.'

Eastwood was equally ready to talk about love, though not about love for Locke. 'Of course everybody's in love in the sack. The question is, "Are you in love five minutes afterward?" I guess the line between love and infatuation is pretty slim. The best kind of relationship is one where both people can express themselves freely and where there's mutual respect. I guess it's possible to love a woman and not respect her. But it wouldn't be anything that's gonna hang around for a while.'

Although Locke was going to hang around for a while, she would probably have been surprised to learn that her next film would be her penultimate screen outing with her distinguished lover. It was also her worst, which was much less surprising, as the project was *Any Which Way You Can*, a follow-up to the money-spinning ape-starrer that turned out to be even less than the sum of its parts second time around. Eastwood resumed as Philo Beddoe, with Locke as Lynne Halsey-Taylor, Geoffrey Lewis as Orville and Ruth Gordon as Ma Boggs. The Black Widows motorcycle gang were back on their bikes and the sheriff's men were back on Philo's trail. Clyde, the orang-utan, had a greatly expanded role and a new younger impersonator. 'Two years in the life of an orang-utan is a lot,' Eastwood explained. 'The original had grown as if aspiring to be King Kong, no longer pal-sized.'

Another newcomer was Buddy Van Horn, originally Eastwood's double and stuntman on *Coogan's Bluff* in 1968 and a regular ever since. 'I was at home and I got a phone call,' he recalls. 'It was Clint and he said, "I've got this script here. Why don't you check it out, and if you like it, you can direct it." My jaw dropped. I told him, "I already like it."'

Quite what he liked about it, other than the fact that it gave him a first chance to direct, remains a mystery. It was written by Stanford Sherman for belly laughs, many of them stemming from Clyde's lust for the female that Philo abducted for him from the local zoo. During a night of passion in a thin-walled motel, Philo and Lynne ape the coupling of the apes for our amusement. Having beefed up the sex side of the proceedings, Sherman turned to the action and came up with two more hoary old chestnuts, the Mafia and the bare-knuckle brawl of the decade. The Mafia is represented by two New York gamblers who kidnap Lynne in order to persuade Philo to fight the deadly brawler Jack Wilson for a $25,000 purse. After many ons and offs, the fight finally takes place in Jackson Hole, Wyoming, with Philo overcoming a broken arm and his opponent to collect prizes that include living happily ever after with Lynne and Clyde.

As befitted a director of his background, Van Horn concentrated on high-intensity action, especially in the eight-minute 'slugfest' that forms the climax. Eastwood's hours at the punching bag paid off here with a performance of minimalist athleticism. 'One well-timed punch means more than all the wall-to-wall fighting in the world,' he said. In his opinion, the fight worked well because the story had been building towards it throughout the film. 'I know it's a cliché, but you've got to have people rooting for something,' he explained. 'It's like a suspense film. You can have people coming out of the woodwork with knives, but it's what leads up to it that scares the hell out of you. That's why I think this current glut of films – the ones with all the eye-gouging and hatcheting – don't really work. There's no reason for any of it. You don't care about the characters.'

Predictably, serious critics refused to care about Philo Beddoe and his associates, while the redneck public showed up in droves. As far as Eastwood was concerned, the most welcome elements were a forty-million-dollar domestic gross when the film opened over Christmas 1980, and a soundtrack LP that teamed him with Ray Charles for the song 'Beers to You'. 'I'll tell you, it was a little intimidating singing with a guy like Ray Charles. I mean, no matter if you're talking rhythm and blues, jazz or country, the man is the best.'

Eastwood ascribed the conversion of the masses to country and western music to Charles's songs 'Born to Lose' and 'I Can't Stop Loving You' on his *Modern Sounds in Country Western Music* album. As the 'Any Which Way' films tapped into the resulting vogue for urban cowboys, he had reason to be grateful, as he readily acknowledged. 'Country music owes him a big debt. I've always liked country though I'll have to admit that back in the old days my favourites were people like Nat Cole, Sinatra or Perry Como. Now, though, country singers have taken over where those guys left off. They can tell a simple romantic story and people seem to be relating to that.'

On the face of it, the next Eastwood film, *Firefox*, is another departure, this time into the realms of science fiction mixed with aerial fantasy. This was the winning formula for the late seventies, with *Star Wars*, its sequels and spin-offs racking up stratospheric profits that made Eastwood's eyes gleam. George Lucas and Steven Spielberg were younger film-makers in his own image, good house-keepers in total control of their careers. Like him, they told simple romantic stories in which right conquered wrong. Their lead actors, Harrison Ford and Mark Hammill, were decent clean-cut WASP Americans, just as he was. Why, then, could he not direct and star in a high-budget, high-skies special-effects spectacular? By doing so, he would be breaking his cardinal rule that no production should cost more than four million dollars, but rules are made to be broken and inflation had already ensured that sooner or later this one would be. Why not make it sooner and go for the eighteen-million-dollar adrenalin burn?

Unfortunately, *Firefox*, a gung-ho novel written by the British teacher Craig Thomas, was much too close to the realms of fact to take what Eastwood planned to throw at it. Lucas and Spielberg placed their *Star Wars* trilogy in places so far removed from the real world that they had only been seen first hand by a dozen or so space pilots. *Firefox*, on the other hand, was set specifically in Cold War Russia, with its climax unfolding over the Arctic. As the film couldn't be shot *in situ*, Eastwood replaced verisimilitude with exotic locations in Finland, Austria, Greenland, Alaska, Montana and California. Where the studio tricks used to open up *Star Wars* excited the imagination, *Firefox*'s meticulously miniaturised aerial battles only served to blunt it. Everyone had seen this kind of thing done better before.

The story offers Mitchell Gant, a fighter pilot traumatised by his experiences in Vietnam, stealing the prototype Firefox, an advanced plane being built by the Soviets. The theft involves Eastwood in assorted disguises – ageing businessman, American tourist, driver's mate – as he dodges security services and the KGB to infiltrate the air-force base where the plane awaits its final test run. Once in the driving seat, he becomes anonymous as he engages a second Firefox, piloted by the pride of the Soviet airforce, in a dogfight to the death. When the film came up for judgment, it didn't help that Eastwood was unrecognisable for most of it, nor that the story presented America as unfailingly right in stealing a high-tech plane from another nation state. With the exception of the honourable and courageous Jewish dissidents – Britain's Ronald Lacey and Nigel Hawthorne – who assist Gant in his mission, the citizens of the Soviet Union are presented as neo-Nazi thugs.

Like other Eastwood protagonists, Gant is a flawed personality who redeems himself through what he and his bosses see as service to the nation. At the outset, he is a burned-out case, lost to the world in a hideaway in Alaska. When the Firefox proposition is put to him, he rejects it outright, only to change his mind when the messengers point out that his cabin stands on government land. As his motive for saying no is fear and his motive for saying yes is greed, it is hard to see him as any kind of hero, yet that is exactly what *Firefox* presents him as. And Eastwood, ever the unthinking patriot, agreed with this interpretation. 'Gant is a loner and the very best at what he does. He has conflicts to deal with, problems to solve outside his area of expertise, but he never doubts himself. He is a professional, a technician and a patriot. I liked the guy and wanted to go through the changes he experiences.'

Eastwood, a first-time producer as well as director and star, has no one to blame but himself for *Firefox*'s shortcomings. But then he would probably ask 'What shortcomings?' in genuine puzzlement. In any case, he had no cause to lose any sleep over it. Despite its World War II-style jingoism, a particularly unfortunate element in Britain where its opening coincided with the Falklands War, *Firefox* made enough friends worldwide to turn a small profit when it opened in June 1982. Although Warners were sad to have netted a minnow where they hoped for a shark, Clint Eastwood had more interesting fish to fry.

13

One For Me, One For You

In 1982, Clint Eastwood started on a series of alternating films that would bring him critical recognition and keep Warner Bros happy, though not at the same time. He'd been working on the principle of payback for some years, pandering to studio greed with high earners like *Magnum Force* and *Every Which Way But Loose*, then demanding his own pound of flesh for cherished projects like *The Outlaw Josey Wales* and *Bronco Billy*. Up to this point, the scales had been tipped in favour of the megabucks, but from now on he would use his power to balance each action movie with an 'adult' one. 'I made an awful lot of movies back in the fifties and sixties,' he told me in 1990, 'and a lot of them weren't very good. Now it's a cyclical thing. It's not a formal arrangement with the studio but I know they find shoot-'em-ups appealing and they know I like to strike out, not always do the same thing.'

Whichever way you look at it, *Honkytonk Man* is a film for grown-ups, if only because it is long, slow and maudlin. It is also both the climax and the end of Eastwood's five-year concentration on projects featuring country and western music. As this period coincided with his most romantic years with Sondra Locke, it may be that the ballads, with their seductive tunes and their sentimental lyrics, provided a fitting accompaniment to the love that would prove all too transitory. If so, it would be appropriate, because his first contact with country and western when he was a teenager working at a pulp mill in Springfield, Oregon was inspired by a search for girls. 'It was always wet, dank, really depressing, and I didn't know anyone,' he recalled. 'Someone told me to go out to this place where there was a lot of country music. I wasn't very interested, but this guy told me there were a lot of girls there. So I went. I saw Bob Wills and his Texas Playboys. Unlike most country bands, they had brass and reeds and they played country swing. They were good. It surprised me a little bit, how good they were. Also, there were a lot of girls there, which didn't surprise me at all. So I guess you could say that lust expanded my musical horizons.'

Be that as it may, there was no role for Locke in Clancy Carlile's screen adaptation of his novel about a tubercular would-be country and western singer called Red Stovall. Realising that he may die without singing in the ultimate country and western mecca, the Grand Ole Opry in Nashville, Tennessee, he sets out across Middle America at the height of the Depression accompanied by his nephew, Whit. As he is a penniless alcoholic with few qualifications for his chosen profession, his prospects are bleak, but in the end he dies happy after touching fleetingly on his dream. 'He is based a bit on some self-destructive people I've known,' said Eastwood. 'He's wild and funny, but he's been a coward in his time. He won't face up to his ambitions. He's not that great a singer, but he writes some interesting things. When he gets his moments, he's already destroyed himself.'

Red Stovall is an intensification of Bronco Billy, a failure with no place to go but down. His family is smaller, just Whit and his curmudgeonly grandfather who shares a part of the last journey. His purpose is much less humourous, with the laughs laid sparingly on the tragic reality of the drama. And he dies, which Eastwood knew was unacceptable to the mainstream of his audience. The last film he'd died in was *The Beguiled*

and it had bombed at the box office. The same fate awaited
Honkytonk Man, but why should he care? 'We shot it
in five weeks for very little money and we had great
fun doing a period thing. When you get to the end,
you don't want to have 'em say, "Well, he did fifteen
cop dramas and twenty westerns and that was it." It's
nice to have those others too.'

Honkytonk Man also gave him the opportunity to launch
his son, Kyle, in a profession that would prove less than
eager to receive him. When he cast him as Whit and gave
him equal billing, Eastwood laid himself open to charges
of nepotism, but again, why should he care? 'He's a very
natural kid and he's been totally immersed in film. He
was always obsessed with it. When other kids would be
watching cartoons, he'd be watching *Of Mice and Men* –
the original 1939 version. That's why I thought he'd be
able to handle that size of part. Kyle kept asking me to
let him have a part in a film and I realised that the boy in
Honkytonk Man was just his age at the time so I let him
have a go.'

Like *Firefox*, *Honkytonk Man* was both directed and
produced by its star. The shoot took place in a selection of
downbeat bars in northern California and Nevada, before
moving on to Nashville for the mournful climax. Eastwood
did his own singing and accompanied it by strumming on
his guitar, but his musical input was outclassed by Marty
Robbins's recording of the title song, a fitting memorial for
the legendary country and western singer who died after
a heart attack just before the film opened. Sondra Locke
found herself a role of a kind as acting-coach to Kyle,
a fourteen-year-old with his father's looks and immobile
expression. Allegedly it served him ill when he wanted
to build on *Honkytonk Man* by playing the title role in
The Karate Kid. Columbia was so reluctant to cast him
that Eastwood offered to direct the film and to star in

another one of the studio's choice, but even these en-
ticements proved insufficient to win Kyle the part that
eventually went to Ralph Macchio.

The reviews for *Honkytonk Man* were mixed, with the
Motion Picture Product Digest describing it as 'a folksy
boring movie that will be a real test of the loyalty of
Eastwood's fans'. Janet Maslin took much the same view
in the *New York Times* when she condemned the Eastwoods
as unconvincing relations and their roles as simple clichés,
then added, 'The story's musical angle offers Mr Eastwood
another chance to do something new, and once again it
is something that doesn't quite suit him. No audience,
already distracted by the hard-to-believe pretence that the
Eastwoods are actually uncle and nephew, is liable to take
Mr Eastwood for a hard-drinking singer with dreams of
making it to the Grand Ole Opry. The film comes across
sympathetically but unconvincingly, as an attempt by a
well-established movie tough guy to reveal his tender side.'

It took *Time*'s Richard Schickel to set the record
straight: 'Clint Eastwood has fashioned a marvellously
unfashionable movie, as quietly insinuating as one of Red's
honkytonk melodies. It is a guileless tribute not only to the
plain values of plain people in Depression America, but
also to the sweet spirit of country and western music. As
both actor and director, Eastwood has never been more
laconic than he is in this film.'

Although Eastwood started work on his next film, *Sudden
Impact*, before *Honkytonk Man* was released, he must have
realised that he was going to need a high grosser because he
agreed to yet another resurrection of Harry Callahan. Not
that the San Francisco detective had ever been definitively
buried. 'Sure, I'd do Harry again,' Eastwood had said in
1980, 'if the story was exciting, if it was a real gripper.
Harry's a strong character and I enjoyed playing him. But
you know, you've got to have a change of pace every now

and then. At a certain point, I said to myself, "You can't just go around blowing people away with a .44."'

Maybe you could, maybe you couldn't, but what was indisputable was that Harry Callahan had been moribund since *The Enforcer* in 1976 because Eastwood believed he had no new places to go. 'It's a little ironic that some of the critics who didn't like what I was doing in the sixties say they don't like what I'm doing now because it's not as good as the stuff I was doing in the sixties. They said Harry was on the edge of being a fascist. Now they ask why I'm not going to do Dirty Harry again. But where would you take him now? Without the very good writing the Harry films had, there's no point doing it again except for monetary reasons.'

Sudden Impact would prove these comments absolutely correct in all respects, but that didn't stop Eastwood producing and directing part four from a screenplay by Joe Stinson, a scriptwriter who compensated for a lack of original thought with the bloodiest Harry yet. 'The script just sort of came about and I thought, "Well, it's fun, let's do it." There's only so much you can do with a character but it's fun to reprise now and then. Dirty Harry is a character who is contemptuous of people who stand in the way of solving murders. He's obsessed with solving his cases. I don't think he cares that much about other people's choices in life. The whole trick to the Dirty Harry films is that there is a certain humour in the irony of the way the guy handles it. And the audiences expect that. They want him to do outrageous things. It's like every cop's dream, "Boy, would I like to handle it like that." It's also every person's dream, "I'd like to be that self-sufficient and still be able to say the right thing."'

Sudden Impact was the film that gave Dirty Harry his Dirty Harriet, a soulmate plucked not from among his crusading colleagues, as Tyne Daly had been in

The Enforcer, but from among the ranks of freelance avengers with scores to settle with extreme prejudice. While Harry is dispatching fourteen members of the scumbag classes, Harriet, also known as Jennifer Spencer and played by Sondra Locke, shoots three men and one woman in the groin and then the heart. The film endorses this as a fitting punishment for those who raped Ms Spencer and her younger sister ten years earlier.

The unsavoury couple meet when Harry is sent to a small Californian coastal town called San Paulo to investigate the background of one of Harriet's victims. In the course of his enquiries, he runs into Spencer, a young artist who paints anguished canvases in the style of Edvard Munch, one of several clues that leads him to the conclusion that she is responsible for the crimes. Except that when he learns why she turned into an avenging angel, he no longer considers them to be crimes. Instead, he puts her in much the same category of innocent victim as the girl who is kidnapped and buried alive in *Dirty Harry*, someone he is pledged to defend, no matter what the cost in human life or the abuse of human rights.

When Harry is not tangling with Harriet, he is tripping over alternative evildoers who are not billed as worthy of his help. Many of them are black or Hispanic but, mindful of earlier accusations of racism, there are a few blond thugs out on the streets as well. Harry runs into his first gun fodder at his favourite San Francisco lunch counter, three armed robbers who fire on him and are fired on in their turn. Two of them fall to the ground, leaving the third to grab a waitress, put his gun to her head and demand a getaway car. As Callahan lines up his Magnum on the man's head, he speaks the legendary words 'Go ahead. Make my day', at which point the criminal throws his weapon to the ground in capitulation. The line was written by Joe Stinson in the spirit of typical Harry catchphrases like 'Do you feel lucky, punk?' As had become his custom in earlier films, Callahan subsequently repeats his key line, but with a different outcome. 'I saw the line as a goodie, so I used it a second time,' said Eastwood.

Despite its double standards and its broken-backed morality, the public loved *Sudden Impact*. This was partly because the country was in ferment over the 'exclusionary rule' that had come into force in the sixties when the Supreme Court, under the chairmanship of Chief Justice Earl Warren, had altered the relationship between the prosecutors and the police on one side and the criminals on the other. As a result of the Miranda decision in 1966, a police officer had to spell out the criminal's rights at the point of arrest. These included the right to remain silent and to refuse to answer questions and the right to have an attorney present during questioning. In the eyes of right-wingers, the 'exclusionary rule' added further insult to this injury by invalidating evidence gathered by any methods that didn't conform with the exact letter of the law.

It was because *Dirty Harry* presented these factors as contrary to the interests of the law-abiding American public that the film received such hostile criticism from liberal reviewers, most of them based in New York. By the time *Sudden Impact* came out for the Christmas season in 1983, Ronald Reagan was in the White House and his supporters had no wish to find excuses for wrongdoers in a society in thrall to a drug culture masterminded by criminals. The administration had already backed a bill that would suspend the 'exclusionary rule' provided the police had acted in 'good faith' and individual states were in the process of voting 'good faith' bills into law or making plans to abolish the 'exclusionary rule' altogether.

As a result of this change of climate, *Sudden Impact* did unexpectedly well all over the country, not just in the established Eastwood strongholds in the west and south.

'Harry stands out because of what he represents,' the actor-director commented, 'especially now that the pendulum seems to be swinging in a more conservative direction. People are a little edgy about the rights of criminals with courtroom procedures and legal delays. I think the public is interested in justice, and that's what Harry stands for. He's unique because he's stood for the same principles from the beginning, when it wasn't terribly fashionable.'

Eastwood picked up an estimated thirty million dollars as his share of the proceeds, adequate compensation for savage reviews on all fronts. The *New York Times*'s Vincent Canby said that the screenplay resembled Michael Winner's *Death Wish*, especially in its promotion of vigilante lore over the system of justice by which most people lived. Pauline Kael also returned to the attack with a sardonic mention of the racially 'integrated scum' and a crack about the 'sledgehammer slow pacing', but overall her review reads as if she can't be bothered to sink her teeth into a target she sees as limp as roadkill. Having noted that Locke 'out-deadpans' Eastwood, she concludes that the picture 'is like a slightly psychopathic version of an old Saturday afternoon serial, with Harry sneering at the scum and cursing them before he shoots them with his king-size custom-made "44 Auto Mag". He takes particular pleasure in kicking and bashing a foul-mouthed lesbian; we get the idea – in his eyes, she's worse than her male associates because women are supposed to be ladies.'

Kael would not be so lacklustre about Eastwood's next movie, *Tightrope*, probably because it was not only number one at the box office for several weeks when it opened in September 1984, but because it won what she may have considered to be more than its fair share of adulation from her peers. For Eastwood, the role of Homicide Inspector Wes Block was partly an extension of Harry Callahan and partly a steamy sexual journey into a darker part of his psyche than he had exposed to his public before. Unlike Harry, Block is not a simple brutal killing-machine. When his wife abandons him and their two daughters, he is full of self-doubts as he tries to come to terms with life as a single parent. 'My wife didn't want tenderness,' he says sadly, and rather than look for it with a more sympathetic woman he allows himself to be tempted into a bleak routine of drunkenness and kinky sex with prostitutes.

The key to this particular door is presented to him when he is assigned to a case involving a series of dead hookers. At first, he rejects opportunities to tie up the survivors or handcuff them to the bedstead for his pleasure, but once he recognises his need for this kind of sexual excitement, he is easily persuaded. At every stage, he is watched by his quarry, a masked psychopath who becomes his alter ego through their shared experiences. Soon it can be established that Block's hookers die through more extreme forms of the deviant sex he last had with them. In a classic film noir device, Block's quarry is also his hunter, so that they become mirror images of good and evil. Wherever Block looks for the killer, he finds himself, so that they are locked together in a vicious and increasingly claustrophobic spiral.

Or is Block himself the masked psychopath? It hardly seems likely, but first-time writer-director Richard Tuggle keeps his options open as the brutalised female body-count mounts. Tuggle sent his script to Eastwood with the rider that he should direct it and the expectation that he would receive a sharp 'no' for being so presumptuous. Instead he received a buoyant 'yes' in a thirty second phone call. 'Clint has tremendous confidence in himself,' he commented. 'He's very personal and very shy but he's an incredibly comedic person. There's an intelligence and substance, a strong character in him. If you were in an alley and three guys were coming at you, Clint's the guy you would pick to back you up.'

As Eastwood had liked Tuggle's screenplay for *Escape from Alcatraz*, he now gave him carte blanche to do his own thing. His reward was a role that stretched him in new ways. 'Block is not as superheroic as some guys I've played,' the actor explained. 'He's a more vulnerable and self-destructive type. The hunter becomes the hunted, and there are these parallels between the two. I think of it as an adult suspense story meaning that blood does not spurt from the frames. We're not doing the obvious axe-wielding kind of thing. I like the fact that most of the killing is done off screen. Otherwise it becomes just a horror story.'

So that there could be no question of confusion between Callahan and Block, *Tightrope* was moved from its original location in San Francisco to New Orleans. Behind the delicate wrought ironwork of the French Quarter, Wes Block finds the sleazy bars and the steamy bordellos that feed his post-marital habits. Eastwood's regular cameraman, Bruce Surtees, surpasses himself as he creates a lurid nightmare out of red lights in the darkness, a corrupt and corruptive hothouse in which the killer gradually targets Block's home. As he tires of watching the detective squirm after the hookers die, he re-defines his ultimate goal as the rape of the elder daughter, a rare symbol of purity in a world in which sex is both brutal and paid for in money and blood. The message is the more striking because the girl is played by twelve-year-old Alison Eastwood, promoted as Kyle had been in *Honkytonk Man* to a strong role opposite her father. 'I thought it was only fair to let her have a turn at being in a film too.'

As Sondra Locke had had her last shot at being his leading lady in *Sudden Impact*, it was Genevieve Bujold who got the call this time. She plays Beryl Thibodeaux, the founder of the New Orleans Rape Crisis Center. She becomes a thorn in Block's side when she leads a vociferous protest over the unsolved crimes, but eventually the harassed detective has no choice but to ask her for help. As she understands the related compulsions of the killer and the cop, she is well qualified to give it, and she is also generous enough to offer Block a simpler form of sex which he willingly accepts.

It required fast footwork from Tuggle to direct Eastwood through these uncharted sexual waters. At one stage, Block is propositioned by a male prostitute. 'How do you know you don't like it if you haven't tried it?' he asks when he is turned down. 'Maybe I have,' Block replies. And yet Block must be clean enough to tangle honourably with Bujold's straightforward campaigner. It is a fine line, but Tuggle drew it accurately in a picture that earned the first-ever suggestions that Clint Eastwood could be an Oscar contender. No way, the actor insisted, he was much too successful at the box office to make the grade in the country club. 'The Academy Award group is political and so often gives Oscars to actors who don't have popular appeal and therefore aren't threatening – people like F. Murray Abraham or Ben Kingsley. I'm not putting these people down, they did a great job. I'm just saying that a popular movie star like Paul Newman, who competes for jobs with Academy members, doesn't have a chance against them.' On this occasion, his instincts proved right, but there is no doubt that *Tightrope*, coming so soon after *Honkytonk Man*, started the change of perception over his status that would eventually bring him two Academy Awards for *Unforgiven*.

David Denby of *New York* magazine admired Tuggle's competence and Eastwood's 'genuinely spooked performance', but regretted that he stopped short of displaying open enjoyment in moments of sexual domination. 'I've resisted Clint Eastwood for years,' he concluded, 'but it's time to stop making jokes. Long ago, he got hold of a powerful conservative theme – the dishonour of living in a society out of control – and it's beginning to pay off for him. He works hard. In a community devoted to fashionable time-wasting (workout books, salad dressing), he does something very peculiar: he makes movies. Directs them, produces them, stars in them. More and more, he's beginning to look like the last serious man in Hollywood.'

Pauline Kael did not agree. 'If there's anything new going on in Eastwood's performance, it's that he seems almost to be punishing himself for wanting to act. At times, he seems to be trying to blast through his own lack of courage as an actor. But the picture just grinds along, and it's like an emanation of Eastwood's dullness. He seems to want to be fiery, but he doesn't have it in him – there's no charge to his self-disgust.'

Any suggestion that Eastwood was the last serious man in Hollywood took a knock in his next film, *City Heat*, one of the worst he has even been involved with. The idea was to team America's two current top box-office attractions, Clint Eastwood and Burt Reynolds, in a Prohibition comedy. In 1983, Eastwood had deposed Reynolds from the number-one spot in the Top Ten list and he'd retained his supremacy in 1984. It followed that he was in a position to demand top billing and a higher fee, a reported five million dollars compared to Reynolds' four million. The initial deal was that Reynolds's name would appear first on the credits and Eastwood's in the advertisements but, before the cameras rolled, Reynolds capitulated in the face of greater fire power and gave Eastwood the top line on all fronts.

City Heat, or *Kansas City Blues* as it was originally known, was conceived by Blake 'Pink Panther' Edwards as a buddy-buddy movie in the Lancaster–Douglas, Newman–Redford mould. Eastwood played a cold-eyed cop with a deadly finger on the triggers of assorted period weapons, with Reynolds as his ex-partner, now turned private eye in the hope of keeping out of the crossfire. Their humourless adventures re-united them in a colourful underworld of speakeasies and shootouts in slums ruled over by gangsters and their molls.

Edwards was slated to direct the screenplay he'd written with Joe Stinson, but backed out after a stormy start involving the replacement of the leading actress, Clio Goldsmith, with Madeline Kahn. No sooner had Richard Benjamin taken over from Edwards than Marsha Mason quit, to be replaced in her turn by Jane Alexander. The old pros, Eastwood and Reynolds, merely shrugged and carried on, as good friends on the set as they'd been for years off it. Their fees plus the need for elaborate period sets and props resulted in a bill for twenty-five million dollars, money ill spent on a project that had been a mistake from the outset. 'My sanity wouldn't have lasted through *Heaven's Gate*,' Eastwood had said. 'I'm a little more patient than I used to be but not that patient.' However, he survived *City Heat*, with its fatal lack of chemistry between the stars and its loss-making extravagance, with equanimity, if only because he had more important things on his mind.

14

Better Late Than Never

For years, the size of the Eastwood divorce settlement was a talking-point at all the best Hollywood parties. Would the man acclaimed as the world's richest actor make the woman who stood by him for over a quarter of a century into the world's richest divorcee? Not if he could help it, but the other question, just how much?, was never answered by either party. Estimates as to the size of the settlement that was finalised in 1984 range from twenty-five to fifty million dollars, but they are only estimates. On this topic, Maggie has always been as silent as Clint. 'Everyone speculates about how much money is involved, and I don't think it's really anyone's business,' she commented at the time. 'I just know that I have enough to live on.'

She also had more than enough to re-marry, a consideration as the man she chose as her second husband had a fairly unpromising financial record. The Dutch-born Henry Wynberg took up a career as a second-hand car salesman when he emigrated to America at the age of seventeen. In the classic manner, he was fined one thousand dollars for winding back the clocks on four cars he sold in 1972–3, after pleading no contest to the charge. A year later, he got lucky when he sat next to Elizabeth Taylor at dinner at the Beverly Hills home of Peter Lawford, the British actor who had been married to President Kennedy's sister. Taylor was between Burtons at the time and ready to party with the man who described himself as 'a nice-looking ex-used car salesman who happened to meet a charming lady'. The couple toured the world for fourteen months, only to separate when Taylor re-married Burton. When Burton–Taylor floundered for the second time, Wynberg–Taylor re-grouped for a while, despite charges that Wynberg had supplied underage girls with drugs and alcohol in return for sex. In 1977 he pleaded guilty to statutory rape and was sentenced to three months in prison.

Shortly after this, he met Maggie Eastwood at another Beverly Hills dinner. By October 1980, he was claiming in public that he'd been with Maggie for eighteen months, which suggests that the first encounter took place when she was at her most vulnerable in the immediate aftermath of the legal separation from Clint in February 1979. 'Functioning as a single person after being married for twenty-six years is one of the most difficult parts of the whole thing,' she explained. 'After all that time, you find yourself single and supposedly independent, whether you ever felt independent or not. When you first separate, it's like a part of your life is gone. Not a very comfortable feeling. I found it shattering.'

Small wonder she sought consolation with Wynberg, although they lived three hundred miles apart, she in the Pebble Beach house and he in Beverly Hills. 'We meet as often as we can, usually a couple of times a month,' he said. 'We spend our time together skiing, swimming, playing tennis. That's one reason I like her so much, she plays a hell of a game of tennis. Sometimes we just take long walks and do some talking. We also love to cook and have friends over for a dinner party. That's one reason she likes me, I'm a great cook. As for now, we have no plans to marry. We're just good friends.'

After two years of separation, Maggie proved that she was capable of building a life after Clint. She opened a health studio in Monterey called Transitions, an establishment that offered seminars on marriage problems, career changes, and investments, as well as classes in yoga, meditation, and aerobics, this last under the instruction of Kim Novak. 'I'm very happy now and I'm discovering many new things,' she commented. 'For the first time in my life, I've come into my own. I have my own space that I can move around in and call my own shots. I'm beginning to feel like a complete person and it's very comfortable. I think I'm coping fine now.'

Unfortunately, the one habit she couldn't kick was marriage. 'I've been married most of my life and I'm much happier that way. I want to share my beautiful home with someone.' Early in 1985, Henry Wynberg became that someone in a simple outdoor ceremony on the lawns of the Manua Kea hotel on the Big Island of Hawaii. Kyle and Alison were among the fifteen guests, but Clint heard nothing about it until it was all over. 'He'll have to read about it in the papers,' said Wynberg on an unpleasantly triumphalist note. 'For Maggie and me there's no one else now. We're sure this is it for the rest of our lives.' In the euphoria of the moment, Maggie agreed. 'There's only one man in my life now and that's Henry. I just want to cry with happiness.'

While the briefly happy couple returned to the palatial Eastwood home, Clint and Sondra were discovering that their love was not to lead to the altar. As Locke has never divorced Gordon Anderson, the assumption is that she always recognised Eastwood's reluctance to marry again. There has never been any reported animosity between the two men, which suggests that Sondra's declaration that she and Anderson were 'tantamount to brother and sister' has more than a grain of truth in it. After all, a man with Eastwood's libido would be unlikely to tolerate a direct sexual rival. 'Gordon and I are very happy,' Sondra said shortly after the Eastwoods had separated. 'We happen to have a wonderful relationship. We're alike. We grew up together in a small town so we're like family. It's a close bond. We're best friends and nothing has changed.'

'I still think of myself as a child,' she continued, struggling to explain the inexplicable. 'Not that I'm immature. I feel I was born old, in one way, in that I have always been independent. I have always felt that I had to be responsible for myself and take care of myself because of a lack of rapport with my parents but at the same time that I crave independence, I don't really want it. I want someone else to have control. I want someone else to take care of the situation.' The odd trio often went out together and Eastwood was generous when it came to buying Anderson's objets d'art, if only as a means of supporting the man who provided such an effective smokescreen for his extra-curricular activities.

When Clint and Sondra first lived together in 1977, it was in the Sherman Oaks house the Eastwoods had bought and extended with the money the actor earned from the 'Dollar' trilogy. 'People are always asking me why we don't move to Bel Air,' Eastwood had said in 1969. 'I'd go crazy in a pretentious house, so would Mag. But a nice place with a lot of land around it, that's for us. I'd like to stay as I am and be able to go where I want in jeans and a t-shirt.' These preferences would not survive once Sondra felt that her position was secure enough to complain about living with the ghosts of her lover's marriage. In a flush of uncharacteristic largesse, Clint replied that if she could find a house she liked, he'd buy it for her. She had no difficulty in singling out a two-storey Spanish-style stucco property in Bel Air and he had no difficulty in meeting the price tag: $1,125,000. Over the next three years, he allowed Sondra to re-decorate it to her own tastes. As Locke never forwarded her new address to her parents in Tennessee, they

assumed that success had gone to her head. 'Who wants
to be associated with a couple of old hillbillies, anyway?'
her father asked plaintively, but Locke cited their Baptist
principles as a reason for not divorcing Anderson.

The first rumours of trouble between 'Eastwood and
Locke came as early as 1980 when the actor was spotted
flirting with assorted young women while skiing in Vail. The
ensuing dispute led to a short separation but they were soon
together again, living amicably within the confines of their
bizarre triangle. In February 1984, unbeknownst to Locke,
Eastwood became a grandfather when Kimber gave birth to
a son she rather tactlessly called Clinton. 'My father didn't
approve of me having the baby. I was nineteen and perhaps
he thought I was too young.' She claimed the father was
her boyfriend, Anthony Gaddie, and, although he never
confirmed it, he married her before the child was born.
'I knew about Clint before I met Kimber because I was a
friend of her mum,' he said. 'After we married, I wanted to
forget all about him but you couldn't escape him. Finally
it helped to break up our marriage.'

As the second Reagan administration got into its stride,
the change in the critics' perception of Clint Eastwood
began to register with those who organise retrospectives and
give awards. For years, he'd been too successful to appeal
to those who took cinematic artistry seriously. Sure, he'd
won prizes, but mostly from organisations like the National
Association of Theater Owners who were naturally in
favour of a man who earned them big bucks. When they
gave him a distinguished career award in February 1980,
he agreed to accept it from William Holden, the veteran
actor he'd directed in *Breezy*. 'There are few careers in
Hollywood as solid as Clint's,' said Holden in what would
be one of his last public performances before his death
from a fall later in the year. 'He's gone beyond being an
actor. He's one of the most respected directors we

have with his own production company and, in short, he's a filmmaker concerned with maintaining an image of strength and honesty, as did Gary Cooper and John Wayne with whom he has every right to be bracketed.'

After thanking Holden, and saying how easy his job would be if he always had actors of his stature to direct, Eastwood paid a gracious tribute to the people who bought the tickets. 'No way I can thank you except to try and do entertaining films in the future,' he concluded. 'I've been here for twenty-six years and I ain't won nothing – but this is nice!'

Nicer still was the retrospective of his work put on by the Museum of Modern Art in New York in 1980. 'It wasn't one of those promotional things. No campaigns, no ads, no fake gold medals. Those folks back there are very serious. They ran it very well.' And, to his satisfaction, they wrapped it up with *Bronco Billy*, a personal favourite rather than a box-office blockbuster.

In early 1985, it was Europe's turn to re-think Clint Eastwood during a tour that started grandly in January with a retrospective at the Cinémathèque in Paris and a minor award, Chevalier des Arts et Lettres, from the Ministry of Culture. Jacques Lang, the Minister of Culture, was not there to give it nor Eastwood to receive it, which suggests that there were still some reservations in high French intellectual places. Certainly there were works that never crept into the proceedings, among them *Firefox* and *City Heat*, but overall the serious press was quick to praise where formerly it had only blamed. The self-regarding *Cahiers du Cinéma* approved Eastwood's 'self-parodying subtlety' and his 'perfectly sincere humility', adding portentously that the losers in *Bronco Billy* 'have transcended the boredom of daily life and chosen to live in a universe of poetry and the imagination.' The rival magazine, *Positif*, admired the actor-director's ability to 'totally control his audience and his own universe, both stylistically and mythologically.'

The next stop for the Warners Gulfstream jet was Munich where the Filmmuseum hosted another retrospective. Then Eastwood went to London to deliver a *Guardian* Lecture at the National Film Theatre. 'A Die-Hard Liberal Behind the Magnum Image' ran the headline on an article designed to enlighten the readers of Britain's only serious left-wing newspaper as to the reasons for the sea-change. The text beneath described Eastwood re-born as alienated, vulnerable, sensitive and self-deprecating, but conveniently forgot to mention that he had telephone conversations and the occasional lunch with President Reagan, the *Guardian*'s perennial *bête noire*.

In less liberal quarters, which meant almost all quarters in the yuppified mid eighties, Eastwood's re-birth was a logical sign of the times. Where Dirty Harry had been a political anathema among the thinking classes when he first pointed his Magnum at ethnic wrongdoers, he was now perceived as a champion of truth, justice and the American way. 'I don't have an explanation,' said Eastwood, with the resigned air of a man who has gone over the same ground too often before, 'other than the fact that maybe there were certain prejudices in the times of *Dirty Harry* in 1971 that don't exist now, or are changing now, or times are changing now. Maybe I'm older, more mature, maybe the audiences are changing and I'm changing. It's just circumstances.'

After an arrival heralded in the *Daily Mail* by the headline 'Dirty Harry Goes Arty', Eastwood gained further immortality when he was photographed at Claridge's by Lord Snowdon. 'One of the most respected portrait photographers working today,' he quipped, 'and his family connections on his wife's side are also not to be sneezed at.'

This tour, with its unaccustomed intellectual razzamatazz, paved the way for the three major Eastwood films that have come since, *Bird*, *White Hunter*, *Black Heart* and *Unforgiven*. There is no doubt that Eastwood and his support team planned it that way, nor that their strategy worked, as John Vinocur, then the Paris bureau chief of the *New York Times*, eloquently pointed out. 'As enterprises go, the tour was an intriguing one, bones being consciously fitted under the flesh of Clint Eastwood's new, public embodiment as a very important American filmmaker. As cultural, or political, phenomena go, it was plain fascinating. Until a couple of years ago, Eastwood, actor or director, had been consistently reviled as a cinematic caveman, a lowbrow and lunkhead credited with a single frightening trick: his Dirty Harry cop pictures seemed to tap straight into the part of the American psyche where the nation's brutal, simplistic and autocratic reflexes were stored. The great foul audience, guzzling diet cola and wolfing down whole cartons of Milk Duds, had been seduced into roaring with base delight as Dirty Harry cleaned up murderers the authorities would have left free.'

Then, Vinocur's argument continued, the times caught up with Clint Eastwood and turned him almost overnight into everybody's artistic high-achiever. Acting that had once been likened to 'a sphinx trying to make sense of a sandstorm' was now acclaimed as 'spare and economical'. Even more gratifying was the change in attitude to the subject-matter, especially when it became the perceived wisdom among the chattering classes in America as well as in Europe.

One who jumped on to the bandwagon was Norman Mailer who met the actor and described him as 'a very nice man' before delving into the nature of his appeal. 'These films come out of the old, wild, hard, dry, sad, sour redneck wisdom of small-town life in the Southwest,' he wrote. 'All of Eastwood's knowledge is in them, a sardonic, unsentimental set of values that is equal to art for all it would grapple with the roots of life itself.' Mailer went on record as liking *Every Which Way But Loose*, so giving a quasi-respectability to one of Eastwood's most absurd movies, but in his opinion the film that best illustrated his virtues was *High Plains Drifter*.

Of course, there were those who dared to doubt the rehabilitation, citing some of the old chestnuts about refusing to appear with strong name actresses or to work for strong name directors. When Gene Siskel of the *Chicago Tribune* asked him about this in June 1985, the reply was frosty. 'This is one of the things that does bother me about the business. Everybody's after the same actors of the moment. The point is there are dozens of fine actresses out there who are as talented – and some more talented – than the three women who were nominated [for Academy Awards] for those save-the-farm movies [Jessica Lange, Sally Field, Sissy Spacek] but these other actresses are not the gals of the moment, the fad of the moment, so nobody hires them. I hate the way they discard people, particularly the women. One minute they're given all this praise and the next minute they're dustmops. It's a real shame.'

No, he insisted, he had never been afraid to play opposite forceful females. What about *Play Misty for Me*, once seen as an anti-feminist picture but now revered as a women's picture? What about Geraldine Page in *The Beguiled*, Shirley MacLaine in *Two Mules for Sister Sara*, Sondra Locke in *Sudden Impact*? 'I give women strong roles out of selfish reasons. If the character I play appears next to some coy little angelic creature, well, I think it would be a real drag both for me and the audience.'

No, he continued, he wasn't too cheap to hire famous names. Had he not paid big money to Genevieve Bujold for *Tightrope*? Nor was he too cheap to spend whatever it took to get a decent script. 'If it's good, I'll pay for it, but I'm not going to hire somebody just because he's got

a great name. Even the most expensive guys turn out crap.'
Nor was he about to change his approach to filmmaking
to please his critics. 'I've always been rebellious that way.
I think it had to do with how I was raised. My father used
to say to me, "Show 'em what you can do and don't worry
about what you're gonna get. Say that you'll work for free
and make yourself invaluable." That approach builds your
confidence. If I hadn't been brought up that way, I might
have reacted differently to the criticism I received early
on in my career. I might have said, "Well, I've had some
success, I'll do something a little more middle-of-the-road
and not offend anybody." But by not offending anybody,
you do offend somebody – yourself.'

As nearly a decade had passed since *The Outlaw Josey
Wales*, he decided the time had come to revive the classic
western. His choice was *Pale Rider*, a natural extension of
High Plains Drifter in that it provides a saviour in the form
of an ethereal but ruthlessly efficient Stranger. Like many of
his kind, he has hung up his guns in a fit of remorse
so that he arrives in an independent mining community
terrorised by corporate thugs as a peaceful preacherman.
This is appropriate because his coming is in response to
the prayers of a desperate woman as she seeks inspiration
in the Book of Revelations. 'And I looked, and behold, a
pale horse,' she reads, while requesting a miracle to put an
end to the community's troubles, 'and his name that sat
on him was Death, and Hell followed with him.' At this
point, she looks up and behold, there is Clint Eastwood
silhouetted against the skyline on a grey horse. If, as has
been reported, the gap in his western career was due to a
midlife allergy to horses, he certainly made a rod for his
own back with a plot that requires him to spend much of
his time astride this handsome beast.

One of his stated aims for *Pale Rider* was to express contemporary concerns about corporate greed and mercenary

enterprise within the framework of traditional mythology. 'If you consider film an art form, as some people do, then the western would be a truly American art form,' he mused. 'In the sixties, American westerns were stale, probably because the great directors – Anthony Mann, Raoul Walsh, John Ford – were no longer working a lot. Then the Italian western came along, and we did very well with those; they died of natural causes. Now I think it's time to analyse the classic western. You can still talk about the spirit, about the love for the land and ecology. And I think you can say all these things in the western, in the classic mythological form.'

Pale Rider marks a departure from Eastwood's customary *modus operandi* in that he selected the theme, the stranger-comes-to-town one that had been embroidered for a number of westerns including *Shane*, then had a script written to fit it, rather than developing an existing script. The writers, Michael Butler and Dennis Shyrak, returning to the Malpaso fold for a second time eight years after *The Gauntlet*, set the story in the Californian Gold Rush in the 1850s. As the genre dictates, they provide the Stranger with an adversary, the Marshal, a ruthless mercenary hired by the mining conglomerate. The two men have unspecified unfinished business to complete, so providing the story with a climactic final confrontation.

As was the case in *High Plains Drifter*, the Stranger teaches the miners, under Michael Moriarty's soft-spoken leadership, to defend themselves, and once again, there are intimations of ghostliness about the proceedings. Eastwood has described this Stranger as a horseman of the Apocalypse, one of God's avengers, whereas the Marshal represents the devil. 'Clint was obsessed with the project,' said his producer and childhood friend Fritz Manes. 'His whole bent was westerns from the start, and I can't tell you how many fans have asked him or written to ask when he would do a western again. You can't feel as secure with *Pale Rider* as you would with, say a sequel to *Dirty Harry*. However, my feeling is that there is going to be no problem. I guess themes just run in cycles – detective movies, then cars, drugs, outer space and whatever. But everybody loves cowboys. They know the hero always comes out on top. It gives people a good fantasy to live with.'

The film was shot in five weeks and two days in the autumn of 1984 near Sun Valley, Idaho, a convenient location as Eastwood already had a holiday home in the resort. After the rigours of night shooting on *Tightrope*, he was relieved to be out in the sunlight in the clear mountain air. Even on as tight a schedule as this one, he demonstrated his priorities by leaving cast and crew standing around doing nothing for several hours while he and his camera team climbed a hill to get the shots of dying autumn leaves he required for the opening sequence. Despite the money-wasting delay, he had an instinct that the leaves would be gone the next day when he was scheduled to shoot them and he was right.

The set was fairly elaborate, an authentic mining camp with twelve buildings, including a dry-goods store stocking the sledgehammers, picks and panning equipment required for extracting gold in the mid nineteenth century. Like its predecessors, it had interiors as well as exteriors, which went up at lightening speed over four weeks. 'You learn from everyone you work with,' said Eastwood. 'I'm surrounded by the best crew around and we all like to move at the same tempo. I think if the director is slow and ponderous, it can hurt the final product. The movies might not be as satisfying and, besides, I'd get bored.' 'Yeah,' adds Manes cryptically, 'as a leader, he doesn't want to look over his shoulder to see if the troops are following. He knows they're following – or God help them.'

In May 1985, Clint Eastwood hired a yacht to launch *Pale Rider* in the official competition at the Cannes Film Festival. He was the toast of the festival, hounded by paparazzi whenever he went ashore, but as the prize-givers hadn't caught up with his change of status, he went home empty-handed. When the film opened in America at the end of June, it took $21.5 million in its first ten days, a vindication for the man who made it 'out of gut instinct'. 'It just seemed like the right thing to do,' he elaborated. 'I can't think of any profound reason for it except that I grew up on westerns, I like them very much. It isn't in my history not to make westerns.'

Better still, it won recognition for his change of status from Vincent Canby in the *New York Times*. 'I'm just now beginning to realise that, though Mr Eastwood may have been improving over the years, it's also taken all these years for most of us to recognise his very consistent grace and wit as a filmmaker.' There were doubters, of course, among them *Vanity Fair*'s James Wolcott, who mounted a virulent two-pronged attack on the Eastwood oeuvre, as it was now being called, and the critics for their mealy-mouthed about-turn.

By 1985, Locke was getting restless. Although Eastwood saw the female lead in *Pale Rider* as a thin, wispy thirtysomething blonde, he cast Carrie Snodgrass in the role rather than Sondra. As she was well aware, when he worked, he worked full time. 'Once he starts filming, he moves like a machine and when he throws the gears, he likes everything to go.' This meant that when she wasn't in his films, she was left with a lot of time in which to ponder on his elusive nature and his habitual unfaithfulness. As the praise mounted after a decade in a working relationship in which he supplied the homespun American instincts while she injected intellectual stimulus, she may have added professional jealousy to her list of complaints.

Her reaction was positive: she would make a movie of her own. Her choice was *Ratboy*, 'a comic fable' about a window-dresser who tries to exploit a rat-like boy. Warner Bros had bought the project years before but it was Locke who dug it out and brought it to their attention second time around. As she worked out of an office at Malpaso on the Warners lot, charges of nepotism were inevitable. Well, said Sondra in defiant reply, being with Clint was 'a double-edged sword'. 'My starring roles with him didn't make me the toast of the town. I became his append-age. Everything I did was in his shadow. People want to know, "What is she capable of?"'

Whether they did or not, they were about to find out because Warners green-lighted her project. The snipers were quick to suggest that lavishing money on the mistress to keep the master happy was good studio economics, but Locke was having none of that. 'Warner Bros aren't going to do something crazy and just throw away millions of dollars because someone has a contact. Sure, it got me in a position – maybe, probably – to get in there. That's the name of the game. A son or daughter of someone famous will get a break, but once they're in there, they're on their own. They may listen to you but they're not obliged to go for it. I got in there and put myself on the line. Let my critics direct a movie if they think it's so easy.'

Like her mentor, she put aside initial doubts and decided to direct herself as the reprehensible window-dresser. She laid herself open to further charges of nepotism by using Eastwood's crew, available at the time because he was pre-occupied with his campaign to become Mayor of Carmel. She thought it would be sensible to limit her problems as a first-time actor-director by working with people she knew. The crew were surprised at her determination to make every decision herself, a reversal of the norm as first-time directors tend to ask for advice from the experts. Locke claims that even without formal training, going behind the cameras came easily because she'd always taken an intelligent interest in everyone else's job. 'I was terrified to direct but at the same time it seemed natural because in my mind I'd directed so many times.'

Although Eastwood saw some of the rushes, he wasn't consulted on the nuts and bolts of the production, nor asked to give his opinion on the results. This was good thinking on Locke's part, because *Ratboy* had no pretensions to the box-office success that he believed should underpin a director's career. It was essentially a small offbeat film, a sub-*Elephant Man* but with a satirical rather than a heavy moral message. When it was released, it won few friends, even on the art-house circuit to which it ostensibly belonged, but Locke was convinced that she'd found her true calling after years of being crushed by the twin juggernauts of Hollywood and Clint Eastwood.

'I found an outlet to express a lot of my own persona. I'm kicking myself that I waited so long to direct. Had the world been different when I was a teenager, I might have pursued directing instead of acting, but the only women I could relate to then were on the screen. I've been a disgruntled actress for a number of years. I understand what it's like to be overlooked, stereotyped, taken for granted and labelled as something I'm not. Yet I found it easy to sit back and not try to control my career. Often we don't start finding ourselves until we see others finding themselves. I started seeing other women directing. Then I found some material that inspired me to want to direct. I now understand how necessary it is to take the bull by the horns.'

When he did give his verdict, her lover was predictably 'very proud of her'. 'I thought she did a great job but then she's never been the kind of actress to rush back to the trailer after her scene was over. She always hung around the set asking questions, learning what everybody did.' A bit lukewarm as a tribute to the woman you love, but Eastwood was grateful to *Ratboy* in that it kept Locke occupied while he pursued a radical change of direction of his own.

15

His Worship the Mayor

'The City of Carmel-by-the-Sea is hereby determined to be primarily, essentially and predominantly a residential city wherein business and commerce have, in the past, are now, and are proposed to be in the future subordinated to the residential character.' This 'Magna Carta', drawn up by city attorney Argyll Campbell in 1929, was still enshrined in poster form in the chambers of the City Council in 1986, the year Clint Eastwood beat three opponents to become Mayor of Carmel. It contains the essence of the disputes that have divided the picturesque square mile, with its wild shore and its pine-covered hills, since it first became a thriving artistic community in the early part of the century.

The impetus for Carmel came first from Spain, eager to add this part of California to its empire before the Russians, then making inroads in Alaska, or the English, who were well established on the Atlantic coast of North America, could beat them to it. So it came to pass that Father Junipero Serra, a Franciscan priest who'd worked as a proselytiser in Mexico for seventeen years, set up the Mission San Carlos Borromeo in Monterey in 1770. The next year he moved it to its present position on the fertile banks of the Carmel River. It was the first of a chain of Spanish missions designed to convert the Californian native Americans to the Catholic Church. After the mission system fell into decline at the start of the nineteenth century, Carmel was left more or less to its own devices until the coming of tourism near the end of it. When California's first resort hotel opened in Monterey in 1880, a popular excursion was the spectacular Seventeen-Mile Drive round the peninsula via Pebble Beach to the Carmel mission, but it was the real-estate developer, James Franklin Devendorf, who ensured that there would be a town to put on the map.

Like many immigrant Californians at the time, Devendorf was a Midwesterner with a strong egalitarian streak. His first visit to Carmel Bay was for a picnic with his wife and daughters in the early 1890s, an occasion that gave him an enduring vision of the land's resort potential. Ten years later, he found himself in a position to set up the Carmel Development Company with his partner, a San Francisco lawyer called Frank Powers. Devendorf's Jeffersonian heritage prompted him to go not for the millionaire's-row development that later took place in Eastwood country on Pebble Beach, but for affordable community property in a natural setting. Although he used a conventional grid pattern, he replaced all the trees that had to be cut down to make it. Even today Carmel employs its own 'city forester' to maintain an estimated 45,000 trees within the city limits.

The modest lots attracted professors from Stanford University, followed by refugees from San Francisco in the aftermath of the 1906 earthquake. Devendorf provided the fledgling community with amenities, a reliable water supply, the Pine Inn, the Carmel Bath House, a school, a library, and a lot for the first Methodist Episcopal Church. In 1910, he helped found the Forest Theater, a focus for the artists, writers, poets and academics who gave the town a folksy air in contrast to neighbouring Monterey, with its fishing fleet and sardine canneries.

In 1951, when the twenty-one-year-old Clint Eastwood first fell in love with it, Carmel was still an unpretentious outpost on a coast that was embracing mass tourism.

Thirty-five years later, it retained many of its old embargos – no mail boxes, no house numbers, no neon signs, ultra-discreet street signs, no public toilets at the beach, no stiletto heels or eating ice-cream cones in the streets, no snogging in cars parked along the front between dusk and dawn – but by now they had become anachronistic rather than quaint. The residents were rich, elderly and ultra-conservative, the roads were crammed with Rolls-Royces and Mercedes and the shops with over priced luxury goods that barely dented their Amex Gold cards. They liked Carmel the way it was and fervently believed that that was the way it had to stay. Their figurehead was Mrs Charlotte Townsend, the grandmotherly mayor who hoped to win a third term in the 1986 election after victories in 1982 and 1984. When faced with the accusation that she never said yes to progress, she replied, 'Well, I'm proud of that. It's what we don't have that attracts people in the first place and keeps them coming back – and makes them want to live here.'

As the motels went up on the landward side of Highway One, the main coastal road between Los Angeles and San Francisco, there were those who appreciated Carmel's potential as a tourist honeypot. Many of them owned businesses, mainly restaurants, art galleries, antique shops and upscale outfitters, in the town but were not eligible to vote for the mayor because they were not among the 4,700 residents of the magic square mile. One of them was Paul Laub, a natural entrepreneur with a silver 1937 Bentley drop-head coupé and a cocky accumulator's drive that was an anathema to the Townsend brigade. His philosophy was that tourists should be treated as God-given bounty. 'I will return free enterprise to Carmel. I will bring Carmel back into the United States,' he pledged when he bought a house in the town in January 1986 so as to be eligible to stand against Townsend in the mayoral race that April.

The third element in the election – and in the 'to change or not to change' equation – was Tim Grady, an ardent young environmentalist who wanted to turn back the clocks on almost everything. His agenda included a pesticide-free organic garden and a wildlife sanctuary within city limits so that 'going outside would be like a religious experience'. 'I will tell everyone to use their energy, money or whatever, to promote love and peace,' he added, but as a member of the underclass – he worked as a dishwasher – he was never going to draw in the voters in one of the wealthiest enclaves in the United States.

If the Planning Commission had not dared to tamper with Clint Eastwood's plans in 1983, one of these candidates would have been the next mayor of Carmel. His entry into the business lists in the town began in 1972 with the opening of the Hog's Breath, his much publicised eaterie on San Carlos Street. It consists of a restaurant and bar facing each other across a split level courtyard. In the early days, the outdoor space was dominated by a mural of a many times life size Cowboy Clint squinting down on the hordes below. This has now been replaced by a pastoral scene that suggests a vast open air barbecue, an effect that is boosted by several giant log heaters.

However the menu still lists Eastwoodian attractions: a Sudden Impact Polish sausage and jalapeno pepper sandwich, an Eiger 'mountain of roastbeef' sandwich, a Coogan's Bluff New York strip steak, a Gauntlet green chile and sour cream or a Magnum Force ham and cheese omelette and, the most popular choice of all, a Dirty Harry burger. The press had fun with that one when the restaurant fell foul of the health inspectors in August, 1987, while Clintmania was still running high in the middle of his term as mayor. 'A total disgrace,' said Walter Wong, the environmental health director for Monterey County. The refrigeration was legally inadequate, the conditions were unsanitary, the food storage improper and there were structural problems that made it difficult to clean an 'extremely dirty kitchen'. As the restaurant contravened a total of 122 health regulations, Wong had no hesitation in closing it down until the correct standards were met. When The Hog's Breath received a clean bill of health two weeks later, the owner was there to take guests' coats, escort them to their tables and invite them to check out the new walk-in freezer and the immaculate kitchen. Although the incident was embarrassing at the time, it did no lasting harm to business, not judging by today's prices, which are extremely high for this type of cuisine. Nevertheless they are paid gladly in a rich tourist town in case mine host should pass this way.

The rather unattractive name represents Eastwood's notion of an English pub and the low, heavily beamed premises have a wooden board bearing the legend PUB, as a means of reassuring anyone who doubts its authenticity. Clint has always liked bars. He sees them as places to play pool and hang out with the old schoolfriends who have remained as close to him through the good years as they were in the bad. Fritz Manes is the best known but by no means the only one of a gang that puts loyalty very high among the essential virtues. Rule one is no tittle-tattle: 'There are certain things we just don't talk about,' said Manes. 'That's one reason we've been able to remain close friends. We don't advise each other on personal matters. I don't know the personal matters.'

Bars became pubs for Eastwood in 1968 when he spent several weeks at Pinewood Studios filming *Where Eagles Dare*. His mentor was Richard Burton, a world-class toper if ever there was one, but it is unlikely that he would have been proud of his pupil's choice of name or premises. Eastwood has claimed that Newcastle Brown is the best beer in the world but there is no trace of this or any other foreign brew in The Hog's Breath. The hogs, however, are out in force, a row of stuffed boars' heads breathing heavily down on a listless crowd of Californians sipping Bud Lite while watching live sports on a giant television screen.

By 1983, Eastwood was the owner of the site overlooking The Hog's Breath, distressed premises occupied by the Shell Fisher art gallery and the Nishi Nursery. His plan was to demolish the existing buildings and erect a two-storey U-shaped commercial property, with ground-floor units to be let out as shops and first-floor ones as offices. 'The whole intention of the project is to do a quality building and keep the scale relative to the residential character of Carmel,' he said as he submitted his plans to the Planning Commission that June. If they had been approved, construction would have started that autumn and that would have been that, but they weren't. Eastwood modified them and re-submitted them but again they failed to make the grade, so he issued a writ against the city's 'arcane planning laws'. In due course, the two parties settled out of court and the Eastwood Building rose on San Carlos, but the negotiations gave him pause for thought.

'It's true,' he commented, 'I did have a problem with the city. It could have been settled a year earlier. The out-of-court settlement we got was the exact settlement I wanted a year earlier. I kept saying, "Tell me what your objections are and I'll fix it." They wouldn't tell us what they would accept, only what they wouldn't accept. The whole thing was a learning experience. I started thinking, 'If this can happen to me, who has visibility and access to the press, imagine what happens to the little guy who is trying to get a project through. Imagine if that project was my whole life, if my whole life savings and my family's future were riding on it. It doesn't take too much imagination for me to put myself in that position. You're dealing with people's lives and they deserve respect.'

Politician's words indeed, but Eastwood has always insisted that he didn't pick up the gauntlet lightly, and that he did not do it on behalf of Carmel's greedy business community. As the rift between commerce and conservation was the topic of the moment, he pressurised his friends to go in against Charlotte Townsend so that she would face tougher opposition than she had in 1984. 'They said, "If you're so concerned, why don't you run yourself?" At first I thought, "Well, maybe there would be some resentment to the high profile." Then I decided I had to try it. I'm not pro-business; I don't want more motels, hotels, condos, that sort of stuff, but I do feel the business community has to be included in decisions. We can't put our heads in the sand and scream and yell that the business community is the cause of all the problems. The only way we're going to weld this community together is for someone to be mayor of the whole community, not just one segment.'

On 30 January 1986, Clint Eastwood made headlines around the globe by announcing that he would run for mayor of Carmel. 'I've lived here a lot of years and I want to put something back into the community,' he said with the sanctimoniousness that comes naturally on such occasions. 'This mayor and this council have just been too unreasonable in trying to thwart growth, trying to stop everything, but we can't stand still forever.'

With the exception of the no-hoper, Grady, all the contenders were registered Republicans, but where Paul Laub was quick to pull out of the race and pledge his support to Eastwood, the sixty-one-year-old Charlotte Townsend dug in. As the world's camera crews flooded into town to record the great event, she must have known her cause was hopeless, but she gave it her best shot, showing up for interviews whenever her famous adversary was absent. 'Mr Eastwood is just incredibly naive,' she told reporters. 'He's made no effort, in all the time he's been in the area, to get involved in civic affairs, and now he wants to be mayor. If he was interested in our little village, why didn't he evidence it? Can he only operate in front of a camera? I think he's still upset about The Hog's Breath. He's a man used to getting his own way. If we had approved the plan he submitted, it would have looked like something off Rodeo Drive. Two storeys of glass!'

Predictably, Clint Eastwood, the star of dozens of films in which he almost always came out the winner, had no intention of losing a grassroots election in his hometown. 'I said I'd do it after a few glasses of wine,' he joked. 'Being a very determined person, I decided to win.' If victory required folding money, then so be it. Even before he agreed to run, he'd hired the services of Eileen Padberg, an experienced political consultant with Republican credentials, to conduct a telephone poll of Carmel voters to see whether they would support him. Having got the green light, he threw more money into the arena, an estimated $34,000, compared to Townsend's $6,300. Unlike his opponent, he had his own campaign headquarters and he was to be found doorstepping the residents to encourage them to vote for him. Over an often bitter ten-week campaign, he also attended fifty-five informal social functions which he remembers best for the amounts of 'very weak tea' that he consumed. He would, he assured them, take the fifty-dollar-a-week full-time job seriously, drastically reducing his commitment to his career to put in the hours required to make it work. 'I just don't intend to do it wrong,' he insisted. 'I have that kind of positive feeling about life.'

When the election took place on 8 April there were 2,166 votes, or 72.5 per cent, for Clint Eastwood and 799 for Charlotte Townsend, a landslide victory that brought congratulatory telephone calls from James Stewart and Ronald Reagan. 'What's an actor who's played with a monkey want to be doing in politics?' asked the President, a reprise of a question he'd been asked himself with reference to his co-starring role with a chimp in *Bedtime for Bonzo*. After hosting a cork-popping celebration for the party faithful far into the night, the mayor-in-waiting had a week in which to reflect before he was sworn in on 15 April. On a drizzly day, six hundred people collected in the temporary stands in front of City Hall to watch Eastwood, formally dressed in a grey suit and a red tie, receive the gavel from Townsend. His mother, Ruth Wood, and his sister, Jean Bernhardt, looked on as he took the oath of office in a seven-minute ceremony.

Three hundred miles to the south at the Warner Bros headquarters in Burbank, the mood was glum as the golden goose went on a sabbatical that would last for most of his two-year term. Frank Wells, ex-Eastwood lawyer and president of the studio through many of his most profitable movies, expressed mild surprise when he first heard of the mayoral contest. 'He needs this job like he needs a hole in the head. There's no reason for him to burden himself with the politics of a small town. Then I thought about it and saw it was consistent. Clint has very strong convictions. When he's made up his mind, he jumps in with both feet. I don't think he enjoys the business of business – he hasn't gone out and started a chain of restaurants, for example. He got into producing and directing because he had strong feelings about the cost of making a motion picture. Most people who make the shift to producing and directing do it to control the process. With a star of his magnitude, control is axiomatic. Clint did it because he thought he could make pictures more efficiently, and he has.'

True to his word, he now turned this efficiency on Carmel, with the assistance of a personal aide, Sue Hutchinson, who had masterminded his campaign. She dealt with the mail that arrived by the sackful after his inauguration, directing fan letters towards his regular service and reading the rest herself to avoid burdening city staff. Although the normal monthly council meeting had to be moved from the fifty-seat city chamber to the 250-seat Women's Center to accommodate the Clint-gawpers, he always showed up for his starring role.

Within four weeks of taking office, he'd replaced four of the seven planning commissioners who'd blocked his office building, effectively giving himself carte blanche to develop the town as he wished. 'Most everybody was enthusiastic over that,' he said with satisfaction. 'The commission had a rude, ruthless attitude. For every complaint, I have had twenty letters in support.' After the sackings, his only adversary on the commission was Councilman James Wright, who suggested that he didn't know how to handle criticism, then added, 'He has made no move whatsoever to be a team player in the time I've known him.' By way of reply, and perhaps of proving his adversary's point, the mayor dubbed him 'Councilman James "Lone Wolf" Wright. Wolf or coyote, both are pack animals who tear their victims apart.'

During an administration that had its fair quota of pluses and minuses, Eastwood never allowed the feelings of those who disagreed with him to stand in his way. On the positive side, he cut through red tape like a knife through butter, speeding up construction on a much-needed second set of public toilets in Devendorf Park in the heart of the business district, expediting an old plan for a library annex, and authorising the landscaping of the Scenic Avenue beachfront. He also won the ice-cream-cone war that never was. In 1985, Carmel had been christened Scrooge City by the *Los Angeles Times* because the planning commissioners refused to allow an ice-cream take-out shop to replace an existing fast-food outlet which was giving up its lease. Mayor Eastwood, always an ice-cream-lover according to his ex-wife, now gave permission for a shop called Chocolate Dreams to sell take-out ice-cream cones, so winning credit for lifting a ban that hadn't existed in the first place.

On the negative side, planning ran riot during the Eastwood regime, with chain stores opening up in the town for the first time. 'Eastwood is not villainous or vicious,' said former mayor and arch-conservationist Gunnar Norberg. 'He sincerely believes that any developer or businessman with enough money should be able to do as he pleases. Unfortunately this meant that his term as mayor was a disaster. He turned a peaceful forest by the sea into Coney Island.'

Norberg was far from unbiased, but it is still undeniable that Eastwood's business perspective resulted in decisions that played into the hands of speculators: during the Eastwood term, the Planning Commission granted sixteen commercial building permits as compared to four residential ones, hardly a balance within the spirit of the 1929 'Magna Carta'. 'During the Eastwood era water moratorium on new construction,' wrote Harold and Ann Gilliam in their book, *Creating Carmel*, 'the city continued to issue permits for work to be done when the water situation improved. When the moratorium was lifted, Carmel began to experience its greatest building boom since the motel invasion of the 1950s. After Eastwood left office in 1988, some of the Eastwood commissioners and council members were horrified when they began to see the collective impact of separate projects they had routinely approved during the era of permissive regulation.'

Ironically, the other factor in the deterioration of Carmel was the tourist boom inspired by the mayor himself. On this front, he proved ready to countermand his own permissive business climate by stamping on the rampant 'Clintabilia' that swept through the town. The worst offender was his erstwhile opponent turned ally, Paul Laub, who opened a shop called Clintville to peddle vulgar souvenirs, an enterprise that had generated twenty thousand dollars by October 1986. Laub's best-sellers were cheap t-shirts bearing badly printed slogans like 'Go ahead and jaywalk – make my day!' or 'No punks! Go ahead punks – make my day!' Even more offensively, there were panties reading 'Go ahead, Clint – make my night!' At first, Eastwood asked the merchants to split their profits on such items with his favourite local charity, the Carmel Youth Center, but later he instructed his lawyers to write to the offending merchants and ask them not to re-stock. As most had made their killing by this time, they agreed. 'At first it seemed nice to donate money to the Youth Center,' Eastwood commented, 'but it has gotten out of hand – people are suing each other over the use of the name, Clintville. Besides, I have the feeling that people here don't like it. I think it's time to end it.'

In this, he was right. 'Clint's real impact has been that we have some pretty tacky-looking tourists, infinitely lower than any we've had before. They're t-shirt, ice-cream people,' said Sandy Swain. She was hardly a dispassionate observer as she was one of the sacked planning commissioners, but she was not alone in her protests. 'I think it was almost impossible for him to accomplish anything,' commented Jane Mayer, the president of the residents' association. 'We wanted to eliminate traffic and parking problems, not make more with hordes of tourists. He brought a lot of notoriety that we didn't need. Some people thought he was charming, but I disagree. He didn't know anything about the issues. People are giving him credit for things that were on the table for years. He also hired a public relations woman and kept an unlisted phone number. He was totally inaccessible. I don't think that's being a good mayor.'

No doubt many community stalwarts agreed with these opinions but there were others, like Hariette Rowntree, an inveterate joiner of committees for improving Carmel, who took a more progressive view. 'Clint has learned a little diplomacy and tact, that you can't ride into town and shoot things down like he does in movies. The real story is that he has galvanised the community and caused the younger people to wake up and save their community.'

By 1988, he'd decided that enough community service was enough, so he passed his mayoral mantle to his friend Jean Grace, who saw off her anti-commerce opponent, Clayton Anderson, by 1,444 votes to 868. 'I stood for office because, at a time in my life when I was no longer totally satisfied with my celebrity, I was tempted to go in a new direction. When you know that you already have the audience waiting for you, the temptation is very great. I didn't stand for a second term because I have children, Kyle, aged twenty, and Alison, aged sixteen, and I want to spend time with them. They are at an important age and I don't want to live with regrets over not sharing as much as possible with them at this stage. Raising children in the present atmosphere of drugs and teen suicide is frightening. Nobody wants to be the fathers you read about in the papers. You are probably talking to the one person in Hollywood who has never even tried cocaine. Beer is fine for me.'

Before he handed over the gavel to Grace, a glamorous athletic fifty-two-year-old blonde whom he counted among his closer women friends, on 18 September 1987, Mayor Eastwood was one of twenty local political and clerical dignitaries who welcomed His Holiness Pope John Paul II when he landed at Monterey airport. On a less serious note, he contributed his recipe for Hearty American Apple Pie to *The Mayor's Cookbook*, a publication that also included a blueprint for Pasta Primavera from Ed Koch, then mayor of New York, among its three hundred delicacies.

In 1987, Eastwood won the unchallenged approval of all Carmelites by dipping into his pockets and coming up with

$5.5 million to buy the Mission Ranch, a twenty-two acre site overlooking the estuary of the Carmel River just outside the town. It had originally been part of a two-hundred-acre estate established in the mid nineteenth century by a Scottish immigrant couple called Martin. Later it became a dairy farm, then an officers' club, complete with swimming-pool and polo field, for nearby Fort Ord. Eastwood remembered it from his army days as a good place to get a cheap meal, but by the time he was mayor, the straggle of buildings had deteriorated into a transient's hotel, a 'seedy refuge for travelling salesmen and illicit couples', as the *Architectural Review* put it. At this point, developers moved in with intent to cash in on the spectacular view by building condominiums.

'I'd always loved the place and they were just going to flatten it. They said it was obsolete. I thought it should be preserved as what it was,' Eastwood commented. His first solution was to put together a financial package to rescue it, but when that failed he bought it himself. Whether he would have come to the same decision if he'd known exactly what was involved is open to question, but so far he has remained true to a project that he will consider a success if it breaks even in his lifetime. Over the years, he has replaced the wiring and the plumbing and built thirty-one luxurious guest rooms of the kind favoured by small conferences.

Alan Williams, an architect from the Carmel Development Company, oversaw the restoration, and Eastwood supplied some of the furnishings from his movie sets. The rest was designed by his golfing pal, Edgar Broyhill, a manufacturer from North Carolina who was responsible for the Mission Ranch Collection. The results are solid and comfortable, with lots of deep cushions to keep customers lounging at their ease. Eastwood's current partner, Frances Fisher, has enhanced the effect with pretty quilts and blueprints for elaborate flower arrangements. 'She cares more about details. I see the big picture,' was Clint's verdict.

In the grounds, the renovated bar and restaurant provide a lively meeting place when local pianists play on Saturday nights, and tennis courts and a fully equipped gym are currently under construction. 'I don't buy anything I don't love but when you open up a place like this, it's like the bear who climbs a hill to see the next hill and the next hill. It never ends. There's a big difference between doing preservation and advocating preservation. It's different to put your money where your mouth is.'

As his term as mayor came to an end, speculation grew as to whether Eastwood would do a Ronald Reagan and expand his career into national politics. There were rumours that both he and Charlton Heston, a fellow Republican, might challenge for the governership of California, the Reagan route to the White House, in the 1990 election. In the end, neither did, and Clint has consistently denied that his political horizons ever extended beyond his own parish. 'That was said by a lot of people but never by me,' he told me in 1990. 'My ambitions were only for my own community. I think I achieved quite a bit by winning with a large margin and approaching the problems from a business point of view. Previously all the councillors were schoolteachers. There's nothing wrong with schoolteachers but they haven't had any business experience.'

On an earlier occasion, he confessed to a level of boredom with the parochial discussions in the council chamber. He also hinted at what is probably the real reason for his decision not to take any further steps down the road to the White House. 'Most of the offices beyond being mayor of a small community require retiring from the motion picture business and I had no intention of doing that.' They also require digging deep into a personal fortune, and he had even less intention of doing that.

16

Jazzing It Up

No one denies that Clint Eastwood gave Carmel his best shot during his term as mayor, but a 'nitpicky' monthly council meeting and an annual salary of $2,400 were nowhere near enough to satisfy his appetites for work and profit. During his term of office, he found time to make three films which illustrate the ambiguities that underpin his choices. The first was *Heartbreak Ridge*, a gung-ho drama based on the training of the US Marines but with a soul-searching role for its star. The second was the Charlie Parker jazz biopic *Bird*, a long-cherished labour of love. The third was *Dead Pool*, featuring Harry Callahan.

As actors who make their names with cowboys and cops invariably do, Eastwood had found occasion to diversify into the armed forces. The randy Yankee soldier in *The Beguiled* was one of his better early roles, but his twentieth century excursions into the military, *Where Eagles Dare* and *Firefox*, were way off target. As he didn't fight in Korea and he was too old for Vietnam, he has no personal experience of combat but, as a lifelong Republican, he had a degree of sympathy for his country's chosen role as global policeman. In 1982, he'd put his money where his mouth was by donating thirty thousand dollars to help finance a search for American prisoners of war listed as missing in action in South-East Asia.

According to newspaper reports, a much-decorated ex-Green Beret, Lt–Col James 'Bo' Grits, led three of his fellow US Army veterans and fifteen Laotian guerillas on a commando raid codenamed 'Lazarus'. Its purpose was to locate one hundred Americans said to be imprisoned on the borders of Laos and Thailand and it was known to, but not authorised by, the US Defense Department. When it failed after one mercenary died and three were seriously wounded in a mortar attack, Grits remained in South-East Asia while his three colleagues returned to America to sell their stories to *Soldier of Fortune* magazine. *Star Trek*'s William Shatner claimed that his donation of ten thousand dollars was paid solely in return for the film rights to Grits's life story, but Eastwood, who had no such fallback, remained silent.

Heartbreak Ridge was just the kind of movie that a man who sympathised with American intervention, legal or illegal, in the affairs of smaller nations might be expected to make. Eastwood directed himself as Gunnery Sergeant Tom Highway, a veteran of Korea and Vietnam who'd won a Congressional Medal of Honor for courage in the face of enemy fire. Highway is typical of the Eastwood characters of the eighties, a man past his prime who has kept professional control while allowing disappointment to take its toll of his private life. Like his predecessors in *Honkytonk Man* and *Tightrope*, he is a drinker and a womaniser facing a lonely and unfulfilled old age. 'Yeah,' said Eastwood, 'he's a bit of a screw-up. He's been a problem solver, a brawler, a fighter from the old infantry school, and he's all scarred up. Now he's at a crossroads in his life and career, approaching mandatory retirement and trying to come to terms with the world he'll be facing after the service.'

According to a scenario that borrowed heavily from earlier movies – most obviously from the 1949 John Wayne genre classic *The Sands of Iwo Jima* – Tom Highway has one last chance to make good by moulding a band of undisciplined and foul-mouthed recruits into a tight-knit fighting unit. In a military extension of his Dirty Harry mode, Eastwood is in perpetual conflict with his superiors and also with what he sees as his low-calibre raw material. Where are the standards of yesteryear, he demands as he sets out to win the respect and loyalty of the recruits through the vicious authoritarianism that is customary in such movies. And, come the inglorious American invasion of Grenada in 1983, his strategy in vindicated.

Heartbreak Ridge went before the cameras in 1986 shortly after the Carmel victory. The producer-director-star spent a lot of time selecting supporting players who include Everett McGill, Moses Gunn and Bo Svenson from tests taped by his casting director, Phyllis Huffman. 'Basically, I can't interview actors because I've been in their position myself. I've been there too many years of my life, sat with producers who didn't know their ass and had no idea what they were looking for. I just can't put actors through that, and I hate to build up people to think that they're really close to something and then have to turn them down.'

For the wife Highway is trying to win back after years of infidelity, he chose Marsha Mason. She'd walked away from *City Heat* when her part was re-written so drastically that she could no longer relate to it, but now she responded eagerly to Clint's call. 'He's extremely down to earth, very unspoiled, very modest, with a great sense of humour. He's certainly not Dirty Harry. He has none of that character's intensity, wariness or sense of menace. He's very relaxed on the set but, if things should ever get a little tense, he knows how to take the edge off with a little wit. And he just exudes self-confidence, a confidence that is very infectious.'

Behind the cameras, it was business as usual, according to Jack N. Green, elevated to director of photography for the first time. After fifteen years as camera operator for Bruce Surtees, he'd learned how Eastwood liked to work. 'There's no trick to lighting,' Surtees once said. 'You turn on a light, and if it looks good, you use it. If it doesn't, you turn if off and put it some other place.' Green has taken this philosophy to its limits on a string of Malpaso films which now includes *Unforgiven* and *A Perfect World*. He's also learned to appreciate his employer's kindness and loyalty. 'Every person working on the set is important to Clint. Even after all this time, the depth of his concern for people's feelings still surprises me. One crew person had to leave the set of *Heartbreak Ridge* because of a family problem and Clint came over to me, right in the middle of the picture, and asked, "Jack, what happened? Is there anything we can do?"'

Heartbreak Ridge started out with the full backing of the US Defense Department. When Taylor Hackford's *An Officer and a Gentleman* opened in 1981, it was noted by the military that the deprivations endured by Richard Gere as he trained under a sadistic sergeant proved to be an unexpectedly powerful recruiting aid. In a sponsorship-conscious age, they decided to co-operate with selected films by providing access to military bases and equipment in return for presumed benefits to come. In 1986, they struck the jackpot with Ridley Scott's *Top Gun*, a banal story linked to breathtaking aerial sequences which triggered flyboy mania among Tom Cruise wannabes nationwide.

When they saw *Heartbreak Ridge* at a special screening on 14 November 1986, they were not so amused. Why, they demanded, did these supposedly wholesome role models use language fit only for the gutter? 'We were told by a general and a civilian lady in the Pentagon that this is the new military, the new army,' Eastwood explained. 'They seemed to feel that back in World War II and Korea, it was a different era, a different military. And now it's a whole new deal, and the new people talk this way or do this or that which is all bullshit. I said, "I imagine that people who served in World War II and in Korea and Vietnam might resent that. Are you putting down all those people who fought and died for their country? That was all crap and this is all so great and new now?" And they said, "Oh, no, no, no." But they really were in a way. It's all built on more of a glamorous high-tech public relations deal.'

Although members of the Marine Corps confirmed the film's authenticity, the big brass withdrew their support. As a result, tributes to the Marines were removed from the credits and benefit screenings were cancelled. From Eastwood's point of view, military action was a cause for some financial celebration. After positive publicity resulting from what was seen as official heavy-handedness had pulled in massive crowds, his share of the pay-off was estimated at six million dollars.

Kurt Jacobsen of the *Guardian* put *Heartbreak Ridge* into the *Tightrope* rather than the Dirty Harry mould, praising Eastwood for his portrayal of a macho man plagued by self-doubts and the realisation that he has destroyed his wife's love for pleasure. 'Despite a conventional storyline and a sequence celebrating the US triumph over mighty Grenada,' he wrote, 'Eastwood miraculously made Sergeant Tom Highway a poignant and affecting character, a man a little lost in the present, who earnestly leafs through women's magazines for clues to help him win back and "mutually nurture" a sceptical ex-wife he still loves. In these memorable roles, Eastwood has the courage to appear as a confused and hurt man and works through that pain to new insight and understanding.'

From the outset, Eastwood knew that *Bird* would never make a comparable return on its capital investment, but ever since Joel Oliansky's screenplay had surfaced at Columbia eight years earlier, he'd been putting pressure on Warner Bros to buy it for him. Eventually they traded it for *Revenge*, a project that later became a failure for Kevin Costner. Eastwood's fascination with Charlie 'Bird' Parker began in 1945, the year the fifteen-year-old Clint first lied about his age to play ragtime and blues on the piano at the Omar Club in Oakland in exchange for free meals and tips. 'I was proficient for my age but I didn't have the discipline at the time. I was too busy chasing chicks and doing the things kids do.' Although his musical taste had shifted towards country in the intervening years, his memories of the Oakland concert at which he heard the legendary saxophonist transforming familiar favourites through soaring flights of improvisation was undimmed by time.

Parker's short life mixed triumph and tragedy in equal measure. In his childhood, he learned to play the saxophone on the porch of the family home in Kansas City, Missouri, then left school at an early age to pursue a career in music. He spent much of his adolescence trying to get into the Reno Club where Count Basie used to play. It was here that he was first called Yardbird, a nickname that was corrupted to Bird when he went to New York. By Eastwood's account, the name was an affectionate tribute to his tenacity – like a chicken in a hencoop, as he put it – but others ascribed it to the large quantities of chicken he ate during his vigil outside the club. If so, his excessive appetite was an early sign of an addictive personality that soon branched out into drugs and alcohol. At fifteen, he was hooked on heroin, at sixteen, he was married, and at thirty-four, he was dead. When he was found slumped in front of the television in March 1955, the doctor said he had the physique of a sixty-year-old man. The official verdict was pneumonia exacerbated by ulcers, but the reality was heroin: despite several periods in detoxification clinics, he had taken so many shots that he hadn't a vein left to inject.

For Eastwood, Parker's experiences evoked the well-worked phrase from Scott Fitzgerald's *The Last Tycoon* – 'there is no second act in an American life' – and his film was designed to emphasise Bird's struggle with his demons. Eastwood himself had never had any truck with demons – his youthful guideline was 'if there's anything better than a woman and a cold beer, you better not tell me about it because it might kill me' – so it can be assumed that he felt an attraction of opposites for Parker. On one level, he explained it by saying that America, in all its long history, had only produced two genuinely original forms of expression, jazz and the western. 'Sometimes we treat them as a joke which is ridiculous because they are an integral part of our culture and they bridge the gap between our present and our past.'

By taking this analysis a step further, he decided that he had a mission to explain one of America's great jazz icons to his own people. 'I felt I was destined to make *Bird*, though I doubt I could have done it ten or fifteen years earlier,' he commented. 'Charlie Parker was living in the fast lane. Everything he did was to excess. He was going to soar high and fast but it was going to be a short existence. He knew he was hooked but he went out of his way to stop others from getting into the same thing. He was acutely aware that he was adversely affecting a whole generation of jazz saxophonists who felt they had to indulge in drugs to play like him.' As a health and exercise freak, Eastwood stressed the 'do as I say, not as I do' aspects of Parker's philosophy in a sombre, brooding film that pulls no punches on the agonising detail of his spiral into despair.

The basis of Oliansky's screenplay was a memoir written by Bird's common-law wife, Chan Richardson, his companion through his last seven years. When they met in the late forties, she was a New York model with an apartment that soon became a meeting place for the luminaries of the be-bop movement. From the outset, their relationship was turbulent, with Parker moving out whenever the going got too rough. On one occasion, he decamped to Los Angeles, on another to Chan's mother's house in the country.

Even before *Bird* got the green light from the studio, Eastwood tracked Chan Richardson down to her house outside Paris to invite her contributions. As much of Parker's later life was seen through her eyes in a script that played a lot of tricks with time and place, it was a logical move, but the director had no idea that she held the key to Eldorado. Over the years, he'd heard rumours of lost Parker tapes but it was only when he asked Chan where they were and she answered him by unlocking her bank vault that he learned the truth. Time had resulted in deterioration, but Parker's original saxophone solos were in good enough condition to build into the film's soundtrack. Using state-of-the-art technical wizardry, Lennie Niehaus faded the piano and string-bass sounds out of the recordings and replaced them with music for new instruments. Niehaus, a friend of Eastwood's since they first met as corporals in the US Army in 1952, had scored his last four pictures. On *Bird*, his expertise received its just reward: an Academy Award for Best Achievement in Sound.

As Eastwood hadn't directed a film in which he didn't appear since *Breezy* fourteen years before, he had to be more meticulous than usual about casting the title role. Although he toyed with the idea of using a jazz musician, as Bertrand Tavernier had used Dexter Gordon in *Round Midnight*, his final choice was Forest Whitaker. Best known at this early stage of his career as the kid who hustled Paul Newman in *The Colour of Money*, he had the physique to suggest gargantuan appetites, if not heroin addiction. With the help of Lennie Niehaus, he learned the techniques for playing the saxophone, and there was an added bonus in the shape of a younger brother who stood in for him as the adolescent Parker in the Kansas City scenes. 'Forest is an excellent actor and undoubtedly underrated,' Eastwood offered. 'He has a natural spontaneity combined with a charismatic calm that is very similar to Charlie's.

He understood exactly what we wanted to do with the film so he was able to invest an enormous amount of himself in the part.' Diane Venora, who'd cross-gendered as Hamlet at the New York Shakespeare Festival in 1982, played Chan, with Sam Wright as Charlie Parker's fellow be-bop pioneer Dizzy Gillespie.

Bird was made in the studio and on location in New York over nine weeks in the autumn of 1987 for less than ten million dollars. As was his habit, Eastwood ran a tight but happy ship. 'He was sweet-tempered when I knew him in the Army and he's the same gentle man now,' said Niehaus. 'You never hear him yell.' His opinion was warmly endorsed by *Bird*'s executive producer, David Valdes, a Malpaso team player since he worked as second assistant on *Any Which Way You Can* in 1980. 'Tempers never flare. You're never walking on eggshells. On a lot of sets, there is always a panic. I always schedule tight but Clint always gets ahead. It's never "let's get one more shot for insurance."'

It came as no surprise that the American critics loved *Bird*. It prompted *Time* magazine to describe Eastwood as 'a major American director'. Pauline Kael got in her crack, 'the picture looks as if Eastwood hasn't paid his Con Edison bill', in reference to *Bird*'s muted lighting. Nor was it unexpected that the American public shunned it so thoroughly that it only took $2.2 million domestically. It broke new ground in the matter of awards, winning Eastwood a Golden Globe from the Los Angeles Foreign Press Association for Best Direction and an NAACP (National Association for the Advancement of Colored People) award for the way he treated ethnic minorities in his work. This was a tribute to the on-screen romance between Charlie and Chan, a rare example of a relationship between a black man and a white woman in American films in the late eighties. 'I never saw that as a problem,'

Eastwood commented. 'I just did it straight.' Nevertheless, his acceptance of the prize at a televised ceremony raised a few quizzical eyebrows among those who recalled the range of ethnic scumbags who had been blown away by Dirty Harry in his prime.

The plaudits continued at the Cannes Film Festival in 1988. Eastwood, in buoyant mood in his new role as non-acting director, held court in the Eden Roc beach restaurant at the exclusive Hotel du Cap in Antibes. He wore his uniform jeans, shades, trainers and t-shirt, his pumping-iron muscles bulging out of the sleeves. 'I like being a director so I can dress like a bum, my usual fashion,' he told the world's press gathered eagerly around him for a rare Eastwood audience. Later that day, sleek, even aristocratic, in dinner jacket, pleated shirt and black tie, he trod the red carpet up the Palais steps with Sondra on his arm. 'I've loved her for ten years,' he said firmly at what would prove to be their last public display of togetherness. When the winners were announced, they included Forest Whitaker as Best Actor.

Even before this peak, the seeds of the next Eastwood trough had been sown in the form of *The Dead Pool*, a fifth, worst and hopefully final outing for Inspector Harry Callahan of the San Francisco Police Department. Eastwood's excuse for this blatant exercise in commercialism was that he was now the same age as the character written nearly twenty years earlier for Frank Sinatra, so he'd finally grown into him. Then again Harry had become such an old and valued friend that it was nice to look in on him now and again just to see how he was getting on.

The title refers not to a stagnant pond but to a list of San Francisco celebrities – no doubt it appealed to Eastwood's sense of humour to make one of them a film critic – who have died or are slated to die on the orders of a crime lord. As this arch-villain has just been put behind bars by the force's finest, the name of Harry Callahan is rapidly promoted to the top of the list and the television crews latch on to his every move in the hope of catching it live if it should be his last. Harry romances a TV newswoman and blows away a gang of would-be assassins who dare to interrupt his meal in a Chinese restaurant, but the best of this torpid show is a chase in which his car is pursued by a radio-controlled model packed with explosives.

After his stint in the sticks in *Sudden Impact*, Harry returned to the streets of San Francisco in February and March 1988. Diane Feinstein, approaching the end of her term as mayor just as Eastwood was, gave permission for the cameras to turn in the face of vociferous protest from citizens who objected to Harry Callahan as a representative of their forces of law and order. Perhaps because he'd enjoyed directing without acting on *Bird*, Eastwood now chose to act without directing in *The Dead Pool*. This opened the door to the ex-stuntman Buddy Van Horn. He'd already directed Eastwood in *Any Which Way You Can*, one of Malpaso's least satisfactory pictures in any except the commercial sense. Van Horn now confirmed his ability to touch the lowest common denominator with *The Dead Pool*, a film of no artistic merit which nonetheless took eighty million dollars at the box office.

It fell to Kurt Jacobsen to provide a fitting obituary for a cop whose deftness with a long-barrelled .44 Magnum made him an archetypal symbol of potency for men and women alike. '*The Dead Pool* rounds up the usual story elements, puts the surly inspector though his violent paces, and you like the result or you don't. At this juncture, one suspects that Eastwood himself is among those who don't. Just look at the tediously macho role. Here's a cop who takes every street crime as a personal affront and reacts accordingly. Again and again he has proven impervious to small-arms fire, self-doubt and soft emotions

– which is hardly challenging for an actor, unless you are Arnold Schwarzenegger.'

Not so, said Eastwood. 'If I am convincing as Harry, it is because I am a good actor. Harry is a bitter man, a bastard who fights against laws that he considers too flexible, and I believe that's a role I play well. On the screen, that is, not in real life.'

He may have been saying farewell to Harry Callahan but he endorsed Buddy Van Horn's treatment of him by hiring him to direct his next picture, *Pink Cadillac*, a comedy action drama set in the contemporary American West. In physical form, this translated into the desert of Nevada and northern California, with its stretches of open scrubland and pine-covered hills. Clint's character is a latter-day bounty-hunter who makes a living out of delivering bail-jumpers to justice, but there is no trace of The Man with No Name in contemporary clothing. Tommy Nowak is more of a Philo Beddoe re-born without his orang-utan, a drifter who dons a number of disguises in the course of his duties, including the big red nose of a rodeo clown. The title refers to his favourite car, a 1959 convertible De Ville stolen at the outset by Bernadette Peters but later regained after the appropriate romantic sparks have been struck.

Before shooting, Peters had been worried by her co-star's well-known reluctance to spend time and money on a lot of takes, but she was quick to revise her opinion. 'I soon fell into the swing of it which is to capture every moment of what happens. You can't do that with every actor but Clint is so right there that he makes it easy to work off each other. It was a good lesson he taught me.'

Although the American critics universally loathed *Pink Cadillac*, it showed a healthy profit by making the top five in the box-office ratings. Despite this, it is the only Clint Eastwood film not to be released theatrically in Britain.

Allegedly Warner Bros were reluctant to spoil Clint's image with such a lightweight movie in the run-up to the prestigious *White Hunter, Black Heart*, so fans had to wait until it surfaced in the video rental market in September 1991. 'It's something different,' he said defensively.

More importantly, it introduced him to Frances Fisher, the English-born strawberry blonde who has a minor role in the movie. As the daughter of a construction superintendent, she and her brother and sister spent their childhood moving between sites in Bogotá, Milan and Rio de Janeiro. Eventually the family settled in Orange, Texas, but Frances went to New York when she was nineteen to marry a man she has always refused to talk about. When they divorced two years later, she built up a low-profile career on the New York stage, then re-located in Los Angeles in the mid eighties with a view to getting into the movies. She managed to keep going with roles in *Patty Hearst* (as the terrorist Emily Harris) and *L.A. Story*, but there is no doubt that *Pink Cadillac* was her big break. When she saw Clint Eastwood at the kick-off party, her first impression was 'he doesn't look so tough'. 'He's got such a gentle bearing in real life,' she added. 'We had a very good connection right away.'

Was this because she was a tiny, fragile blonde like Sondra Locke or because her wandering youth had given her an independence that appealed to him? A bit of both, perhaps, but he knew where to turn for consolation as he moved into one of the most turbulent years of his life.

17

White Lover, Black Heart

Throughout their love affair, Clint and Sondra had spent Christmas in Sun Valley, the first glamour resort in the Rockies. It owes its existence to the Union Pacific Railway, which ran some miles away from the Idaho mining town of Ketchum, Sun Valley's big brother. By 1932, the decline in mining meant that most of the passenger cars were empty, much to the chagrin of Chairman Averell Harriman, especially as the Interstate Commerce Commission insisted that they continue providing the loss-making service. His solution was to throw $685,000 and a branch line at a mountain selected by an Alpine skiing pal, Count Felix Schaffgotsch.

The result was Sun Valley, named by a canny publicist and embellished with one of the world's earliest chairlifts, a device that applied the techniques used for shifting stems of bananas on to ships in the Panama Canal area to the human frame. For bananas, read skiers, but unfortunately no one thought about snow when the world's first chairlift was installed on Dollar Mountain in August 1936. Come the winter, the chairs were embedded, even without the bodies. No matter. Hollywood, lured by freebies and intrigued by a novel sport, flocked to Sun Valley Lodge, still a veritable hall of photo fame for the likes of Bing Crosby, Gary Cooper, Marilyn Monroe, Clark Gable, Judy Garland, Katharine Hepburn and Spencer Tracy. Ernest Hemingway wrote *For Whom the Bell Tolls* in Room 208, then built himself a permanent home in Ketchum. He committed suicide there in 1961, but his granddaughter, Margaux, still lives in his house.

And Hollywood still comes to Sun Valley. There are no names on the letter boxes along Prospector Road, an exclusive residential street overlooking the golf course, but if there were, they would read like a studio roll-call: Schwarzenegger, Willis, Dreyfuss, Lee Curtis, Shields, Zanuck, and, discreetly tucked away at the very end of the loop, Eastwood. Schwarzenegger and Zanuck have gone for conspicuous opulence, with homes lit up like casinos in full fiesta, but the Eastwood house is as understated as its owner, a dark, silent wood-clad building in which the money is where the people are: inside. However, it wasn't silent over Christmas 1988, not anyway on the day Clint and Sondra had the row that broke the camel's back. It ended with Clint ordering her out of the house.

Back in Los Angeles in January, the couple set about untangling their lives with the minimum of fuss. Over the years, there had been newspaper reports that Sondra was pregnant, that Clint had given her a $200,000 diamond engagement ring, and that they would marry, but the reality was that she was still Mrs Gordon Anderson, dividing her time between the Bel Air mansion she shared with Clint and the $650,000 Crescent Heights home he'd bought for her to share with her husband. The early negotiations in January 1989 seemed amicable enough, with Locke receiving an assurance from her attorney, Norman Oberstein, that there would be some sort of settlement for her.

Three months later, when she was directing her second film, *Impulse*, a thriller about a cop (played by Theresa Russell) who was working undercover as a hooker, Locke learned that her lover wasn't nicknamed Skinclint for nothing. Early in the morning on 3 April, a phone call informed her that Eastwood was on his way to their Bel Air home. When he arrived, he was brief and to the point: Locke was 'sitting' on his only real estate in Los Angeles and he wanted her out. 'I told him that I couldn't believe that was all he had to say to me after thirteen years,' said Locke in the written declaration she filed on 26 April in the Los Angeles Superior Court. She also claimed that this was her first intimation that their romance was irrevocably over. She'd only had four hours' sleep the night before and she was due on the set, so she asked Eastwood to delay matters until filming was completed. 'Clint told me that he understood, that I should just put it "in the back of my head" and that we would talk about it again after I finished *Impulse*.'

A week later, a letter arrived on the set addressed to Mrs Gordon Anderson. It was from Eastwood's lawyers and its message was succinct and brutal: 'Mr Eastwood has asked you to vacate the premises. You have refused to do so. This is to let you know that in view of your intransigence, the locks on all the entrances to the house have been replaced. Your possessions accordingly have been placed in storage.' By her own account, Sondra fainted. When she revived, she had no option but to return to her husband. Because she was too busy to get her clothes out of storage, she had to borrow from friends. She was also distressed that Eastwood had taken her pet parrot, Putty, and her 1971 Mercedes.

By her account, Eastwood had talked frequently about marriage without ever getting to the point of naming a day. However, they had lived as man and wife for thirteen years, whereas Sondra and Gordon had an unconsummated marriage and a relationship 'tantamount to brother and sister'. During their time together, Locke claimed that Eastwood persuaded her to have two abortions and then a sterilisation operation. He denied this, saying that Locke had told him on several occasions that she never wanted children. 'I felt so disappointed and the disappointment was with myself,' he said with an egotism that must have infuriated Locke.

'How could I have been such a bad judge of character?'

On a more official level, he denied the allegations through his lawyers. 'I adamantly deny and deeply resent the accusation that either one of those abortions or the tubal ligation were done at my demand, request or even suggestion. As to the abortions, I told Locke that whether to have children or terminate her pregnancies was a decision entirely hers. Particularly with regard to the tubal ligation, I encouraged Locke to make her own decision after she had consulted with a physician about the appropriateness of and the necessity for that surgical procedure.' Given that he has fathered children by three different women, in and out of marriage, this has the ring of truth, though it does rather beg the question as to why two such intelligent people should have been so inept at contraception.

Locke's declaration insisted that Eastwood had said that their partnership would be permanent from an early stage and that he would always look after her. She also said that her career had failed to develop because she was in his shadow, an unjust accusation in that he'd given her prominent roles at a time few people wanted to employ her and had helped her to get the money to make her own films at Warner Bros. 'Clint repeatedly assured me that regardless of whether we were married, everything he had was ours together,' she said.

It is easy to imagine that the rift was caused by Eastwood's term as mayor of Carmel. Maggie and Clint had always been a popular couple, eager participants in pro-am golf and tennis tournaments and supportive of local causes. As Maggie was a permanent resident, it is hardly surprising that a town as small and cliquey as Carmel failed to extend a warm welcome to Sondra. 'Ten years ago, Clint was out on the town several evenings a week,' said mine host at the popular Jack London bar in October 1993. 'He'd have a few beers with some of his mates but Sondra was never with him.

We hardly ever see him now but then he's old, isn't he?'

Locke herself said that being mayor meant that her lover spent a lot of time in Carmel while she remained in Los Angeles. 'During this period I began to sense some increasing tension and estrangement in our relationship. I frequently tried to speak to Clint about these problems, but he never wanted to do so. He would often discourage me from accompanying him to Carmel, and over the past year or year and a half he has stayed in Los Angeles only infrequently.' No doubt she suspected infidelity during his absences in Carmel, especially as the easy-going holiday town had always been described as his happiest hunting ground for casual sexual encounters. According to journalist Simon Kinnersley, every wannabe in the area who could conceivably become a fragile blonde lookalike took the steps necessary to do so.

Given the nature of her complaints and the wealth of her lover, Locke's initial demands seem modest. Topping the list were the houses in Bel Air and the Hollywood Hills, now valued at four million and one million dollars respectively. She also asked the court to ban Eastwood from the Bel Air house because 'I know him to have a terrible temper and he has frequently been abusive to me'. In addition, she wanted a one-off payment of $250,000, plus $15,000 a month for four years, $12,500 a month in the fifth year, $10,000 a month in the sixth year, and $7,500 a month in the seventh year, in total just over $1.3 million. 'It would have been easy and tempting to inflate Sondra's settlement request for negotiating purposes or to be simply opportunistic,' Oberstein wrote in a letter to Eastwood's lawyers. 'Our objective is neither to gather the last dollar nor to obtain a settlement in light of Clint's substantial ability to pay; rather, it is to meet Sondra's minimum expectations in light of a thirteen-year-relationship, Clint's promises and the emotional and economic time and effort

Sondra put into the relationship and into the two properties which she selected and developed.'

Eastwood's legendary financial acumen should have dictated that he accept these terms, but being stubborn and tight-fisted by nature and totally unaccustomed to not getting his own way, he didn't. Locke's reaction was to file a palimony suit demanding a quoted seventy million dollars, still substantially less than the fifty-fifty split of the huge Eastwood fortune that she could have claimed under Californian law. The precedent for palimony had been established by Marvin Mitchelson in 1975 when he represented actress Michelle Triola in her case against Lee Marvin. However, Locke's case was complicated by the fact that it was the first time a married partner had sued a common-law lover. 'I'm deeply disappointed and saddened that she's taken this kind of action,' said Eastwood through his publicist on 27 April. 'It will soon come to light that these accusations are unfounded and without merit. However, this matter will be dealt with in an appropriate legal arena.'

And so it was. The first hearing took place on 31 May 1989, in front of an unnamed Superior Court judge hired privately by the contestants. The private hiring of judges was a relatively new but increasingly popular tactic, especially in high-profile civil disputes like this one. Although the legal documents in the case were ordered sealed, the *Los Angeles Times* acquired copies of the whole of Locke's deposition and part of Eastwood's. In an article entitled 'In the Matter of Locke vs Eastwood', which appeared on 8 May 1989, Claudia Puig reported extensively on the whole affair.

In a second article published on the day of the closed hearing by the same writer, Eastwood expressed anger that correspondence between counsel and details of settlement proposals should have fallen into the hands of the media, especially when the court had sealed the file. Locke and her lawyer must have realised that the only weapon she had was the tale she had to tell, at least at that time. Before the matter was finally settled in a private out-of-court agreement on 28 March 1991, she survived two operations for breast cancer. She ascribed the disease to stress over her break-up with Eastwood, but whether or not her illness moved him to generosity is not known as the details of the settlement have never been disclosed. If the quoted figure of $5.5 million, some of it in real estate, is correct, it is close to Locke's original demand. Certainly her lover understood that his privacy was at risk because she promised not to write a book about her Eastwood years, nor to speak about them to the media, in return for whatever sum she received. 'The matter was amicably settled to the mutual satisfaction of both parties,' said Norman Oberstein conclusively.

The cynical might think that 'amicably' was window-dressing, but the fact that Locke signed a three-year deal with Warner Bros later in 1991 suggests otherwise. The non-exclusive contract gives the studio first look at all projects initiated by Locke's newly formed Caritas Films. As Clint Eastwood is responsible for a massive eighteen per cent of the studio's revenue, they would never have signed his ex-lover without his approval, so it can be assumed that the animosity dissipated fairly rapidly once the settlement was finalised. Even in the absence of her lover's shadow, Locke's career as a director has yet to take off; she has just one credit, the television movie *Death in Small Doses*, to her credit in the intervening years. In Hollywood terms, her approach is relatively cerebral, with none of the populist touch that underpins the Eastwood canon.

For the actor, 1989 was a year that didn't get any easier. The world's press, already hot on his trail over the palimony suit, found more fuel for scandal when their investigations revealed the existence of Roxanne, Kimber and Clinton

Tunis. The reporters who hit the jackpot, Annie Leask and Mike Kerrigan, got hold of Kimber's birth certificate which named her father as Clinton Eastwood Junior, then tracked her down to the Avenue Grill in Denver where she worked as a waitress. She allegedly told them, 'Yes, Clint Eastwood is my father. I must speak to him about this. I am partly shocked and partly glad it is all out in the open. I don't know what he will think about this. I have to talk to him and find out how he feels about it all.'

In recent years, Clint's eldest child had divorced Anthony Gaddie and made plans to marry twenty-eight-year-old Doug McCartney. Originally trained as a construction engineer, he now ran a valet parking business in Denver. He was also something of a sports jock, teaching soccer and playing for a local team, which gave him something to talk to his future father-in-law about. By all accounts, they got on very well when they first met early in 1989. According to McCartney, there had never been any secret about the identity of Kimber's father through the two years he'd known her. 'I'm fond of her for who and what she is in her own right. She's really a lovely person,' he said, adding that young Clinton was a shy child who seldom strayed from his mother's side and preferred reading to racing around playing cowboys and Indians.

Hardly a chip off the old block, but Eastwood never denied that he was his grandson and saw him whenever he could until his true identity was made public. It has been reported that Kimber's eagerness to claim her father and her decision to change her own and her son's surname to Eastwood has led to a cooling of relations between them. Naturally it is not a topic he will discuss, but she has no such reservations. At their first meeting after the news broke, a dinner in an expensive restaurant, she begged him to spend more time with her and he promised he would. 'I felt sure he meant it but I have tried to make an appointment to see him and he always has other commitments.'

It is not known how the journalists got on to the story, but one who claimed to be the source was Frances Stevenson. In the *News of the World* on 9 July 1989 she said that she went in fear of the actor after spilling the beans and warned him that she was armed and dangerous. She described him as obsessed with sex, with a special preference for bondage, citing as examples his making love to Roxanne in her apartment and later sitting on a chair with his hands tied together with a golden sash. This was too much even for Eastwood who promptly slapped a writ for libel on the newspaper. They paid a 'large sum' in an out-of-court settlement and published a retraction, 'We're Sorry, Clint!', on 9 August. 'The apology was the most important thing to me,' he said. 'I have not embarked on this to make a profit and whatever money I end up with, after all this, I shall pay over to various charities, including the Cinema and Television Benevolent Fund here in Britain.'

Meanwhile Maggie Eastwood was having romantic troubles of her own, triggered by the discovery that Henry Wynberg was a spendthrift, a drinker, and a womaniser. Kyle and Alison were old enough to express forcible opinions on his behaviour – and to enlist their father's help in convincing their mother that she should divorce him. It may be that her decision became final during a holiday with Clint in a luxury villa owned by a film tycoon in St Tropez in August 1989. During the break, they swam and sunned by day and partied by night, so relaxed and happy that reporters had no hesitation in declaring them in love and predicting a second marriage.

In fact they were just good friends, as they had always been once the pain of separation receded. Maggie filed for divorce from Wynberg when she returned to California. In her petition, she described him as 'hotheaded and verbally

abusive towards me, especially when he has been drinking'.
As he went on to marry a nineteen-year-old Costa Rican
girl in 1992 and to sue his old friend and drinking partner
Elizabeth Taylor for a share of the profits from her best-
selling perfume Passion, on the grounds he'd provided the
inspiration for it back in 1973, Maggie Eastwood was well
out of her rebound marriage.

All these troublesome happenings unfolded against the
backdrop of one of the best Eastwood projects, *White
Hunter, Black Heart*. It was an adaptation of Peter Viertel's
novel, first published in 1953 two years after the shooting of *The African Queen*. As it was about a flamboyant
megalomanic director called John Wilson who held up
shooting on a film about a querulous couple on a Congo
riverboat while he pursued his dream of shooting an elephant, it didn't take an Einstein to identify him as John
Huston. Viertel, the young screenwriter chosen by Huston
to accompany him to Africa to work on James Agee's
script, had made good use of the times the director was
pounding the bush with his big-game rifle to record his
behaviour with deadly accuracy. The resulting novel was
both graphic and amusing. 'It didn't have a prominent
place on our bookshelves,' said Anjelica Huston, who was
born the year it came out.

Although *White Hunter, Black Heart* was obvious film
material, it passed through the hands of many producers
over three decades before it arrived at the Malpaso offices
in 1988. 'A friend asked me to read an existing script,'
Eastwood observed. 'It was remarkably well written and
the subject was absorbing. I find the idea of a man believing that an elephant has his name on it to the extent
of endangering a film he's supposed to be making very
moving.'

Moving and horrifying in equal parts, presumably, because it is hard to think of two directors whose methods are

more diametrically opposed than John Huston and Clint Eastwood. Where Huston was mercurial, difficult, subversive and, according to his detractors, overrated, Eastwood's laid-back efficiency had resulted in his being underrated for years. 'I'd never be able to leave a project for the sake of some outside activity,' he told me in Edinburgh where the film opened the Festival in 1990. 'I'm a work or play sort of person. If I'm not ready to do the job, I'll stay away from it until I am. Huston needed a little bit of release from the pressures of directing a film – a girl, a horse running at the track – maybe these did just enough for him to keep going.'

Their respective attitudes stemmed directly from diverse childhoods. Huston was the son of a Canadian-born vaudevillian, Walter Huston, who later became a star of both Broadway and Hollywood. As in all the best fairy stories, his career peaked with the 1948 Academy Award for Best Supporting Actor in *The Treasure of the Sierra Madre*, part of a family treble in that his son won the Awards for Best Director and Best Screenplay. After his parents divorced in 1913 when he was seven, John divided his time between the vaudeville circuit with his father and the horse-race circuit with his gambling-addicted mother. These unchildlike activities gave him a lifelong passion for damaging, and sometimes dangerous practical jokes at other people's expense and an easy come, easy go attitude to money, his own or anyone else's.

Compare this with the Eastwoods, locked into their blue-collar poverty and their Protestant work ethic through the bitter deprivations of the Depression, and it is easy to appreciate Clint's fascination with the brittle giant whose mixture of poetry and madness was so far outside his own range of experiences. Throughout his career, his characters had been ordinary Americans – cowboys, cops, soldiers, and assorted oddball lowlifers – but now he was faced with a Hollywood aristocrat who'd bought himself a castle in Ireland, made and spent a succession of fortunes, and lived a life of self-indulgent decadence until his death during pre-production of *White Hunter, Black Heart* at the age of eighty-two.

'I never knew the man and I felt it was not really necessary to know him,' said Eastwood, but he went to considerable lengths to research him before the cameras rolled. He had a meeting with Peter Viertel, several discussions with Anjelica, and as much input from people who'd worked with Huston as he could get. He also read his autobiography and trawled through his television interviews. 'After all that, I had a pretty precise idea of the way he thought and acted. He was fantastic, disconcerting, a mixture of contradictions. One moment, he'd fight physically to defend a young black boy, the next he'd behave disgracefully to his collaborators. He was excessive in everything he did but that was because he believed that stimulation came from constantly taking risks. He was also a skilled manipulator who loved to disconcert people. However, I didn't really want to create an accurate portrait of Huston. What was important was to suggest him rather than ape him, which would anyway have been impossible because he was so complex.'

Huston was forty-five when he directed Humphrey Bogart as the drink-sodden riverboat trader and Katharine Hepburn as the prim missionary in *The African Queen* in Uganda and what was then the Belgian Congo in 1951. The producer, Sam Spiegel, had mortgaged his house in London and borrowed far beyond good sense to raise the four-million-dollar budget. With hindsight, his investment was inspired because the film grossed ten times as much and it's still earning, but when he arrived in Uganda to find that his director was AWOL in elephant country rather than re-writing the script with Viertel, he went ballistic. Even when Huston was rounded up and installed in the jungle camp on the banks of the Ruiki River with Bogart, Bacall and Hepburn, he would cut loose to pursue his obsession. There must have been many times when Spiegel wished that Huston had a better eye so that the matter would be over, but he was not to be so lucky.

'Your friend, John, is not William Tell,' Bogart warned Hepburn when she was considering accompanying Huston on yet another elephant hunt. 'In fact, when you get on that goddamned boat, you'd better throw a few cans over the side and see how good or bad he is. And if the elephant charges, take my advice and run.' A few days later, Huston and Hepburn threw a few cans over the side and the actress saw that Bogie was right. 'He – John – had beautiful guns and a passion for *le sport*,' she wrote in her memoir, *The Making of the African Queen*. 'Not a great eye but I was with him all the way. Adventure.'

Eastwood, who had been credited with a long-held secret ambition to do a re-make of *The African Queen*, was fifty-nine when he took on John Huston in *White Hunter, Black Heart*. The two men shared a beanpole leanness and Clint's relatively abstemious lifestyle and his relentless fitness allowed him to bridge the age gap with conviction. Eastwood assembled his customary low-profile cast for the shoot which began in Zimbabwe, standing in for the Congo, in June 1989. Its best-known member was Marisa Berenson in the Hepburn role, with Richard Kanstone as Bogart, Jamie Koss as Bacall, and Jeff Fahey as Viertel, renamed Peter Verrill. As many of Huston's crew were British, Eastwood hired a number of British character actors for the minor roles, selecting them, as was his custom, from tapes rather than face-to-face audition. They included Alun Armstrong as Huston's harassed unit manager, Ralph Lockhart, and Clive Mantle, who found fame of a kind by being the first man to beat up an Eastwood screen character without repercussions. When the fight scene was staged, he was mortified to find that although he was half Eastwood's age, he was panting for breath before his adversary had broken sweat.

The cinematographer was Jack N. Green and Viertel himself was in attendance after writing the script in collaboration with James Bridges and Burt Kennedy. 'I never loathed John Huston,' he told me. 'In fact, I liked him more than I admired him. He had the ability to do what he wanted no matter what, which is admirable but it can get in the way of a friendship. Writing the novel allowed me to say things that I couldn't have said any other way and we remained friends until his death. As for Clint Eastwood, I found him aloof on the set. We always had the feeling that he was the boss without any shouting or tantrums. In my opinion, he's a very shy man down deep, but a man driven by tremendous ambition.'

Most of the African sequences were shot on the shores of Lake Kariba, the 180-mile man-made lake formed by the damming of the Zambezi River in 1958. It was here that production designer John Graysmark, a previous Eastwood collaborator on *Firefox*, converted part of the Kariba Breezes Hotel into the Lake Victoria Hotel, circa 1952. Additional sets were built on Fothergill Island, a reserve in the middle of the lake for protected herds of zebra, water buffalo, elephant and antelope, as well as lions and innumerable species of birds. As the island was a forty-five minute commute by boat through crocodile-infested waters, the crew took over the wooden cabins normally used by tourists on safari. Shooting also took place at Hwange, known internationally for its domed forest areas and its elephant herds, and the Victoria Falls.

'It wasn't tough for us like it was for Peter and John in the Belgian Congo,' Clint explained, 'because there'd been a lot of films in Zimbabwe. We saw a good amount of elephants. When you get close to an elephant, even a domestic elephant, it's an awesome experience. All they gotta do is accidentally step on your foot and you got a frisbee for a foot. We spent a lot of time getting up to the animals in the game park because these guys are family-oriented and they'd stomp all over you if you scared them. The worst thing that happened to me was a buffalo stuck its head into my tent, a Cape buffalo which is the most dangerous kind. If you shock them they attack fast and furiously, so I just let him go where he wanted. Where does a two-thousand-pound animal sleep? Wherever he wants to . . .'

Eastwood was in his most vital hands-on mode throughout the shoot. When it was time for Wilson to confront the elephants, he took over the controls of the helicopter to track the herds himself. When Wilson was to film the *African Queen* shooting the rapids, he was in the director's place behind the camera as the boat went over. When there were native dances to be recorded, he cut short rehearsals to film immediately and pronounced himself satisfied after one take. 'I am very flexible,' he said. 'The start of the rehearsal was so beautiful and spontaneous that it would have been a shame not to record it. Jack never objects to a change of plan so I can take decisions at the very last minute, knowing that I won't be disappointed.'

After two months in Zimbabwe, cast and crew returned to Britain in August for a final two-weeks' shooting at Pinewood Studios, Northolt Airfield and West Wycombe House, the Buckinghamshire home of Sir Francis Dashwood. The house, which is now owned by the National Trust, was closed to the public for a week – and also to the lord of the manor who still lived there. 'I couldn't get in at night because of the security guards and I certainly couldn't get my car into the garage,' said Sir Francis bitterly. 'When it's a closed set, nobody gets in,' Warner Bros replied smugly.

White Hunter, Black Heart was the talking-point of the 1990 Cannes Film Festival, with Clint Eastwood outpointing rival tough guys Sylvester Stallone and Arnold Schwarzenegger in the publicity stakes. This was fortunate because he shut down production on his next film, *The Rookie*, for five days at a cost estimated at $1.5 million to be there. He flew in by private jet in time to install himself at the Hotel du Cap at Antibes and escort Marisa Berenson, in slinky lace decolletage, to the Palais de Festival for the gala screening on the opening night. At the party afterwards, Eastwood fulfilled a career-long ambition to meet Akira Kurosawa, the eighty-year-old Japanese director who'd unwittingly set him on the path to stardom. Talking through an interpreter, they discussed *Yojimbo*, the Kurosawa epic that provided the inspiration for *A Fistful of Dollars*. Sergio Leone hadn't cleared the rights so Kurosawa had sued him and won. The two men laughed in delight.

A few days later, Warner Bros celebrated both the film and their goldmine's sixtieth birthday with a party, featuring a huge pink cake with an elephant on it, at the Moulin de Mougins restaurant. There were less happy moments when French and British environmentalists mounted a protest over the showing of elephant-hunting scenes at a time when ivory trading had just been banned in a global drive to save the species. 'The world was not as conscious of that particular aspect back in 1953,' Eastwood commented, 'but now is the right time for a film about environmental issues. We should know about the demise of wildlife like elephants and rhinos, and that man still gives the impression he was put on this earth to destroy everything.' His apparent unconcern can be justified, in part at least, by his lifelong commitment to not killing animals, large or small, and by the fact that Huston never killed an elephant anyway, on or off the screen. When the prizes were presented at the end of the Festival, *White Hunter, Black Heart* was not among the winners. This may have been due to the controversy or, perhaps, to Anjelica Huston's presence on the jury, but either way it didn't stop the film getting excellent reviews and as wide an audience as a limited-distribution policy could bring.

Back in Los Angeles, filming resumed on *The Rookie*, an inter-generational shoot-'em-up featuring Charlie Sheen in the title role and Clint Eastwood as his veteran partner, Nick Pulovski. The rookie is a cop by choice, a fresh-faced enthusiast from a wealthy family who relishes the excitement of law enforcement, whereas Pulovski is trying to collect his pension after half a lifetime on the streets. In the interests of drama, their relationship is antagonistic, with the older man emphasising the message that only fools rush in where angels – or veteran cops – fear to tread. 'Yeah, I'm an unorthodox police officer,' Eastwood explained, though without any obvious enthusiasm. 'I've had my disappointments. It's humorous, lots of "make my day"-type lines, very good action sequences. Sure I've played this before.'

Their adversaries are a couple of car thieves working the top end of the market in Beverly Hills, which allows a lot of high-priced hardware to roar across the screen. The baddies are played by Brazil's best-known actors: the lean, saturnine Raul Julia is a calculating gangland boss while the short, curvy Sonia Braga is transformed into an efficient killing-machine. For much of the time, she is called on to snort cocaine and kick the shit out of the cops, but her finest hour comes when she rapes her director-star as he sits strapped to a chair. Erotic? Oh yes, and the more so because it was widely claimed that the Brazilian sexpot had had an affair with Robert Redford during the making of *The Milagro Beanfield War*. Oh no, she has always claimed, but those who chose not to believe her probably found confirmation in her sexually aggressive behaviour with a comparable star in *The Rookie*.

Braga's attitude to her craft was intelligently pragmatic: when she was offered parts in Latin American art films like *The Kiss of The Spiderwoman*, she took them for the greater glory of her culture; when she was offered parts in Hollywood movies, she took those too for the greater liberation of her countrywomen. Her theory was that watching her with Eastwood or Redford would make Brazil's darkskinned sisterhood realise that you didn't have to look like Michelle Pfeiffer to be an international sex symbol. One who got the message was Frances Fisher who regularly hung out on set until her lover was ready to leave. For the rest, Braga summed up *The Rookie* as two good guys, Sheen and Eastwood, versus two bad guys, Julia and her. 'When I was four years old, I was watching *Tom and Jerry*. Now I'm nearly forty years old and I'm up there with a gun playing out my earliest fantasy. I'm lucky Clint chose me because he is good in action so people will see the film.'

And so they did, though by no means as many as Warner Bros expected for a simplistic exercise in sex and violence of this kind. Although the Eastwood career had gained prestige from *Bird* and *White Hunter, Black Heart*, it had lost some momentum with the relative failure of the lowestcommon-denominator romps *The Dead Pool*, *Pink Cadillac* and *The Rookie*. 'Was the mine running out of gold?' the studio asked. As always, Eastwood had the answer. Its name was *Unforgiven*.

18

A Strong Man in Tears

'I'm not sure this will be my last western, but if it is, it'll be the perfect one. The fellow I play is living on the edge of hell most of the time. He's really a tormented person.' Clint Eastwood on William Munny, a man with a past that haunts him until he re-embraces it as an antidote to poverty and loneliness. In his heyday in the mid nineteenth century, Munny became cash-rich by robbing trains and destroying towns. He was saved from his life of crime – and the drink problem that accompanied it – by the love of a good wife who turned him into an indifferent hog farmer and bore him a son and a daughter. When she died of smallpox in 1878, he became a New Age father – caring, sanctimonious, ineffective, and out of touch with the requirements of modern crime. Two years later, when he found a would-be bounty-hunter, the Schofield Kid, standing in the mud outside his remote Kansas cabin, he talked of 'the sins of my youth' as he turned down his proposition.

Many traditional westerns end with the concept that old heroes buy into the land they've purged. Even Sergio Leone's trilogy, with its untraditional outlook, suggests that The Man with No Name might end up as a rancher, while insisting that his nature makes it impossible. In general, the implication in western lore is that to farm is to live happily every after, but *Unforgiven* asks the question, what if it isn't? What if farming is unrewarding, uncomfortable and boring? After the Kid leaves, Munny reviews his story of a prostitute whose face has been slashed by a drunken cowboy in Big Whiskey, Wyoming. Outraged that the aggressor has been let off with a whipping and a 'fine' of seven ponies payable to Sheriff Daggett, the madame of the brothel has offered a thousand-dollar bounty on the culprits. 'Is the slashing of a prostitute a just cause for taking up a gun?' Munny asks himself. As he desperately wants the answer to be yes, he ignores warnings from beyond the grave and plaintive looks from his children. Could he protect the Kid and collect his share of the money without pulling the trigger himself? Again he doesn't find it difficult to convince himself that the answer is yes.

For years, Eastwood had been cherishing Will Munny like fine claret until he was mature enough to bring him to life. The original script, *The William Munny Killings*, was written by David Webb Peoples as a 'revisionist' western – he cited Altman's *McCabe and Mrs Miller* and Peckinpah's *The Wild Bunch* as seminal influences – in the mid seventies, a time when raising finance for a cowboy movie was tougher than raising the *Titanic*. In the early eighties, after his screenplay for *Blade Runner* had made him saleable, Webb Peoples sold *The William Munny Killings* to Malpaso. 'I bought it in 1983 and I kind of nurtured it like a little jewel you put on a shelf and polish now and then,' Eastwood explained. 'I figured I'd age into it a little bit, just have something to look forward to. It's a fictional story about a renegade, very stylised, a little different. What appealed to me was the idea that the good guys weren't all that good and the bad guys weren't all that bad. Everything is cyclical in Hollywood. They made an awful lot of westerns back in the fifties and sixties and it followed that a high percentage weren't very good. Perhaps the time is right . . .'

By now, the project had become *Unforgiven*, a starkly uncompromising title that expresses both the vengeful nature of the plot and the ungodliness of the protagonists. Having cast himself in the lead, Eastwood needed three male actors of his own age and calibre to play Munny's old adversary, Sheriff 'Little Bill' Daggett, his old mucker, Ned Logan, and a third veteran assassin, English Bob. When first approached for the sheriff, his erstwhile motor-racing friend, Gene Hackman, refused on the grounds he'd overdosed on violence already. 'Gene, I know exactly where you're coming from,' said Eastwood, at his most articulately persuasive. 'I've been involved in a lot of violent films but I would love to have you look at this because I think there's a spin on this that's different. I don't think this is a tribute to violence, and if we do it right, it's not exploiting it; in fact, it's kind of stating that it doesn't solve anything.' Hackman looked and was won over. 'He was very explicit about his desire to demythologise violence,' he told Peter Biskind of *American Premiere*. 'I'm really glad Clint convinced me this was not a Clint Eastwood film!'

Richard Harris was an actor whose career was in decline but, even if it hadn't been, he would have accepted English Bob unreservedly. 'Clint's idea was that there were no heroes and no villains,' he explained. 'It was to be a slice of American life that debunks the myth of the West. You know, that they couldn't shoot each other from a hundred paces, that they were filthy and that the West was this infinity of rock and burned-out bush. I loved that.' It was in 1993 that Mario Van Peebles attempted to re-define the role of the Afro-American in the settlement of the United States in the black western, *Posse*, so Eastwood was a little ahead of the game when he chose Morgan Freeman for Ned Logan. With characteristic economy of explanation, his colour is never mentioned. 'Every time I would approach the subject, I would say to myself, "I've seen this before", and I wanted to keep to scenes I hadn't seen before. Maybe it's hipper this way.'

In their different fashions, these four grizzled veterans display the dysfunctional personality of the gun for hire as death approaches. Officialdom rarely comes well out of an Eastwood film but even Harry Callahan's corrupt, self-serving superiors can't match Little Bill Daggett, a man with few redeeming features to balance his greed and thirst for revenge. At one time or another, each of his adversaries falls into his hands with brutal or deadly results. Not that the other three have much to offer in terms of virtue. English Bob has made a fortune out of shooting Chinese railroad workers who are surplus to requirements while Logan is a follower, easily seduced by the lure of easy money but reluctant to do the dirty work himself.

And then there is Munny, initially too stiff to mount his horse without falling flat on his back but gradually reverting to type as the showdown with Daggett approaches. Where Josey Wales starts and ends as an honest farmer, with a spell of lusting for revenge in between, Will Munny sloughs off the influences of his wife's ghost and stands up to be counted as the ultimate avenger. When he strides into Big Whiskey with narrowed eyes and flapping coat and snarls, 'Who's the fella that owns this shit hole?', it is clear that his good intentions have gone forever.

Casting the Schofield Kid gave Eastwood the chance to balance his old-timers – none of them a day under fifty-five – with a top-line juve crowd-puller, but instead he chose the unknown Canadian Jaimz Woolvett. 'I cast who's right for the role,' he snapped. 'You just make it the best you can, or don't make it at all. I don't give a damn about demographics and all that crap.'

The function of the Kid in any self-respecting western is to be foolishly impetuous, and the Schofield Kid is no exception. Having chosen William Munny as his fellow bounty-hunter on his past reputation, he is contemptuous of the physical wreck who has lost the will to

pull the trigger. This kid is short-sighted – a poor qualification for a hired assassin – but eager to embrace his
chosen career. Or so he believes until he shoots one of
the prostitute-slashers at point-blank range and discovers
that he can't stand the remorse. Although he has a crucial
role in the story, his purpose in the revisionist scheme of
things is to show us the principals from the other side of
the generation divide. He learns that the ways of the Old
West are moribund while he still has time to take another
direction, but Munny, Logan and Daggett have lost the
chance – and the will – to change.

If there is any righteousness in Munny's crusade, its
origins lie in the defence of women. They are the vengeful
catalysts for the action and the observers of its effects, a
chorus registering approval and shock at the ways of men.
Frances Fisher, by now accepted openly as Eastwood's
lover, had a choice between Delilah, the prostitute whose
face is slashed, and Strawberry Alice, the madame who
instigates the bounty hunt. 'As Delilah, I'd have to play
a victim, but I'd get to play a scene with Clint. What
actress wouldn't want to do that? Then I decided that
Strawberry Alice's feistiness was much more in line with
my temperament. I really felt the way she did in the movie.
I personally wouldn't want to kill someone for hurting a
friend of mine, even though I would have those feelings
inside. Alice starts out with a sense of injustice but she
moves towards revenge when she takes matters into her
own hands because no one else is going to do anything
about it. She definitely goes overboard.'

Unforgiven was shot in Alberta, Canada, an empty
landscape that conformed to Eastwood's mental image
of nineteenth century America. Using Calgary as a base
camp, a predominantly Canadian crew built the town
of Big Whiskey, the Munny and Logan farms, and the
Daggett homestead on sites selected by their boss. Eastwood

shoots his westerns in the autumn when death and decay complement his liking for sombre colours, so the cameras rolled in September 1991. Director of photography Jack N. Green provided the muted tones that implemented the director's pessimistic vision. After seven weeks of shooting, Eastwood learned that winter comes early in these parts. When the first snowfall was forecast for Monday morning at midday on Saturday, he still had two and a half days' shooting to go. Not many directors would be able to persuade a crew to work for twenty-one hours straight through the night in sub-zero temperatures, but Eastwood managed it, beating the accurate weather forecast by fifteen minutes as he wrapped at 5.30 a.m.

'He's very, very, very laid-back. And terribly polite. He knows precisely what he wants on the set,' said Richard Harris. 'He's the most relaxed director I've ever seen. There's never any yelling,' Fisher confirmed. Their comments provide clues to the root cause of such unswerving loyalty in cast and crew. Mind you, Fisher added, he can be 'extremely silly', and she has the home video of him kissing Will Munny's horse on the lips and cuddling his hogs in the mud to prove it. Even with such diversions, he completed *Unforgiven* in fifty-two days for $14.4 million, excluding his own fee. He paid tribute to the professionalism of the top-line actors who rehearsed so expertly that he felt compelled to shoot immediately, a method he favours because it doesn't allow people time to get stale. 'Once in a while you get great start-up actors – Gene Hackman and Morgan Freeman are great examples. They're the kind of guys where you start rehearsal, and it looks so good you say, "Wait a second, stop, roll this thing!", because there's no reason to be wasting it. They're ready to pull the trigger straight away.'

As had become customary in recent Malpaso productions, post-production incorporated a powerful score by

Lennie Niehaus. It also included a dedication to Sergio and Don, a gracious tribute from Clint Eastwood to two men who had died shortly before it came out, two men who'd moulded him as much through conflict as collaboration. After he became successful in America, he lost touch with Leone for twenty years, but when he went to Italy to promote *Bird*, he received a phone call from the Italian. 'We went out one evening and got along better than in all the times we had worked together. I left and he died. It was almost like he called up to say goodbye.' With Siegel, he'd been much closer, at least until the end of the seventies. 'When we met, it was a surly sort of relationship but eventually we zeroed in, started agreeing on a few things and became fast friends.'

Unforgiven opened in the summer of 1992, establishing itself instantly as that magical combination, a critical and commercial success. The *New Yorker*, showing an enthusiasm for Eastwood far removed from its stance during Pauline Kael's reign, summed up the general mood by describing it as 'mythic, revisionist, psychological, elegaic'. Public response resulted in the best-ever box-office returns for an August opening weekend. Over the next few weeks, it raced to the crucial hundred-million-dollar mark in America alone, rather to its maker's surprise, as he had always considered it too personal and too downbeat, especially in its ending, to hit the jackpot. 'I didn't make it with any commercial results in mind. If I had, I'd probably have changed certain things, but I tried not to compromise on it.'

An August opening is seen as premature for a potential Oscar contender – the premise being that the Academicians have too long to forget – but through the autumn of 1992, the groundswell of opinion suggested that Eastwood's turn had come. *Silence of the Lambs*, an even earlier opener the year before, had set a precedent by scooping the Oscar pool

in 1992. Now *Unforgiven* began to make the right noises in
the right places, starting with five Golden Globes, including
Best Picture and Best Direction, from the Los Angeles Film
Critics Association. The National Film Critics followed
with Best Picture, Best Director and Best Actor, and then
came the Oscar nominations, nine in all including Best
Picture, Best Director and Best Actor.

   '*Unforgiven* was released in the normal procedure, not
to get accolades,' said Eastwood during the run-up to the
ceremony on 29 March 1993, 'but it kind of held over in
everyone's memory and there still seems to be a bit of good
feeling. It explores a certain morality, a morality that has
been explored in a lot of other films regardless of genre,
but one that strikes chords at this particular time. We never
had any preview screenings but the head of distribution at
Warners seemed to like it, the exhibitors seemed to like it,
the reviewers around the country seemed to discover it.
As the year went on, it all seemed to multiply.'

   Twenty years had passed since Eastwood's last ill-fated
Oscar appearance as a last-minute replacement for Charlton
Heston, but he hadn't wasted any time fretting over his
rejection. 'I figure that by the time I'm really old, somebody
at the Academy Awards will get the bright idea to give me
some sort of plaque. I'll be so old, they'll have to carry me
up there. I'll say, "Thank you all for this honorary award."
Then splat! Goodbye Dirty Harry.'

   Once *Unforgiven* was in the line-up, Eastwood and
Warner Bros put all the promotional muscle that money
could buy behind it. The campaign included blanket
advertising and personal audiences with the producer-
director-star wherever they might be influential. One
interviewer who couldn't believe her luck was Georgina
Howell. In her opening paragraph in *Vogue*, she tells of
a Texas cattle rancher who'd rung Eastwood recently to
ask if he could honour him by naming his prize stud

bull 'Clint'. 'Be my guest,' Eastwood replied. 'This bull is worth a fortune,' the rancher explained. 'We sell his sperm around the world.' There was a pause before the actor replied, 'Just don't label it Clint's.'

Not his first public jest about sex, but one of a very small handful, which goes to show how badly he wanted those Oscars, no matter how much he dissimulated. This was bad news for smaller rivals for top honours like Merchant Ivory's *Howards End* and Neil Jordan's *The Crying Game*, and time would prove that their fears were well grounded.

In what was designated as the Year of the Woman, Eastwood walked tall into the Dorothy Chandler Pavilion, in dinner jacket and festive red tie, with Frances Fisher, in slinky off-the-shoulder black velvet, on his arm. Although he kept telling himself 'Who needs it?', he knew that deep down he was hungry. 'I went in feeling good, and I was going to try to be graceful, win or lose. But when we didn't win for cinematography or screenplay, I thought, "So here I am with my eighty-four-year-old mother. I brought her all the way down here, and we're gonna go home empty." Your mind plays trick on you. But when I saw Barbra open the envelope and smile, I knew.'

On his first ascent to the podium, the presenter was an effusive Barbra Streisand, the statuette was for Best Director, and his speech expressed routine gratitude to his colleagues over the years. 'This is pretty good,' he concluded. 'I've been around for thirty-nine years and I've really enjoyed it and been very lucky.' On his second, the presenter was Jack Nicholson, the statuette was for Best Picture, and the speech paid tribute to his mother: 'In the Year of the Woman, the greatest woman on my planet is here tonight – and that's my mother, Ruth.' The white-haired lady seated next to Frances Fisher threw him a kiss. And yes, there were tears all round.

There was no third ascent, the Best Actor's Award going to Al Pacino for the blind, embittered military officer in *Scent of a Woman*, a popular result after six previous nominations. However, Gene Hackman won Best Supporting Actor and *Unforgiven* also took the Oscar for Best Editing. When Emma Thompson accepted her statuette for Best Actress for *Howards End*, she dedicated it to the 'heroism and courage of women', adding how thrilled she was to be among the élite of Hollywood. And none more so than her childhood hero, Clint Eastwood. 'For someone like me from North London, it is surreal,' she told chat-show host David Letterman. 'I grew up with Clint Eastwood in the movies. I plonked my Oscar on the table and was staring at it reflectively when suddenly this long, lean body sat down next to me and this long, heavy arm landed on my leg. I said, "Hello, Clint", which sounds incredibly stupid in an English accent. He turned to me, put his Oscar on the table next to mine, and said, "Well, we did it." And I just said, "Yes", instead of going, "Arrrgh, I can't believe this is happening to me. Clint Eastwood has just made physical contact with me and I am alive, I am alive." ' After the Oscar ceremony, Eastwood demonstrated his long-term loyalty by hosting his victory party in a restaurant owned by Nicky Blair, an ex-actor he'd 'starved with' in their *Francis in the Navy* days back in 1955.

Once the dust and the hangovers had settled, the consensus was that the major prizes had gone to the right man as the industry made amends for ignoring one of its greatest icons for so long. However, there is some controversy as to whether *Unforgiven* was the right film or merely a beneficiary of the right timing. Certainly Eastwood overindulges his streak of silliness in repetitive slapstick routines designed to show that Munny can no longer ride or shoot. Does this make *The Outlaw Josey Wales* the better western? For some, the answer is yes, but not for Dilys Powell,

Britain's most respected film critic after many years on the *Sunday Times*.

In a tribute entitled 'Clint, Friend to All of Us', she outlines her responses to a man she has supported through most of his career. Although she condemned the 'Dollar' films because they flouted the traditions of the American West, she sat up and took notice when Eastwood went to Hollywood. After *The Outlaw Josey Wales* established him as a 'major figure in the cinema' she became 'a devoted but not uncritical observer of his work, good or bad; I admired him enough not to be deterred by inferior movies. I saw him sometimes breaking away from the style in which he had succeeded. Once of twice he directed, but it has been as an actor that he has mostly shown his gifts. Now, with the triumph of *Unforgiven*, I can think of him as a true creator.'

By the time *Unforgiven* received its recognition, Clint Eastwood had another film in the can and, although he chose not to direct himself, it turned out to be one of his very best. *In the Line of Fire* is a thriller in the style of *The Day of the Jackal*, a taut confrontation between opponents who are worthy of each other's steel. Frank Horrigan is the secret-service agent who stood closest to President Kennedy on that fateful November afternoon in Dealey Plaza in 1963 and yet failed to save him. Why didn't he move quickly enough? It is a question he has been asking himself ever since, a question that has led to drunkenness, divorce, and a determination to do better next time, no matter how long it takes. His days on the job have been reduced to double figures by the time he isolates Mitch Leary, a professional assassin with an assignment to take out the current incumbent, as the one truly dangerous threat out of the fourteen thousand that come in every year. 'Assign me to the President,' he demands, arrogant certainty disguising inner doubt.

Horrigan is a typical Eastwood character, perennially bitter because a single moment of failure has blighted his life. Like Harry Callahan, he is a dinosaur in the service, loathed by superiors and younger colleagues for his rudeness and his obsession with potential presidential assassins. One of his peers puts it to him straight: 'A lot of guys warned me you were a pain in the ass.' 'And they were right,' Horrigan replies smugly. He is less assured in his confrontations with Leary, who is both smarter and more accustomed to success than he is. At least that's how the scriptwriter, Jeff Maguire, plays it, though there is a certain lack of logic in a plot that has a professional killer goading a presidential bodyguard into taking him on head to head.

For Clint Eastwood, *In the Line of Fire* was a rare departure from the regular business practice that has served him so well. Although Maguire wrote the script with Eastwood in mind and submitted it to Warner Bros, the star never received it. It was then bought by Castle Rock Entertainment, who set up a production with Columbia Pictures. They approached Eastwood who agreed to play Horrigan, provided he had director approval. His selection was the German-born Wolfgang Petersen, who made his name with *Das Boot*. His first English-language picture, *Shattered*, suggested that he had the right credentials for Hollywood and *In the Line of Fire* confirms it.

'I loved *Das Boot*,' Eastwood explained. 'Some of his later films have been better than others, but I always felt he had a certain size and that he brought a certain scope to his films. I got the feeling that he prefers John Ford to television.' He also believed that a European might throw a different light on what was essentially an engaging but fairly routine story. In consultation with his star, Petersen chose John Malkovich for Mitch Leary and Rene Russo, building on her recent career breakthrough in her late thirties opposite Mel Gibson and Danny Glover in *Lethal Weapon III*, for his romantic interest.

Like *The Day of the Jackal*, *In the Line of Fire* is a cat and mouse game, with Leary setting up his presidential attack with painstaking attention to detail and a level of ingenuity that deserves to succeed. Why he wants to kill the President is not an issue, but his dedication as he develops his security-proof handgun and his means of access to a fundraiser's banquet is never in doubt. The film has its fair share of action but its impact comes from the powerful interaction between the two principals. Eastwood and Malkovich share a spare, understated style that racks up the tension as the denouement approaches. Eastwood gets the opportunity to show a lighter side than of late in his scenes with Russo, the secret agent who breaks down Horrigan's reserve with her beauty and wit.

Pensioners everywhere will be pleased to learn that Eastwood still carries the courage of his conviction that he was born to be an action man. When Wolfgang Petersen was working out how to film a dramatic chase across the Washington rooftops, he took it for granted that he'd have to fake the bit where Horrigan hangs by his fingertips on a building near Capitol Hill. It's just not the kind of thing that sixtysomething Hollywood stars do, even with the finest safety precautions. That was until his stunt co-ordinator, Buddy Van Horn, said, 'Why don't you talk to Clint? He might just do it for real.' So Petersen asked and Eastwood replied with characteristic brevity: 'Yes, I think I can.'

David Valdes, the executive producer seconded from Malpaso nods. 'Clint didn't see the locations until the day we shot. I scouted with Petersen and tried to paint a picture for Clint, that the ledge was three storeys up with nothing underneath. He knew we could fake it in the studio, with photographic background plates, or we could have him dangle, which would be a lot less time-consuming.

As some of the crew didn't come from Malpaso, he asked me who the special-effects man and the stunt co-ordinator were. When I told him they were ours, he said, "I'm fine. Just hang me from the building."'

So Clint put on his safety harness and rode up in a basket on a crane to take up his position, attached only by a wire inserted into a hole in the brick façade. Once the wire was tightened so that he was flush against the wall, he grasped the edge of the roof and the basket was lowered away so that he was hanging for real. As the action was shot from above, there could be no safety precautions in the street below. 'If Clint lost his strength and slipped,' Petersen told *Premiere* magazine, 'he would not fall, of course, but he would probably hang upside down on that wall, and it would be very hard to catch him. An extremely scary situation, even to think about.' No doubt there were moments when Clint was scared too as he clung on through ten takes during a long, tense day, but no hint of such an inappropriate emotion crosses the rugged features in what turned out to be one of the film's most powerful scenes.

The film was shot in Washington and Los Angeles on a scale to which Eastwood did not want to become accustomed, as Valdes cautiously confirmed. 'They spent money in areas we wouldn't have, but then again every director has a different vision.' When Columbia executives tried to pressurise Petersen into beefing up the action, the director learned the value of having a top-line star fighting in your corner. 'You know, fellas,' Eastwood told them firmly, 'you liked the story well enough to make it. I like the script. Everybody likes the script. You should let it get made, give us a chance to finish it, and then make your decision.' And that is exactly what happened. When it opened in July 1993, to excellent reviews and queues around the block, it was clear that the money had been well spent. *In the Line of Fire* grossed $102 million in

North America, coming eighth in the 1993 line-up. It was Columbia's highest placing, representing nearly twenty per cent of the studio's total domestic gross.

After this profitable excursion into foreign territory, the Malpaso team re-assembled for a film with Clint Eastwood as director-star. In a year in which no big picture was complete without a pre-teen lead, Eastwood jumped on the family bandwagon with *A Perfect World*. John Lee Hancock's original screenplay tells of an escaped convict, Butch Haynes, who kidnaps a seven-year-old boy to ensure his own safety on the run. This is 1963, shortly before traditional family values were fragmented forever by the changing social mores of the sixties. Even by the standards of the time, the hostage is an exceptionally sheltered child owing to his parents' religious objections to anything connected with fun. For Phillip Perry, raised to stand and watch enviously while other children enjoy the corruptive pleasures of funfairs and trick or treat, life on the road with Butch is a release from bondage.

In the course of their adventures on the highways and byways of Texas, the boy comes to love his captor for his flights of fantasy and the way he makes his dreams come true. Though he sees him kill, he knows he is kind; though he sees his dangerous mood-swings, he believes he is good. In this respect, Butch Haynes is an extension of many an Eastwood character, a dark mixture of conflicting emotions. The problem is that he is not played by Eastwood, who thought he was too old, but by Kevin Costner, who is certainly too wooden to express emotional complexity on this scale. 'I think it's always good to stretch,' said Eastwood of a casting decision that was widely criticised when the film opened in December 1993. 'You can't really hit the ball out of the park unless you step up to bat. He's been in a few successful films and he's proved he can do that. Now it's his chance to move out to things he really wants to do, to become more versatile.'

For himself, he chose the smaller role of Texas Ranger Red Garnett, the man who originally put Butch behind bars. Now he directs the re-capture operation from a state-of-the-art silver trailer lent by the Governor of Texas. As we are within two weeks of JFK's death, this must be John Connolly, soon to be crippled in the Dallas crossfire. Red has a sidekick, a criminologist played by Laura Dern, with whom he trades sexist insults in a desultory fashion as they track Butch and Phillip through the Texas Panhandle.

Shooting took place in the environs of Austin in the long, wet summer of 1993, a time when much of Middle America was flooded. Not that it mattered because no one sits around waiting for the light on an Eastwood picture. Even when four and a half inches of rain fell in twenty-four hours, the cameras kept turning. When producer David Valdes looked out of the hotel window, he saw racing clouds rather than the filtered sunlight required to match earlier footage for the end of the movie. With a forecast of continued rain, he was prepared to declare a wash-out day.

Not so his boss. 'Ninety-nine directors out of a hundred would have stayed indoors, but Clint made it work for as long as he could. When it got too dangerous to use the electricity out of doors, he moved into the studio and used some old tricks to fake Kevin and the kid driving at night. It was a poor man's process, using lights to make the stationary car look as if it was moving. When actors are told there's an emergency change of plan, brilliant things can happen. Everyone was covered in mud and wet through, but Clint saved the day.'

19

A Perfect World?

Clint Eastwood sits in his regular corner in the Pioneer Saloon, Ketchum, Idaho. He is alone, beer in hand, rib-eye on the table, grey-green eyes squinting at the noisy crowd. Mine host approaches without deference and asks a familiar question. Eastwood nods, the minimal nod of The Man with No Name, and another beer appears as if by magic. The Pioneer is a stuffed-head steakhouse where diners eat red meat under the wide glass eyes of their victims. Eastwood, who once dined with the health-conscious Maggie on salad and sunflower seeds, cuts deeply into the flesh but only I, the gaping tourist, take note. I learn the reason why from a pool player in Grumpy's saloon: 'Idaho men leave folks alone.' He adds that Clint Eastwood can ride the ski lifts and push his trolley around the supermarket without interference. And that he does both those things frequently.

Nowadays he is accompanied on the Sun Valley slopes, some user-friendly, some with intimidating names like Exhibition and Inhibition, by Frances Fisher, who took up the sport after they met. 'A natural,' said instructor Rod Jones, who gave her her first three lessons. In summer he lives a few hundred yards away from the golf club, just as he did in his first home outside Carmel. The game exercises an enduring fascination over him. According to David Valdes, his obsession with it has grown tenfold over the past five years. One of his future projects is a trip to

St Andrews, the cradle of golf, to film *Golf in the Kingdom*, based on a novel written by Michael Murphy, a fellow fanatic from the Pebble Beach clubs. Over the years, it has become a cult classic, translated into five languages and selling steadily to aficionados all over the world. It is not a sports book, more a metaphysical tale that uses golf as an analogy for a personal drive towards perfection. Like *High Plains Drifter* and *Pale Rider*, it has a ghostly element, a Merlin figure who hovers over the thirteenth hole to prompt questions on the meaning of life. In the early stages of production, Eastwood was slated to direct but not act. 'Things change,' said Valdes, with a shrug.

Malpaso also has plans to expand by producing films with no hands-on Eastwood connection. First off the blocks is *The Stars Fell on Henrietta*, a small story about hope – the hope of striking it rich in the Texan oilfields in 1934. For actor turned television director James Keach, it is a chance to move into features. For Malpaso, it is 'a real departure', though not one that is likely to change its policy towards moviemaking. Keach's budget will be modest and he will be expected to keep to it. 'What makes us unique?' Clint stands, relaxed and casual, at the heart of his empire as he ponders my question. 'Respect. Respect for the person putting up the money. If they have enough faith in you to put up the money, whether it's personal or a bank or a distribution company like Warner Bros, you should have enough respect to watch their money as if it was your own. For them, you are a gamble. You should make sure they don't lose.

'I better get outta here before my reputation gets tarnished,' he adds, turning elegantly to exit left while Valdes takes up the cause. 'He's very frugal, a very unique businessman. He prides himself on being a lean, mean machine. There are only six of us at Malpaso and most of us wear two hats. A lot of people in this business are quite piggish in the way they spend their money. Movies don't have to cost as much as they do. You don't need perks, masseurs, physical trainers, drivers, secretaries, five or six employees for each actor.'

And on a Clint Eastwood movie, you don't get them, though he does hire the best caterers in the business to keep morale high at mealtimes. 'Our business is old-fashioned in that it relies on a lot of old-fashioned ethics – honesty and loyalty and allegiance,' Valdes continues, 'things that our mom and dad taught us, the golden rules that are out of fashion in the nineties. Unlike a whole lot of Hollywood films, we're real commonsensical and we have fun.'

On the acting front, Eastwood has been asked to play Robert Kincaid in the film based on Robert James Waller's *The Bridges of Madison County*. Once it became clear that the book was going to be a runaway best-seller, Steven Spielberg's Amblin Entertainment was quick to buy up the rights. Eastwood and Spielberg have similar attitudes to filmmaking – they both keep the keenest possible eye on the bottom line – but at first glance, their approach to their subject-matter is poles apart. At the most obvious level, Eastwood's terse style rarely brings even the threat of tears, whereas Spielberg doesn't rest easy unless the hankies are out in force.

This makes the prospect of this odd couple collaborating on such an overtly sugar-coated project all the more intriguing. Kincaid is a fifty-two-year-old photographer whose assignment shooting the covered bridges of Iowa for the *National Geographic* leads to a four-day fling with hot-to-trot Francesca, a frustrated Italian-born housewife. What next? Well, nothing really. Should she stay with her farmer husband or leave with her rootless lover? Opinions differ but either way their brief union is dignified as love until death do them part. Kincaid is certainly an Eastwood character, at least in the sense that he is man with no roots, a wanderer who zaps in with a camera instead of a gun, takes what he needs to make money and leaves without a trace of regret. Except, of course, on this occasion. As Spielberg will play up the Mills and Boon factor in Waller's work, Kincaid is likely to be even less hard-edged on the screen than he is on the page.

Will this suit Clint Eastwood? Until recently, the answer would have been an emphatic no, but his 1993 releases suggest that he is moving into a more heart-warming mode. At the end of *In the Line of Fire*, he is seen with a soppy grin on his craggy features as Rene Russo trots off into the Washington sunset. At the end of *A Perfect World*, he goes soft on the killer and softer still on the kid. Maybe he is ready for Steven Spielberg after all.

Time will tell, but meanwhile Hollywood's actresses are lining up for Francesca, a rare romantic lead for a fortysomething actress. America's supermarket tabloids have reported that Frances Fisher has been pleading with her lover to allow her to take a role that would put her up there among the big guns, but this would be unlikely casting for a character of Italian origin. Perhaps it's just that she likes the name, as she must because she called her first child Francesca. 'I was thrilled at having Clint's baby,' she said, 'but I know how he feels about marriage. He told me early in our relationship that he never wanted to marry again, and I won't use our baby to force him into doing something he doesn't want to do. At my age, I wasn't sure I could have a child, but now I'm the happiest woman alive.'

The new baby gives Eastwood another opportunity to put his parenting principles into practice. 'For me, being a father was always rewarding. I was just a garage mechanic when Maggie and I married but we will always be friends. Kyle and Alison had both discipline and love when they were young.' Now in his mid twenties, Kyle is struggling to establish himself as a musician. To date, the only professional help he has received from Eastwood is a commission to compose one of the background themes for *The Rookie*. He lives in a million-dollar house in Hollywood which his father bought for him in May 1992. Although the Mediterranean-style home was only twelve years old, it was renovated throughout before he moved in. It has five bedrooms, maid's quarters, and a music room, plus a huge master suite with sweeping views over the Canyon.

Alison has had more difficulty coming to terms with referred fame and unlimited wealth. Her problems began in 1989 when she was stalked by Mike Joynson, a New Zealander who'd become obsessed with her after seeing *Tightrope*. He tracked her down to the Eastwood house at Pebble Beach, then sent flowers and gifts accompanied by a request to see her. He camped in the woods outside the house and, on one occasion, broke into it in an attempt to confront her face to face. He also lay in wait for her outside Robert Louis Stevenson School until security guards chased him away. Neither a Monterey County police restraining order forbidding him to go within five hundred yards of Alison nor a warning by Clint Eastwood, delivered with due menace in a bar, had any effect, so he was arrested and his bail set at two thousand dollars. After five days in Monterey County prison, he pleaded guilty to a disorderly charge and left America.

In 1990, when Alison was in her graduation year, photographers were lining up to capture her elusive beauty. The camera loved her lean five-foot-nine-inch body, her long blonde hair, her creamy skin, and her father's greenish eyes. When Tom Hollyman, who photographed her for the cover of *Town and Country* magazine, took his preliminary shots back to the office, everyone said, 'God, she's gorgeous', then sent him back for more. 'I have my dad's squint,' she told him. 'All I need is a cowboy hat and a little stubble.' She was joking, but in a way she was right, because she has inherited the headstrong character that the image implies.

After less than a term at the Santa Barbara City College, she dropped out in favour of a modelling career, then settled into a wild routine of dating older men and attending heavy-metal rock concerts. Matters came to a head in October 1990 when she skidded the 1988 BMW her father had given her across a three-lane highway after an evening spent listening to Johnny Monster and the Nightmares in a Hollywood club. When she failed a breath test, she spent the night in jail. Her mother bailed her out the next day but two months later she was fined $846 and sentenced to three years' probation for drink driving. Under the terms of the probation order, she was only allowed to drive to work or college, but her father prevented even that by confiscating the BMW. The next year, she was back in the gossip columns when she dated Chad McQueen. At one stage, they were said to have marriage plans but they came to nothing and Alison's life has stabilised since her father persuaded her to resume her studies.

Eastwood had reason to sympathise with Alison over the Mike Joynson affair because he's been on the receiving end of obsession himself. As a result, he is a firm believer in self-defence, especially his own. In 1983, he applied for a permit to carry a concealed weapon on the grounds that he was 'the victim of various threats against my life, including that of kidnap in 1978'. That incident was investigated by the FBI, but no details were released. However, the permit was issued, one of only 162 in Monterey County, and Eastwood habitually packs a .38-caliber handgun. Hardly Magnum Force, but quite enough to do the job. 'I stay armed most of the time,' he confirmed shortly before his Oscar victories in March 1993, in response to a story that a neo-Nazi group had put a $100,000 reward on his head. In April, he faced more threats from thirty-year-old Brian Keith Neun, a Baltimore nutter who made forty-three 'obscene and threatening' phone calls demanding five million dollars. He didn't speak to his quarry but the calls were recorded, complete with his name and address, on the voice mail at Malpaso. When he was arrested, he said he'd been a fan since he was eight and he felt he was owed the money for three of Eastwood's movies. 'The calls were prompted by God,' he claimed, then added, 'You kept trying to keep the lights out of my life. I will kill you.'

Married or not, Eastwood seems happy with Frances Fisher. She lacks Locke's neurotic drive, which makes her a more peaceful companion, and at forty-three she's the right age to sustain his interest as well as his passion. 'The prospect of dating someone in her twenties becomes less appealing as you grow older,' he told Stuart Fischoff of *Psychology Today*. 'At some point in your life, your tolerance level goes down and you realise that, with someone much younger, there's nothing really to talk about. And I think we're at a point now where a lot of older women take better care of themselves, compared to the 1940s and 1950s when women were programmed to figure it's all over after thirty. I find a lot of appeal in a woman if she's kept herself well in her forties and beyond. I have a friend who's been dating women of the same age since he was twenty. I told him, that's great, but what to you say to her afterwards? If you don't smoke, what do you say? Do you talk about the weather or Jon Bon Jovi? I don't know.'

Fisher is an enterprising woman, always ready to travel to locations or to the Eastwood homes in Carmel and Sun Valley by helicopter, stopping off for picnics on the way. Many film contracts include clauses forbidding actors to drive cars until all the footage is in the can, so what Warner Bros thinks of their star attraction piloting his own chopper defies belief. 'They cringe a bit, I think,' said Valdes, in what must be the understatement of the decade, 'but Clint's always been fascinated with helicopters and now they've become an obsession.'

In other words, try and stop him. For Clint Eastwood money and power are the liberating forces that allow him to do exactly as he pleases. With a personal fortune that is probably underestimated at one hundred million dollars, he can buy anything he wants but, in the context of this kind of wealth, he doesn't want all that much. A few homes, a bit of land, a new helicopter, a state-of-the-art pick-up truck, security for his children, and clothes that are readily affordable by the majority of his compatriots. No art collection, no yacht, no island in the Pacific. Fine wine? His Sun Valley supplier puts it this way: 'I wouldn't describe him as a connoisseur, but when you pay as much as he does, it's hard to strike a bad deal.'

As a self-styled workaholic, his control over his career is absolute. He may make bad movies, even bad decisions, but not bad deals. For the moment, he will go on acting, though he has on occasion threatened to stop. When and if he does, he will go on directing, and even after that he will go on producing movies – and making money. 'I can't have regrets because I don't believe in them,' he says. 'There are many things you can go back and have regrets about, but I don't like doing that. By the same token, I agree that when you get to a certain stage in life, you change. And you should change. I think there's a lot of great things about maturity. You become a little more comfortable with yourself, but sometimes you say, "Boy, I sure don't feel like I did twenty years ago." I guess that comes to everyone, but right now, I have no complaints.'

Filmography

1955

REVENGE OF THE CREATURE

Universal-International. Producer: William Alland; Director: Jack Arnold; Screenplay: Martin Berkeley; Cinematography: Charles S. Welbourne; Music: Herman Stein. Cast: John Agar, Lori Nelson, John Bromfield, Robert P. Williams, Nestor Paiva, Clint Eastwood (uncredited as laboratory technician Jennings). Running time: 82 minutes.

TARANTULA

Universal-International. Producer: William Alland; Director: Jack Arnold; Screenplay: Robert M. Fresco, Martin Berkeley; Cinematography: George Robinson; Music: Joseph Gershenson. Cast: Leo G. Carroll, John Agar, Mara Corday, Nestor Paiva, Clint Eastwood (uncredited as a bomber pilot). Running time: 80 minutes.

LADY GODIVA (UK *Lady Godiva of Coventry*)

Universal-International. Producer: Robert Arthur; Director: Arthur Lubin; Screenplay: Oscar Brodney, Harry Ruskin; Cinematography: Carl Guthrie; Music: Joseph Gershenson. Cast: George Nader, Maureen O'Hara, Victor McLaglen, Edward Franz, Vic Morrow, Torin Thatcher, Clint Eastwood (First Saxon). Running time: 89 minutes.

FRANCIS IN THE NAVY

Universal-International. Producer: Stanley Rubin; Director: Arthur Lubin; Screenplay: Devery Freeman, based on the character Francis the Talking Mule, created by David Stern; Cinematography: Carl Guthrie; Music: Joseph Gershenson. Cast: Donald O'Connor, Martha Hyer, Richard Edman, Myrna Hansen, David Janssen, Clint Eastwood (Jonsey). Running time: 80 minutes.

1956

NEVER SAY GOODBYE

Universal-International. Producer: Albert J. Cohen; Director: Jerry Hopper; Screenplay: Charles Hoffman (based on Luigi Pirandello's *Come Prima, Meglio di Prima*); Cinematography: Maury Gertsman; Music: Frank Skinner. Cast: Rock Hudson, George Sanders, Cornell Borchers, Ray Collins, David Janssen, Clint Eastwood (Will). Running time: 96 minutes.

STAR IN THE DUST

Universal-International. Producer: Albert Zugsmith; Director: Charles Haas; Screenplay: Oscar Brodney; Cinematography: John L. Russell; Music: Frank Skinner. Cast: John Agar, Mamie Van Doren, Richard Boone, Leif Erickson, Clint Eastwood (uncredited as a ranch hand).

THE FIRST TRAVELLING SALESLADY

RKO. Producer/Director: Arthur Lubin; Screenplay: Devery Freeman, Stephen Longstreet; Cinematography: William Snyder; Music: Irving Gertz. Cast: Ginger Rogers, Carol Channing, Barry Nelson, James Arness, David Brian, Clint Eastwood (Jack Rice). Running time: 92 minutes.

1957

ESCAPADE IN JAPAN

RKO. Producer/Director: Arthur Lubin; Screenplay: Winston Miller; Cinematography: William Snyder; Music: Max Steiner. Cast: Cameron Mitchell, Teresa Wright, Jon Prevost, Philip Ober, Roger Nakagawa, Clint Eastwood (uncredited as a rescue pilot). Running time: 93 minutes.

LAFAYETTE ESCADRILLE (UK: *Hell Bent for Glory*)

Warner Brothers. Producer/Director: William Wellman; Screenplay: A. S. Fleischmann; Cinematography: William Clothier; Music: Leonard Rosenman. Cast: Tab Hunter, Etchika Choreau, David Janssen, Clint Eastwood (George Moseley). Running time: 93 minutes.

1958

AMBUSH AT CIMARRON PASS

20th Century Fox. Producer: Herbert E. Mendelson; Director: Jodie Copeland; Screenplay: Richard G. Taylor, John K. Butler; Cinematography: John M. Nickolaus Jr; Music: Paul Sawtell, Bert Shefter. Cast: Scott Brady, Margia Dean, Clint Eastwood (Keith Williams), Baynes Barron. Running time: 73 minutes.

1964

A FISTFUL OF DOLLARS (*Per un Pugno di Dollari*)

United Artists / Jolly / Ocean / Constantin. Producers: Arrigo Columbo, Giorgio Papi; Director: Sergio Leone; Screenplay: Sergio Leone, Duccio Tessari, from the story *The Magnificent Stranger*, by Sergio Leone; Cinematography: Massimo

Dallamano; Music: Ennio Morricone. Cast: Clint Eastwood (The Stranger), Gian Maria Volonte (Ramon Rojo), Marianne Koch (Marisol), Pepe Calvo, José Calvo, Wolfgang Lukschy, Sieghart Rupp. Running time: 100 minutes.

1965

FOR A FEW DOLLARS MORE (*Per Qualche Dollari in Piu*)

Europee / Arturo Gonzales / Constantin. Producer: Alberto Grimaldi; Director: Sergio Leone; Screenplay: Sergio Leone, Luciano Vincenzoni, from the story *Two Magnificent Strangers*, by Sergio Leone and Fulvio Morsella; Cinematography: Massimo Dallamano; Music: Ennio Morricone. Cast: Clint Eastwood (The Stranger), Lee Van Cleef (Colonel Mortimer), Gian Maria Volonte, Klaus Kinski, Josef Egger, Rosemary Dexter. Running time: 130 minutes.

1966

THE WITCHES (*Le Streghe*)

United Artists. Producer: Dino de Laurentis; Directors: Luchino Visconti, Pier Paolo Pasolini, Mauro Bolognini, Franco Rossi, Vittorio de Sica; Screenplay: Cesare Zavattini, Fabio Capri, Enzo Muzzi; Cinematography: Giuseppe Rotunnio; Music: Piero Piccione, Ennio Morricone. Cast: Silvana Mangano (Giovanna) and Clint Eastwood (Mario) in the last of five episodes. Running time: 110 minutes.

1967

THE GOOD, THE BAD AND THE UGLY (*Il Buono, Il Brutto, Il Cattivo*)

PEA (Produzione Europee Associate). Producer: Alberto Grimaldi; Director: Sergio Leone; Screenplay: Sergio Leone, Age Scarpelli, Luciano Vincenzoni, from a story by Sergio Leone and Luciano Vincenzoni; Cinematography: Tonino Delli Colli; Music: Ennio Morricone. Cast: Clint Eastwood (The Stranger), Eli Wallach (Tuco), Lee Van Cleef (Setenza), Aldo Giuffre, John Bartho, Antonio Casale, Rada Rassimov. Running time: 180 minutes.

HANG 'EM HIGH

United Artists / Malpaso. Producer: Leonard Freeman; Director: Ted Post; Screenplay: Leonard Freeman, Mel Goldberg; Cinematography: Leonard South, Richard Kline; Music: Dominic Frontiere. Cast: Clint Eastwood (Jed Cooper), Inger Stevens (Rachel), Ed Begley (Captain Wilson), Pat Hingle, James MacArthur, Arlene Golonka, Charles McGraw, Ben Johnson, Dennis Hopper, Bruce Dern. Running time: 114 minutes.

1968

COOGAN'S BLUFF

Universal / Malpaso. Producer/Director: Don Siegel; Screenplay: Herman Miller, Dean Riesner, Howard Rodman; Cinematography: Bud Thackery; Music: Lalo Schifrin. Cast: Clint Eastwood (Walt Coogan), Lee J. Cobb (McElroy), Susan Clark (Julie), Don Stroud (Ringerman), Tisha Sterling, Betty Field, Tom Tully. Running time: 94 minutes.

1969

WHERE EAGLES DARE

MGM / Winkast. Producer: Elliott Kastner; Director: Brian G. Hutton; Screenplay: Alistair MacLean; Cinematography: Arthur Ibbetson, H. A. R. Thompson; Music: Ron Goodwin. Cast: Richard Burton (John Smith), Clint Eastwood (Lieutenant Morris Schaffer), Mary Ure (Mary Ellison), Patrick Wymark (Colonel Turner), Michael Hordern (Vice-Admiral Roland), Donald Houston, Peter Barkworth, Robert Beatty, Anton Diffring, Ferdy Mayne, Ingrid Pitt. Running time: 155 minutes.

PAINT YOUR WAGON

Paramount. Producer: Alan Jay Lerner; Director: Joshua Logan; Screenplay: Alan Jay Lerner, Paddy Chayevsky; Cinematography: William A. Fraker; Music: Nelson Riddle. Cast: Lee Marvin (Ben Rumson), Clint Eastwood (Pardner), Jean Seberg (Elizabeth), Harve Presnell, Ray Walston. Running time: 166 minutes.

TWO MULES FOR SISTER SARA

Universal / Malpaso. Producer: Martin Racklin; Director: Don Siegel; Screenplay: Albert Maltz, from a story by Budd Boetticher; Cinematography: Gabriel Figueroa, Gabriel Torres; Music: Ennio Morricone. Cast: Shirley MacLaine (Sara), Clint Eastwood (Hogan), Alberto Morin, Manolo Fabregas, Armando Silvestre. Running time: 116 minutes.

1970

KELLY'S HEROES

MGM / The Warriors / Avala. Producer: Irving Leonard; Director: Brian G. Hutton; Screenplay: Troy Kennedy Martin; Cinematography: Gabriel Figueroa, Andrew Marton; Music: Lalo Schifrin. Cast: Clint Eastwood (Kelly), Telly Savalas (Big Joe), Don Rickles (Crapgame), Donald Sutherland (Oddball), Carroll O'Connor, Stuart Margolin, Dick Davalos. Running time: 143 minutes.

1971

THE BEGUILED

Universal / Malpaso. Producer/Director: Don Siegel; Screenplay: John B. Sherry, Grimes Grice; Cinematography: Bruce Surtees; Music: Lalo Schifrin. Cast: Clint Eastwood (John McBurney), Geraldine Page (Martha Farnsworth), Elizabeth Hartman (Edwina Dabney), Jo Ann Harris, Darleen Carr, Mae Mercer. Running time: 109 minutes.

PLAY MISTY FOR ME

Universal / Malpaso. Producer: Robert Daley; Director: Clint Eastwood; Screenplay: Jo Heims, Dean Riesner; Cinematography: Bruce Surtees; Music: Dee Barton. Cast: Clint Eastwood (Dave Garland), Jessica Walter (Evelyn Draper), Donna Mills (Tobie Williams), John Larch, Jack Ging, Irene Hervey, Don Siegel. Running time: 102 minutes.

DIRTY HARRY

Warner / Malpaso. Producer/Director: Don Siegel; Screenplay:
Harry Julian, Rita M. Fink, Dean Riesner; Cinematography:
Bruce Surtees; Music: Lalo Schifrin. Cast: Clint Eastwood
(Inspector Harry Callahan), Harry Guardino (Lt Bressler), John
Vernon (The Mayor), Reni Santoni (Chico), Andy Robinson
(Scorpio), John Larch, John Mitchum. Running time: 103
minutes.

1972

JOE KIDD

Universal / Malpaso. Producer: Sidney Beckerman; Director
John Sturges; Screenplay: Elmore Leonard; Cinematography:
Bruce Surtees; Music: Lalo Schifrin. Cast: Clint Eastwood (Joe
Kidd), Robert Duvall (Frank Harlan), Don Stroud (Lamarr),
John Saxon, James Wainwright. Running time: 87 minutes.

HIGH PLAINS DRIFTER

Universal / Malpaso. Producer: Robert Daley; Director: Clint
Eastwood; Screenplay: Ernest Tidyman; Cinematography: Bruce
Surtees; Music: Dee Barton. Cast: Clint Eastwood (The Stran-
ger), Verna Bloom (Sarah Belding), Mariana Hill, Mitchell Ryan,
Jack Ging. Running time: 105 minutes.

1973

BREEZY

Universal / Malpaso. Producer: Robert Daley; Director: Clint
Eastwood; Screenplay: Jo Heims; Cinematography: Frank

Stanley; Music: Michel Legrand. Cast: William Holden (Frank Harmon), Kay Lenz (Breezy), Dennis Olivieri, Marj Dusay, Roger C. Carmel, Joan Hotchkis, Scott Holden. Running time: 107 minutes.

MAGNUM FORCE

Warner / Malpaso. Producer: Robert Daley; Director: Ted Post; Screenplay: John Milius, Michael Cimino; Cinematography: Frank Stanley; Music: Lalo Schifrin. Cast: Clint Eastwood (Inspector Harry Callahan), Hal Holbrook (Lt Neil Briggs), David Soul (Ben David), Mitchell Ryan, Robert Urich, John Mitchum, Felton Perry. Running time: 124 minutes.

1974

THUNDERBOLT AND LIGHTFOOT

United Artists/Malpaso. Producer: Robert Daley; Director / Screenplay: Michael Cimino; Cinematography: Frank Stanley; Music: Dee Barton. Cast: Clint Eastwood (John 'Thunderbolt' Doherty), Jeff Bridges (Lightfoot), George Kennedy (Red Leary), Geoffrey Lewis, Catharine Bach, Gary Busey. Running time: 115 minutes.

1975

THE EIGER SANCTION

Universal / Malpaso. Producer: Jennings Lang; Director: Clint Eastwood; Screenplay: Warren B. Murphy, Hal Dresner, Rod Whitaker, from the novel by Trevanian; Cinematography: Frank Stanley, John Cleare, Jeff Schoolfield, Peter Pilafian, Pete White; Music: John Williams. Cast: Clint Eastwood (Jonathan Hemlock), George Kennedy (Ben Bowman), Jack Cassidy, Vonetta

McGee, Brenda Venus, Heidi Bruhl, Thayer David. Running time: 126 minutes.

1976

THE OUTLAW JOSEY WALES

Warner / Malpaso. Producer: Robert Daley; Director: Clint Eastwood; Screenplay: Phil Kaufman, Sonia Chernus, from the novel *Gone to Texas*, by Forrest Carter; Cinematography: Bruce Surtees; Music: Jerry Fielding. Cast: Clint Eastwood (Josey Wales), Sondra Locke (Laura Lee), Chief Dan George (Lone Watie), Bill McKinney, John Vernon, Sam Bottoms, Paula Trueman. Running time: 135 minutes.

THE ENFORCER

Warner / Malpaso. Producer: Robert Daley; Director: James Fargo; Screenplay: Stirling Silliphant, Dean Riesner; Cinematography: Richard Glouner; Music: Jerry Fielding. Cast: Clint Eastwood (Inspector Harry Callahan), Tyne Daly (Kate Moore), Harry Guardino (Lt Bressler), Bradford Dillman, John Mitchum, John Crawford. Running time: 96 minutes.

1977

THE GAUNTLET

Warner / Malpaso. Producer: Robert Daley; Director: Clint Eastwood; Screenplay: Michael Butler, Dennis Shyrak; Cinematography: Rexford Metz; Music: Jerry Fielding. Cast: Clint Eastwood (Ben Shockley), Sondra Locke (Gus Mally), Pat Hingle, William Prince, Bill McKinney, Mara Corday. Running time: 109 minutes.

1978

EVERY WHICH WAY BUT LOOSE

Warner / Malpaso. Producer: Robert Daley; Director: James Fargo; Screenplay: Jeremy Joe Kronsberg; Cinematography: Rexford Metz; Music: Steve Dorff. Cast: Clint Eastwood (Philo Beddoe), Sondra Locke (Lynne Halsey-Taylor), Geoffrey Lewis (Orville), Ruth Gordon (Ma), Beverly D'Angelo (Echo), Walter Barnes, Bill McKinney. Running time: 114 minutes.

1979

ESCAPE FROM ALCATRAZ

Paramount / Malpaso. Producer/Director: Don Siegel; Screenplay: Richard Tuggle, from the book by J. Campbell Bruce; Cinematography: Bruce Surtees; Music: Jerry Fielding. Cast: Clint Eastwood (Frank Morris), Patrick McGoohan (Warden), Robert Blossom, Jack Thibeau, Fred Ward, Larry Hankin. Running time: 112 minutes.

1980

BRONCO BILLY

Warner / Second Street. Producers: Neal Dubrovsky, Dennis Hackin; Director: Clint Eastwood; Screenplay: Dennis Hackin; Cinematography: David Worth; Music: Steve Dorff, Snuff Garrett. Cast: Clint Eastwood ('Bronco Billy' McCoy), Sondra Locke (Antoinette Lily), Scatman Crothers ('Doc' Lynch), Sierra Pecheur (Lorraine Running Water), Geoffrey Lewis, Sam Bottoms, Bill McKinney. Running time: 116 minutes.

ANY WHICH WAY YOU CAN

Warner / Malpaso. Producer: Fritz Manes; Director: Buddy Van Horn; Screenplay: Stanford Sherman; Cinematography: David Worth; Music: Steve Dorff. Cast: Clint Eastwood (Philo Beddoe), Sondra Locke (Lynne Halsey-Taylor), Geoffrey Lewis (Orville), Ruth Gordon (Ma), Harry Guardino, William Smith, Glen Campbell, Anne Ramsey. Running time: 116 minutes.

1982

FIREFOX

Warner / Malpaso. Producer/Director: Clint Eastwood; Screenplay: Alex Lasker, Wendell Wellman, from a novel by Craig Thomas; Cinematography: Bruce Surtees; Music: Maurice Jarre. Cast: Clint Eastwood (Mitchell Gant), Freddie Jones (Kenneth Aubrey), Ronald Lacey (Semelovsky), David Huffman, Warren Clarke, Kenneth Colley. Running time: 127 minutes.

HONKYTONK MAN

Warner / Malpaso. Producer/Director: Clint Eastwood; Screenplay: Clancy Carlile; Cinematography: Bruce Surtees; Music: Steve Dorff. Cast: Clint Eastwood (Red Stovall), Kyle Eastwood (Whit), John McIntire (Grandpa), Verna Bloom, Alexa Kenin, Matt Clark. Running time: 122 minutes.

1983

SUDDEN IMPACT

Warner / Malpaso. Producer/Director: Clint Eastwood; Screenplay: Joseph C. Stinson; Cinematography: Bruce Surtees; Music: Lalo Schifrin. Cast: Clint Eastwood (Inspector Harry Callahan),

Sondra Locke (Jennifer Spencer), Pat Hingle (Chief Jannings), Bradford Dillman, Paul Drake. Running time: 117 minutes.

1984

TIGHTROPE

Warner / Malpaso. Producers: Clint Eastwood, Fritz Manes; Director/Screenplay: Richard Tuggle; Cinematography: Bruce Surtees, Billy Bragg; Music: Lennie Niehaus. Cast: Clint Eastwood (Wes Block), Genevieve Bujold (Beryl Thibodeaux), Alison Eastwood (Amanda Block), Dan Hedaya (Detective Molinari), Jennifer Beck, Marco St John. Running time: 114 minutes.

CITY HEAT

Warner / Malpaso / Deliverance. Producer: Fritz Manes; Director: Richard Benjamin; Screenplay: Sam O. Brown (Blake Edwards), Joseph C. Stinson; Cinematography: Nick McLean; Music: Lennie Niehaus. Cast: Clint Eastwood (Lt Speer), Burt Reynolds (Mike Murphy), Jane Alexander (Addy), Madeline Kahn (Caroline), Tony Lo Bianco, Richard Rowntree, Rip Torn. Running time: 97 minutes.

1985

PALE RIDER

Warner / Malpaso. Producer/Director: Clint Eastwood; Screenplay: Michael Butler, Dennis Shyrak; Cinematography: Bruce Surtees; Music: Lennie Niehaus. Cast: Clint Eastwood (Preacher), Carrie Snodgrass (Sarah Wheeler), Michael Moriarty (Hull Barret), Christopher Penn, Richard Dysart, Richard Kiel. Running time: 115 minutes.

1986

HEARTBREAK RIDGE

Warner / Malpaso / Jay Weston. Producer/Director: Clint
Eastwood; Screenplay: James Carabatsos; Cinematography:
Jack N. Green; Music: Lennie Niehaus. Cast: Clint Eastwood
(Sergeant Tom Highway), Marsha Mason (Aggie), Everett
McGill, Moses Gunn, Mario Van Peebles, Bo Svenson, Eileen
Heckart. Running time: 130 minutes.

1988

BIRD

Warner / Malpaso. Producer/Director: Clint Eastwood; Screen-
play: Joel Oliansky; Cinematography: Jack N. Green; Music:
Lennie Niehaus. Cast: Forest Whitaker (Charley 'Bird' Parker),
Diane Venora (Chan Richardson), Samuel E. Wright (Dizzy
Gillespie), Michael Zelniker, Keith David, James Handy, Michael
McGuire. Running time: 161 minutes.

THE DEAD POOL

Warner / Malpaso. Producer: David Valdes; Director: Buddy
Van Horn; Screenplay: Steve Sharon; Cinematography: Jack N.
Green; Music: Lalo Schifrin. Cast: Clint Eastwood (Inspector
Harry Callahan), Patricia Clarkson (Samantha Walker), Liam
Neeson (Peter Swan), David Hunt, Michael Currie, Michael
Goodwin, Evan C. Kim. Running time: 91 minutes.

1989

PINK CADILLAC

Warner / Malpaso. Producer: David Valdes; Director: Buddy Van Horn; Screenplay: John Eskow; Cinematography: Jack N. Green; Music: Steve Dorff. Cast: Clint Eastwood (Tommy Nowak), Bernadette Peters (Lou Ann McGuinn), Timothy Carhart, John Dennis Johnston, Geoffrey Lewis. Running time: 122 minutes.

1990

WHITE HUNTER, BLACK HEART

Warner / Malpaso. Producer/Director: Clint Eastwood; Screenplay: Peter Viertel, James Bridges, Burt Kennedy, from the novel by Peter Viertel; Cinematography; Jack N. Green; Music: Lennie Niehaus. Cast: Clint Eastwood (John Wilson), Jeff Fahey (Peter Verrill), Marisa Berenson, Richard Kanstone, Jamie Koss, Alun Armstrong, Charlotte Cornwell, George Dzundza, Norman Lumsden, Clive Mantle. Running time: 122 minutes.

THE ROOKIE

Warner / Malpaso. Producers: Howard Kazanjian, Steven Sibert, David Valdes; Director: Clint Eastwood; Screenplay: Boaz Yakin, Scott Spiegel; Cinematography: Jack N. Green; Music: Lennie Niehaus. Cast: Clint Eastwood (Nick Pulovski), Charlie Sheen (David Ackerman), Raul Julia (Strom), Sonia Braga (Liesel), Tom Skerritt, Lara Flynn Boyle, Mara Corday. Running time: 121 minutes.

1992

UNFORGIVEN

Warner / Malpaso. Producer/Director: Clint Eastwood; Screenplay: David Webb Peoples; Cinematography: Jack N. Green; Music: Lennie Niehaus. Cast: Clint Eastwood (William Munny), Gene Hackman (Little Bill Daggett), Morgan Freeman (Ned Logan), Richard Harris (English Bob), Jaimz Woolvett (The 'Schofield Kid'), Frances Fisher (Strawberry Alice), Saul Rubinek, Anna Thomson, David Mucci, Rob Campbell, Tara Dawn Frederick. Running time: 131 minutes.

1993

IN THE LINE OF FIRE

Columbia / Castle Rock. Producer: Jeff Apple; Director: Wolfgang Petersen; Screenplay: Jeff Maguire; Cinematography: John Bailey; Music: Ennio Morricone. Cast: Clint Eastwood (Frank Horrigan), John Malkovich (Mitch Leary), Rene Russo (Lilly Raines), Dylan McDermott, Cary Cole, Fred Dalton Thompson, John Mahoney. Running time: 123 minutes.

A PERFECT WORLD

Warner / Malpaso. Producers: Mark Johnson, David Valdes; Director: Clint Eastwood; Screenplay: John Lee Hancock; Cinematography: Jack N. Green; Music: Lennie Niehaus. Cast: Kevin Costner (Butch Haynes), Clint Eastwood (Red Garnett), Laura Dern (Sally Gerber), T. J. Lowther (Phillip Perry), Keith Szarabajka, Leo Burmester, Paul Hewitt, Bradley Whitford, Ray McKinnon. Running time: 138 minutes.

Bibliography

Sources of reviews are mentioned in the text.

Ansen, David, 'An American Icon'. *Newsweek*, 22 July 1985.

Arons, Rana. 'Southern Belle Sondra Locke Is Ready To Stand On Her Own'. *US*, 19 August 1980.

Arrow, John. 'Do You Feel Lucky, America?' *You* Magazine, *Mail on Sunday*, 1987.

Bacon, James. 'French Love Iowa's Star'. *L.A. Herald-Examiner*, 27 April 1969.

Bagley, Christopher. 'Secret Service Man'. *Premiere*, August 1993.

Bates, William. 'Clint Eastwood: Is Less More?' *New York Times*, 17 June 1979.

Bauer, Jerry. 'Clint Eastwood, Still Hanging On In There'. *Petticoat*, 18 January 1975.

Biskind, Peter. 'Eastwood Rides Again'. *Premiere*, Autumn 1992.

Biskind, Peter. 'Any Which Way He Can'. *Premiere*, March 1993.

Bonner, Hilary. 'Clint Plays The Clown'. *Daily Mirror*, 2 December 1988.

Borie, Marcia. 'Eastwood's "Josey Wales" Premiere In New Mexico'. *Hollywood Reporter*, 7 February 1976.

Breskin, David. 'Clint Eastwood'. *Rolling Stone*, 17 September 1972.

Bresler, Fenton. 'Sondra Locke and Clint'. *Woman's Own*, 2 August 1980.

Cahill, Tim. 'Clint Eastwood'. *Rolling Stone*, 4 July 1985.

Caulfield, Max. 'Clint Eastwood's Own Story'. A first-person account published in four parts, *Woman*, April 1969.

Cavan, Frank. 'Clint Eastwood Lives It Up'. *Weekend*, 18 July 1979.

Chaillet, Jean-Paul. 'L'Emotion Intacte'. *Premiere*, May 1988.

Chaillet, Jean-Paul. 'Eastwood'. *Premiere*, June 1988.

Chaillet, Jean-Paul. 'Clint Eastwood, African King'. *Premiere*, 1990.

Chaillet, Jean-Paul. 'Chasseur Blanc, Coeur Noir'. *Premiere*, May 1990.

Champlin, Charles. 'Eastwood: An Auteur To Reckon With'. *Los Angeles Times*, 18 January 1981.

Champlin, Charles. 'A Mellow Eastwood Keeps His Edge'. *Los Angeles Times*, 30 July 1984.

Cole, Anthony. 'Clint's Not Cute When He's Angry'. *Village Voice*, 24 May 1976.

Cole, Gerald, and Williams, Peter. *Clint Eastwood*. W. H. Allen, 1983.

Combs, Richard. 'Shadowing The Hero'. *Sight and Sound*, October 1992.

Dale, David. 'Mayor Eastwood Charms The Councillors'. *Guardian*, 4 September 1987.

Denby, David. 'The Last Angry Men'. *New York Magazine*, 16 January 1984.

Denby, David. 'Good And Evil'. *New York Magazine* 27 August 1984.

De Vries, Hilary. 'His Own Man'. Calendar, *Los Angeles Times*, 2 August 1992.

Disney, Anthea. 'Sondra Locke Enjoys Her Life As Clint Eastwood's Sidekick'. *Herald-Examiner*, 14 April 1978.

Downing, David, and Herman, Gary. *Clint Eastwood, All-American Anti-Hero*, Omnibus Press, 1977.

Ennis, Jane. 'Clint Eastwood: The Tough-Guy Star Who Hates Violence'. *Petticoat* 6 November 1971.

Essoe, Gabe. 'Eastwood Stays Loose With Billy'. Calendar, *Los Angeles Times*, 8 June 1980.

Falk, Roger. 'Dirty Harry Comes Clean'. *Woman's Realm*, 22 November 1980.

Fayed, Judy. 'Just About Everybody'. *Life* Magazine, 1973.

Fenwick, Henry. 'Dirty Harry Comes Clean'. *Radio Times*, 26 November 1988.

Fischoff, Stuart. 'Clint Eastwood & The American Psyche'. *Psychology Today*, January/February 1993.

Galante, Gisele. 'Clint Eastwood – "Je Suis Un Homme Paisible"'. *Paris Match*, 17 September 1992.

Gardner, Michael. 'Clint Eastwood Asks City Nod For San

Carlos Project'. *The Carmel Pine Cone*, 26 May 1983.

Gentry, Ric. 'Charismatic Clint'. *McCall's*, June 1987.

Gentry, Ric. 'Clint Eastwood Interview'. *US*, 26 January 1987.

Gibson, Gil, and Unger, Gustav. 'Interview with Clint Eastwood'. *Hello!*, April 1993.

Gilliam, Harold, and Ann. *Creating Carmel, The Enduring Vision*. Gibbs Smith, 1992.

Grenier, Richard. 'The World's Favourite Movie Star'. *Commentary*, April 1984.

Gristwood, Sarah. 'A Veteran Gunfighter Saddles Up For The Last Time'. *Sunday Telegraph*, 13 September 1992.

Gristwood, Sarah. 'The Man With No Oscar'. *Guardian* Magazine, 27 March 1993.

Harris, Chuck. 'Why Clint Won't Get Close To Women'. *Titbits*, 22 February 1979.

Haskell, Molly. 'Clint Eastwood'. *Playgirl*, November 1985.

Hepburn, Katherine. *The Making of the African Queen*. Century Hutchinson, 1987.

Hodenfield, Chris. 'Clint Eastwood: "Let's Go To Lunch and B.S. For Awhile'. *Look*, 1979.

Howell, Georgina. 'Cool Clint'. *Vogue*, February 1993 (also published as 'A Shot Of Clint'. *Sunday Times* Magazine, 28 March 1993).

Jacobsen, Kurt. 'The Trouble With Harry'. *Weekend Guardian*, 15–16 April 1989.

Johnstone, Iain. *The Man with No Name*. Plexus Publishing, 1981.

Kinnersley, Simon. 'Meet The Sexiest Mayor In The World'. *Woman's Own*, 21 March 1987.

Kleno, Larry. 'Remembering Jean Seberg – A Restless Heart'. *L.A. Herald Examiner*, 14 April 1978.

Lindsay, Robert. 'As Clint Eastwood Runs For Mayor – Small-Town Race Hangs On Big Issue'. *New York Times*, 25 March 1986.

Love, John. 'A Sexy Legend at 50'. *Cosmopolitan*, July 1980.

Luz, Myriam. 'Clint Eastwood, The Quiet Cowboy Who Pulls No Punches'. *She*, August 1969.

Maslin, Janet. 'Clint Eastwood'. *New York Times*, 11 January 1982.

McCarthy, Todd. 'Eastwood Chases Classic Western with "Pale Rider"'. *Variety*, 10 May 1985.

McCooey, Meriel. 'A Faceful Of Dollars'. *Sunday Times* Colour Supplement, 17 August 1969.

Miller, Edwin. 'A Searching Kind of Person'. *Seventeen*, April 1968.

Mitchell, Sean. 'Cool Clint Eastwood Moves On, Again'. *L.A. Herald-Examiner*, 17 August 1984.

Moore, Deedee. 'The All-Purpose, All-American Actor . . .' *Daily Telegraph* Colour Supplement, 1969.

Morgenstern, Joe. 'Is This Any Way To Elect A Mayor?' *L.A. Herald-Examiner*, 10 April 1986.

Munn, Michael. *Clint Eastwood, Hollywood's Loner*. Robson Books, 1992.

Oppenheimer, Peter J. 'Action Hero Clint Eastwood'. *Family Weekly*, 29 December 1974.

Peachment, Chris. 'The Last Lone Rider'. *Independent on Sunday*, 13 September 1992.

Perry, George. 'Eastwood's African Quest'. *The Times Saturday Review*, 18 August 1990.

Pickard, Roy. 'A Fistful Of Fame'. *Annabel*, February 1979.

Pollock, Dale. 'Bare-Knuckle Culture Okays "Comedy" – Providing It's Clint Eastwood's?' *Variety*, 24 January 1979.

Powell, Dilys. 'Clint, Friend To All Of Us'. *Evening Standard*, 30 March 1993.

Puig, Claudia. 'In The Matter Of Locke Vs Eastwood'. *Los Angeles Times*, 8 May 1989.

Puig, Claudia. 'Judge To Hear Eastwood Verdict Today'. *Los Angeles Times*, 31 May 1989.

Reed, Rex. 'Some Of The Folks In Iowa Think She's A Lost Woman'. *New York Times*, 11 August 1968.

Reed, Rex. 'No Tumbleweed Ties For Clint'. *Los Angeles Times*, 4 April 1971.

Robbe, Terri Lee. 'Without Clint'. *US*, 16 February 1982.

Schindler, Marrill. 'Clint Eastwood As Mayor: No Sudden Impact On Carmel'. *L.A. Herald-Examiner*, 2 November 1986.

Scott, Paul, and Mooney, Deirdre. 'Dirty Harry Love Shock'. *Sunday Mirror*, 20 August 1989

Sigal, Clancy. 'Gunfight At The Right-On Corral'. *Guardian*, 22 August 1992.

Siskel, Gene. 'Clint Eastwood: Long-Overdue Respect Makes His Year'. *Chicago Tribune*, 9 June 1985 (also published as 'Eastwood Doesn't Play Dirty – Just Tough'. L.A. Life, *Daily News*, 17 June 1985).

Smith, Paul. *Clint Eastwood, A Cultural Predator*. University of Minnesota Press, 1993.

Stein, Mark A. 'Campaigning With Clint'. *Los Angeles Times*, 30 March 1986.

Stein, Mark A. 'Clint Gets A Call From Central Casting'. *Los Angeles Times*, 10 April 1986.

Thompson, Douglas. 'Clint Eastwood Breaks Loose'. *Daily Mail*, 10 February 1979.

Thompson, Douglas. *Clint Eastwood, Sexual Cowboy*. Smith Gryphon Ltd, 1992.

Usher, Shaun. 'The Good, The Bad And The Elderly'. *You Magazine, Mail on Sunday*, 13 September 1992.

Vecchi, Philippe. 'Le Coeur Est Un Chasseur Solitaire'. *Liberation*, 12–13 May 1990.

Verniere, James. 'Clint Eastwood Stepping Out'. *Sight and Sound*, 1993.

Vinocur, John. 'Clint Eastwood Seriously'. *New York Times Magazine*, 24 February 1985.

Walker, Alexander. 'The Night That Justice Was Done'. *Evening Standard*, 30 March 1993.

Warga, Wayne. 'Clint Eastwood: He Drifted Into Stardom'. *Los Angeles Times*, 22 June 1969.

Watson, Jerry. 'It Has Taken My Breath Away'. *Evening Standard*, 30 March 1993.

Weinraub, Bernard. 'Eastwood In Another Change of Pace'. *New York Times*, 6 August 1992.

Weinraub, Bernard. 'Even Cowboys Get Their Due'. *GQ Magazine*, March 1993.

Wilmington, Michael. 'Eastwood And His Demons'. *L.A. Weekly*, 14–20 September 1984.

Index

Clint Eastwood's films are listed under his name, subheading: films; other films under their titles. Page numbers in **bold** refer to entries in the filmography.